PRAI

# NOT FOR GOD AND COUNTRY

"Wow! I fully enjoyed Bill Murphy's well-articulated, educational firsthand account of his time, service, and respect for all who served in a war that America was not supportive of but instead quickly pushed to history books, to then be brushed over . . . again. This book is not one of glory or a war-time memoir but rather a well-captured, eye-opening look into the war in Vietnam . . . from all angles. A must-read for military and US history."

— **DANIEL "DOC" JACOBS**, HM2 (FMF), USN (Retired), Founder, President and CEO docjacobsfoundation.org

"Bill Murphy has captured the essence of a young Marine infantryman coming of age in a war zone. He and his brother Marines must rely on each other to stay alive for thirteen months in order to return home again. His story of survival during 1968, the bloodiest year of the Vietnam War, will no doubt shock many who have never been exposed to combat. The author has researched and provided a wonderful history and background surrounding the Vietnam conflict, to include the politics that dictated the outcome. All in all, this book is a compelling read."

— **BILL ESHELMAN**, Major General USMC (Retired)

"Grunts who experienced the grueling combat of Vietnam will relate to every step detailed in William Murphy's powerful account of an infantryman's tour in America's controversial war. From the booby traps and ambushes, to facing a determined enemy in an unfamiliar culture and terrain, it resonates and brings back memories. More importantly, it gives the reader who has not experienced the Vietnam War a glimpse into what it was like for those Marines and Army soldiers—the grunts—who bore the brunt of the fighting. *Not for God and Country* is a compelling read from start to finish."

— **JAMES BALLARD**, Author of *Poisoned Jungle*, Vietnam Medic, Mekong Delta, 1969

"A masterfully written firsthand account of a courageous Marine who experienced the most horrific hell of the Vietnam War. The author puts you right there with him as he experiences the danger of snaking his way through an enemy-infested jungle, not knowing if his life would be snuffed out at any moment by a booby trap or a sniper. This story is a captivating, hair-raising chronicle of the suffering endured by our brave fighting men in Vietnam. It starts with the political maneuverings that led our country into a quagmire that turned a former friend into a determined enemy. Interesting statistics about the war are cited throughout the story, making it a valuable reference for current and future generations. It is a must-read for every history student in America; and it deserves wide readership by all who value their freedoms and who believe that sending American soldiers to war should not be the answer to political ineptitude. Once I started reading this story, I could not stop until the end, which left me wanting more."

—GEORGE W. KOHN, Colonel (Ret) USAF, Author of *Vector to Destiny: Journey of a Vietnam F-4 Fighter Pilot*

"Bill Murphy provides an intensely personal account of his combat tour in Vietnam. He brings the reader into the world of an infantry grunt, a close-up view of serving on the front lines of an unconventional war. Murphy's gift is providing a succinct overview of the bigger themes of the war at the same time he describes the tension of being the pointman on a jungle patrol. He provides a context to the entire conflict without taking away from his experience. As an infantry officer commissioned in 1976 just after the Vietnam War, I was taught and mentored by Vietnam veterans, office and noncommissioned officers alike. They were tested on the battlefield and shared their lessons, always with the purpose of making us better soldiers. I got the same feeling from reading *Not For God and Country*. As Murphy says in his foreword, it is important to remember all the men and woman who served in that conflict."

—LOUIS BURGESS, West Point Graduate, Lieutenant Colonel (Ret) US Army, Airborne Ranger

"Murphy did not waste time getting into his very accurate description of the combat conditions in the jungle groundcover of the Vietnam War—the heat, pungent odors, heavy sweating, monsoon rains and the bullets passing overhead but so close that their heat could be felt as they went past.

"We were fighting for our fellow soldiers, who became brothers to us very quickly and were closer to us than some of our own family members. Our combat experiences come back to us almost every night in our dreams.

"This book brings back those memories vividly. It is an excellent read for US military veterans who dare follow along without getting too deeply back into our experiences, and it vividly portrays real combat situations. It is realistic, graphic, powerful, and absolutely intense."

**—L. PATRICK SCHEETZ**, PhD, First Lieutenant (Retired), US Army

## OTHER BOOKS BY WILLIAM M. MURPHY

*Motorcycling Across Michigan*

*Motorcycling Across Ohio*

*Motorcycling Across Indiana*

*Motorcycling Across Wisconsin*

*Grace & Grit: Early Twentieth Century Female Adventurers*

*Ride Michigan*

*Ride America's Heartland*

**www.williammurphyauthor.com**

*Not For God And Country*

by William M. Murphy

© Copyright 2021 William M. Murphy

ISBN 978-1-64663-273-2

Published by

 köehlerbooks™

3705 Shore Drive
Virginia Beach, VA 23455
800-435-4811
www.koehlerbooks.com

# NOT FOR GOD AND COUNTRY

## WILLIAM M. MURPHY

VIRGINIA BEACH
CAPE CHARLES

*Dedicated to all who served in the past
and those that serve our country today—
especially the grunts.*

# TABLE OF CONTENTS

# PROLOGUE

An all too familiar dread was thick in the humid early-morning air. We nervously glanced at one another as we saddled up, gathering all the gear and ammunition needed for a day in the enemy's backyard. Our thoughts were of what we knew awaited beyond the relative safety of the concertina wire fence. Bandoliers of ammunition and spare belts of machine gun ammo hung heavily around our necks. Flak jacket pockets were filled with grenades and C rations. Canteens filled with water tainted with the taste of germ-killing halazone tablets hung from our belts. With quick glances at marines we barely knew, we silently wondered which of us might be killed or maimed today. We snuffed out cigarettes and loaded our rifles, then headed through an opening in the fence into no-man's-land.

It was barely daybreak and yet the heat was stifling. Mist accentuated the already familiar, pungent smell of the surrounding jungle. Not quite rain, but worse, because it resulted in ideal muted conditions for an ambush. In this setting, stealth was on the side of a silent waiting enemy.

As we fell into place in the column, the sergeant whispered to spread out and watch for anything suspicious. We hadn't gone a quarter mile in the sandy soil before sweat began to soak our filthy jungle utilities. Thorny vegetation tugged at our fatigues and elephant grass sliced exposed skin with its razor-sharp edges. Walking at the head of the squad, I didn't need to be reminded to be watchful. My life depended on it, as did the lives of those following behind. We had been in-country only three weeks, but already our ranks were thinned by the deadly efficient work of a seemingly invisible foe. They set mines where we walked and executed ambushes from concealed bunkers in the thick foliage. Snipers in trees and in underground camouflaged spiderholes added to the dangerous reality of the South Vietnamese countryside.

The light rain made the thick brush even darker and more menacing than usual. We used a faint trail rather than clear our way through the thorny brush with machetes. It was easier but more dangerous. A ruthless adversary knew we would use the path rather than fight the underbrush, and we knew he'd be waiting. Our purpose was to locate the foe and engage him, but the opposite was the reality. It was we whose whereabouts were known and we that would be the target of engagement at the time and place of the enemy's choosing. We had no way of knowing when or where. As point man, it was my job to find out.

On occasion I observed questionable conditions and gave hand signals to stop, which were relayed in silent pantomimic fashion down the line. Marines behind me were on high alert as I checked out places or signs along the trail that looked even slightly suspicious. By mid-morning the sun broke through the fog and the heat and humidity soared. Our attention was frequently diverted from peering into the elephant grass and brush to sneaking a quick drink from our canteens. We were used to the strong aftertaste of iodine and chlorine already. In this environment one learned and acclimated quickly. There were no options to what had become a daily routine of seeking out and confronting our adversary in some of the most inhospitable conditions on earth.

At midday we stopped to rest and eat, spread around a perimeter in the brush for protection against attack. We wolfed down whatever flavor C ration packet we happened to grab from the box that morning, and took turns resting for a few minutes. Some rested while others maintained a careful watch. We couldn't linger, as this wasn't a picnic; it was a badly needed break in the middle of enemy-held territory.

With map and compass in hand, the sergeant pointed the way, and we started out once again into the brush, following another faint trail. A dozen marines stealthily followed behind me, hoping for the best but expecting the worst. An hour of tense nerves and eerie silence ended with the dreaded sound of an explosion near the center of the column. The blast was still echoing through the trees when the scream of "*Corpsman!*" was heard. Soon the unmistakable smell of detonated explosives filled the steamy air. As Doc attended to the badly injured man, the rest of the squad took up defensive positions. This booby trap had been activated by electric current, not a footstep. The enemy that pushed the button was nearby. We fully expected the attack that sometimes occurred after an explosive device was triggered. Perhaps for strategic reasons, the foe chose not to press the attack at this time and place.

When the gravely injured man was stabilized, we continued forward, seeking an open area where a medivac chopper could land. Helicopters and foot travel were the only possibilities. There was no overland transportation capability. The wounded man, both legs now mangled and useless, was carried by two marines in the center of the column. We moved out of the thick brush into a somewhat open swampy area, lined with mature trees. Those nearby trees made me nervous.

The squad struggled through the unforgiving mud for only about ten minutes before our greatest fear became a reality. A waiting enemy hidden in concealed spiderholes and bunkers among the trees opened fire. Two marines fell immediately, hit by the lethal fusillade. One was dead before he hit the ground and the other was badly injured, bleeding from a bullet in his chest. I felt the deadly power of bullets passing inches from my body while dropping to the ground. We returned fire at the invisible foe, though at a severe disadvantage from our unprotected positions. "*Doc, get up here! Joe, get your fucking gun set up!*" the sergeant screamed above the din of gunfire.

Only a few seconds passed before the machine gunner and his assistant laid down a deadly stream of bullets directed at puffs of smoke from the tree line. His barrage, coupled with continuous blasts from the rest of us, temporarily stemmed incoming fire and provided cover for the corpsman to reach the stricken men.

Having inflicted the damage they intended and instilling the fear that was part of their plan, the invisible assailants eventually broke off and slipped into the surrounding jungle. We didn't try to follow them into the forest—that would have been folly. We knew we'd encounter them again, perhaps later this day or the next.

This wasn't our first ambush of this type. Over the past three weeks there had been others. There is no getting used to such terror. We all knew that luck was bound to abandon us and near misses would, at some point, be fatal hits.

With two badly injured marines and one dead man, we cautiously struggled forward to an open area awaiting the arrival of the medivac chopper called for by the squad radioman. When an open area suitable as a landing zone was located, we set up a perimeter for security and the dustoff chopper landed while a supporting gunship surveilled the area.

After departure of the birds we continued our patrol to seek out the enemy, eventually making a loop back by the end of the day to the small forward patrol base we called home.

Though in the war zone less than a month, the routine had already become frighteningly predictable. In the relative safety of camp, we cleaned up the best we could and found available shade to rest. We reflected on another day much like others that had already formed a pattern. Our private thoughts were of gratitude that we weren't the ones wounded or killed. We hated the fact that anyone was hurt, but at our cores were glad that it wasn't us. Again, we pondered *why are we here* and *how will we survive this nightmare?* We were thousands of miles from home in an alien land. We had more than twelve months left on our tour of duty on the front lines of the Vietnam War. How could we survive that long? This was just one typical day out of about 400 that had to be survived. *What the hell are we doing in this nightmare*, we wondered.

The feel of that particular day and myriad others like it are still fresh in the minds of every combat veteran of the Vietnam War, a war that destroyed lives and tore our country asunder. One of the earliest lessons a soldier or marine learned on the ground in Vietnam was that this war was different. Unlike the movies we grew up watching and stories we heard from relatives, this was not the noble patriotic cause that World War II represented. Fighters in this strange war did not have the country's support behind them. Much of the American population could not have cared less about our situation. Many actively opposed our involvement and some even considered us the bad guys. We quickly learned what the truth was. We weren't fighting for Mom, apple pie and America. We were fighting to protect the life of the nineteen-year-old grunt next to us on the jungle trail. And he was returning the favor. We were there, not for God and country and a great patriotic cause, but for each other. In that mission we succeeded very well. In that mission we can take great pride.

Michigan Vietnam War Memorial. Photo by author

# CHAPTER 1

# DARK CLOUDS GATHER
# ON THE HORIZON

The Vietnam War was the pivotal event of the latter half of the twentieth century. For many Americans, and in the halls of power in Washington, this historic event is being forgotten in the mix of more recent national traumas and a changing population.

Far too many Americans today have little knowledge of the war and even less understanding as to the how, why, and what of the Vietnam War, an event that once dominated American life like no other. This ignorance of a pivotal event in American history cannot continue. Americans owe it to their country to understand the consequences of decisions that lead to conflict, and they owe those who were sent to war in those faraway Southeast Asian jungles the respect and honor of hearing, understanding, and remembering their story.

The tendrils of the Vietnam War are long and complex. The full story of the war needs telling so that this complex national trauma is understood and the many pitfalls encountered and lessons learned from the war are remembered. The plight of all of those caught in the maelstrom, combatants and noncombatants alike, must be appreciated and honored. This complex story is best told from the viewpoint of participants, not detached observers.

There are three distinct facets to the Vietnam War timetable. To do justice to the telling of the story of America's long and costly involvement in Vietnam one must start at the very beginning, two decades before the 1964 congressional Gulf of Tonkin Resolution that resulted in troops landing on the beaches. There were twenty years of political, diplomatic, and military maneuvering and fateful decisions that led America ultimately into war. The tangled tale of how America became involved in generations-old hostilities in the jungles of Vietnam in the first place requires explanation in order to set the stage.

The decade-long shooting war in which countless thousands died on all sides was the second phase, and the result of those decisions made in the prior twenty years. An inseparable facet of war is the brutality of combat, with its resulting death and destruction. In telling the story of the Vietnam War, one must describe the impacts of this war in the day-to-day lives of grunts in the jungles of Vietnam. War is larger than the blood-and-guts realities of combat, but combat is where the highest terrible price is paid for the failures of diplomacy. War cannot be fully understood unless the realities of combat are understood.

Even after this decade of death and destruction was ended by the 1973 Paris Peace Accords, the trauma didn't end for our nation or for all Americans. For the Americans that fought in Vietnam, the war's consequences lasted a lifetime. Though veterans rarely spoke of it, the war never faded in their minds. At the national government level in Washington, repercussions of the national trauma and so-called lessons of Vietnam affected governmental policies and decision-making for decades. From its earliest embryonic beginnings to the current day, seventy-five years have transpired. And yet the story continues to unfold. But the tale actually begins hundreds of years ago, not mere decades.

The geopolitical, economic and sovereignty issues involving Vietnam extend back to the late 1600s with the entry of France into what was then known in Europe as Cochinchina. French colonialism in Southeast Asia began for the same reasons as virtually all European colonization: for economic and religious purposes. It started with the arrival of the French East India Company and Roman Catholic priests in 1668. Over the next two hundred and fifty years, political and economic control of Southeast Asia by France steadily grew. Total control of Vietnam was achieved in 1885 by the French victory over China in the Sino-French War. To better govern its regional colonies, French Indochina was formed in 1887. After victory in the 1893 Franco-Siamese War, France included Laos as part of its Southeast Asian territories, along with Vietnam and Cambodia.

While the religious focus of colonialism had long ago faded, the economic underpinnings of French control of Southeast Asia grew over time. In the early part of the twentieth century rice production and exports equated to full bank accounts for French overlords and their wealthy native partners. However, this international commercialization of rice growing worsened the plight of Indochinese farmers and peasants dramatically. Small plots of land traditionally used by natives were usurped by speculators, and rice that once fed rural populations was now shipped overseas. Peasants became landless tenants or were forced to eke out an existence on poor land. Many had to look elsewhere, to mines and rubber plantations owned by French interests, for jobs. France's control over the lives of poor and powerless indigenous populations created simmering nationalistic sentiments.

World War II saw additional forces shape events in Southeast Asia with the Japanese occupation of the region. At the beginning of that war, two men entered the world stage in response to Japanese occupation and earlier French colonialism. These men were to have dramatic impacts on the lives of millions for the next two generations. In 1941, a politician and Vietnamese nationalist named Ho Chi Minh, in league with the Indochinese Communist Party, revived an inactive and largely ineffective political and military organization called the Viet Minh. These fighters were originally formed in 1936 under the name The Vietminh League, also known as the Indo Chinese Peoples Independence Confederation. The guerilla organization opposed French occupation before the war and focused on Japanese occupation during World War Two.

Ho Chi Minh oversaw the group's political and diplomatic activities domestically and internationally, turning it into a powerful and effective organization. General Vo Nguyen Giap led the military aspect of the group. Giap's brilliant military strategies and unshakable belief in their nationalistic cause and full confidence in the ultimate success of the Viet Minh, led the guerrilla force through decades of warfare.

In May 1945, Japanese occupying forces ousted the French Vichy government they had allowed to rule in Vietnam during their occupation, installing a puppet ruler named Bao Dai. As part of this overthrow of French rule in Indochina, Japan declared Vietnam, Laos and Cambodia to be free and independent nations, under Japanese imperial influence. From this Southeast Asian base of operations, the Japanese set their focus on China. The situation in Vietnam became desperate as thousands starved due to the shipment of rice harvests out of that country to Japan.

In response, with a mutually desirable goal of defeating and driving out the Japanese, on May 16 the United States Office of Strategic Services, a branch of military intelligence and forerunner of the CIA, formed a pact with Ho Chi Minh and his Viet Minh fighters. The OSS created two special units, called the Deer and Cat teams, for special missions in Vietnam. In July team members parachuted into the jungle northwest of Hanoi. Deer Team members joined directly with Ho Chi Minh and his forces and were warmly received.

The American agents gathered intelligence, sabotaged crucial railroad supply lines, and provided training, logistical, strategic and medical assistance to Ho Chi Minh's fighters. Ho Chi Minh's guerillas fought side by side with the Americans, and Viet Minh fighters, including Ho Chi Minh himself, were friendly and effective comrades. In addition to guerilla actions against Japanese occupiers, Viet Minh forces also helped locate and save American pilots who had been shot down. The Viet Minh proved to be valuable allies and honed their battle and subversive skills during the Japanese occupation against a common enemy. A medic with the Deer Team is credited with saving (or at least playing a major part in saving) the life of Ho Chi Minh in the summer of 1945. Team members returned to the States several months later, after Japan surrendered. OSS members and Ho Chi Minh's government remained on friendly terms through the late 1940s, when it became clear and public that official American policy had tilted toward continued French control in Southeast Asia.

In May 1945, at the founding of the United Nations in San Francisco, US Secretary of State Edward R Stettinius, under pressure from President Truman, assured France that Washington did not question French sovereignty over Indochina. The position was based on an anti-communist, rather than pro-colonial, agenda. On the ground in Southeast Asia, the OSS was largely unaware of these shifts in official American policy away from the prior Rooseveltian stance supporting independence for Indochinese nations.

At the Potsdam Conference in July 1945, following defeat of Germany, the Allies met to discuss post-war geopolitical alliances and boundaries. At that conference France made a claim requesting that their former colonial possessions in Southeast Asia be reinstated following the end of the war in the Pacific. President Roosevelt, who died three months before the conference, had previously made known his opposition to France reacquiring its Southeast Asia colonies when the war was to finally end. Roosevelt felt that native populations had fared poorly under French rule and that their circumstances would be better as sovereign nations. FDR wanted a trusteeship for Indochina, voiced as recently as January 1945 and carried into the Yalta Conference. He had also voiced opposition to American involvement in the decision-making process affecting the future of Indochina. President Truman did not share these sentiments to the degree that FDR did, because Truman faced a new postwar reality as the war was drawing to an end, global communist revolutions. Truman had witnessed the transformation of Russia from a war ally to a postwar adversary.

As part of the Potsdam Conference, China and Britain were given responsibility for disarmament of forces in Vietnam once the war in the Pacific ended. The British were to disarm fighters in the southern portion of the country, and nationalist Chinese troops had the responsibility to disarm fighters in the north.

Following the defeat of Japan in August, a major power vacuum suddenly existed in Southeast Asia. Bao Dai abdicated as ruler of Vietnam and Ho Chi Minh and his forces occupied Hanoi. In September he declared a provisional government for Vietnam. In an action that he hoped would demonstrate his desire for establishment of a free and independent country, Ho Chi Minh quoted the first portion of the American Declaration of Independence as the basis of his government. He was optimistic that the West would support his anti-colonial position. Ho Chi Minh spent four months in France during this period attempting to hammer out an agreement with France but was unsuccessful. He also tried to open communication and cooperation with America after the defeat of the Japanese, but President Truman rebuffed Minh's efforts. One can only speculate as to the different course of history that might have occurred had Ho Chi Minh been successful in his diplomatic overtures with Paris and Washington. Unfortunately, his ties with communist doctrine and revolutionaries doomed his efforts at a time when fear of worldwide communist domination was suddenly the guiding force in political alliances.

Following the surrender of Japan, flames of revenge overpowered prospects of a peaceful transition to normality. Mass recriminations against Viet Minh fighters took place as part of the process of removal of Japanese forces and disarming guerrillas. Many thousands of French still lived in Vietnam and once again tried to assert their former role in Vietnamese society and in economic and governmental affairs. Released French prisoners of war and civilians alike killed many anti-colonial guerrillas and Vietnamese civilians.

The first American to die in the post-WWII history of Vietnam was Lieutenant Colonel Albert Peter Dewey, killed by the Viet Minh near Saigon on September 26, 1945 during the chaos that followed Japan's surrender. Dewey led a seven-man OSS unit called Operation Embankment and deployed to Vietnam in the first week of September for the purpose of rescuing POWs and reporting on political developments. Guerrillas allegedly mistook Col. Dewey for a French officer because he was fluent in French and had apparently spoken in French to some Vietnamese prior to the roadside ambush in which he was gunned down. His body was reportedly dumped in a nearby river and never located. Ho Chi Minh sent a letter of apology to President Truman for the killing and ordered a search for his body. Shortly before his death, Dewey sent a dispatch to his superiors stating that in his opinion "Cochinchina is burning, the French and British are finished here, and we ought to clear out of Southeast Asia." The American military did not begin tallying advisor deaths in Vietnam until 1955, so Col. Dewey is not counted among those killed in the American Vietnam War.

* * *

In October 1945, 35,000 French soldiers arrived in Vietnam to reclaim control of their colony. This action sparked the first opposition by American citizens to our involvement in that faraway land. Merchant Marine sailors condemned the use of American ships to transport European troops "to subjugate the native population" of Vietnam.

Early the next year, Nationalist Chinese forces left northern Vietnam and the French military completed its occupation of the entire country. In July 1946 the Viet Minh began a guerrilla campaign directed against the French. That fall French forces bombed two major cities—Hanoi and Haiphong—forcing Ho Chi Minh and his government into jungle exile. The First Indochina War had begun.

General Giap stated that "The resistance will be long and arduous, but our cause is just and we will surely triumph." In the First Indochina War, as in the second, the American War, the will and determination of

Ho Chi Minh and General Giap, and the millions who followed them, were unyielding and unbreakable.

France was aided in their endeavors to reclaim their Vietnamese colony by America. The United States had political, not economic, reasons to become involved in that faraway corner of the world, however. America wanted to stop the spread of communism. In an address to Congress in March 1947, President Truman declared that the foreign policy of the United States would henceforth be to assist any country whose stability was threatened by communism. This anti-communist policy was known as the Truman Doctrine.

World affairs became vastly more complex, and the American communism phobia strengthened even more, in October 1949 when Mao Tse Tung, the communist revolutionary leader, assumed power in China. He formed the People's Republic of China, a fiercely anti-west communist autocracy.

In 1950 President Truman authorized $15 million in military aid to the French and sent 352 advisors, called the Military Assistance Advisory Group, to help France in their battle against the Viet Minh communist rebels. The decision by Truman to become involved in the internal political and military activities of Vietnam changed everything. America had established a toehold that she would later be reluctant to abandon.

Decision makers no doubt did not think at the time that their actions would explode on the world stage more than a decade later. They could not have foreseen that their policy would result in one of the most divisive and controversial events in American history.

\* \* \*

The brutal guerilla war against France went on for four more years. In the end, French efforts to retain control of Southeast Asia failed as a result of their stunning defeat at Dien Bien Phu in May of 1954. In their battles against French forces, the Viet Minh learned many lessons about successful conduct of insurgency warfare. That knowledge would not be forgotten.

The French defeat in Vietnam resulted in the signing of the Geneva Accords later in 1954 and the full departure of France two years later. In reality, the Accords were just a truce between France and the Viet Minh. French Indochina as a geopolitical entity ended in 1954 with the Geneva Accords.

The Geneva treaty divided Vietnam into two countries near the seventeenth parallel: the Democratic Republic of Vietnam in the north and the State of Vietnam south of the line of demarcation. Along the newly imposed border between the two Vietnamese nations a six-mile-wide demilitarized zone, (DMZ) three miles on each side of the line of demarcation, was created to form a buffer.

After defeat of their French overlords, the Vietnamese can't be blamed for thinking that peace might have finally arrived in their small country after centuries of colonialism and decades of hostility. The Geneva Accords had simply temporarily paused an unsettled state of affairs, however. They gave the French an exit strategy but created a divided Vietnamese people. Vietnamese nationalists in the north were not content to exist as two nations of the same people.

Dividing Vietnam into two states was meant to be temporary. Elections were to be held in 1956 to determine the government of what was intended to once again be a unified country. Ho Chi Minh enjoyed strong support in the north. The communist leanings of nationalists in the new Democratic Republic of Vietnam made them abhorrent to the west, however. The population of northern Vietnam was higher than in the south, and the north was economically more powerful. Because of these advantages, the United States and South Vietnam feared that the northern regime, with backing by Russia and China, would win that election with ease. President Eisenhower therefore did not sign the Geneva Accords.

\* \* \*

When great treaties are signed that dramatically influence world events, repercussions are expected. The Geneva Accords resulted in a mass migration of Christians and anticommunists from northern Vietnam to the new country of South Vietnam. It is estimated that nearly one million people crossed the DMZ into the south through official refugee stations alone. These fleeing Christians became some of America's strongest allies later during the war. They did not want the same kind of persecution they experienced in the north to occur again in the south.

Reunification, of course, did not happen in 1956. North Vietnam almost immediately violated the Accords by failing to withdraw all of their troops from South Vietnam. Leaders in the north had no intention of allowing the division of Vietnam to stand and maintaining a military presence in the south was crucial to their plans. They also interfered with the migration of North Vietnamese refugees into the south. Furthermore, they dramatically increased their military by more than doubling the strength of the new People's Army of Vietnam (PAVN), also referred to as the North Vietnamese Army (NVA). Russia and China were supporting Ho Chi Minh and the disciplined and determined communist nationalists. South Vietnam, however, largely stood alone and was vulnerable because of political infighting as well as their weak economy.

A string of five American presidents were unwilling to see Southeast Asian countries conquered by communist forces. Accordingly, each of them made the same commitment to forestall a communist victory. Presidents Truman and Eisenhower began American involvement by sending military advisers. Eisenhower administration officials felt that this policy of containing communist expansion saved South Korea from occupation by the communist north and China in another proxy war that had just ended. The Korean War guided the decision to continue American intervention in South Vietnam. Hardliner Secretary of State John Foster Dulles led the charge. Personnel from the US Army's First and Fifth Special Forces groups were assigned to Vietnam in 1957 to train and assist South Vietnamese forces so that they could handle the problem themselves. The Army of the Republic of Vietnam (ARVN) was created for national defense.

From the very beginning a simmering hostile environment existed between the two halves of what had been a single nation. In the late 1950s this bad blood, based on incompatible political underpinnings, slowly but inexorably devolved into violence. In 1959 Communist party leaders in Hanoi authorized their followers in the south to rise up against Ngo Dinh Diem, South Vietnam's new, but unpopular, leader. Reacting to these developments, 760 Americans were assigned to South Vietnam in an advisory role by the end of 1959. In an attack on their barracks near Saigon, the first Americans were killed in this burgeoning police action in July of that pivotal year. Undeclared war between the two Vietnamese states had begun.

In 1960 the National Liberation Front (NLF) was formed in South Vietnam with disaffected South Vietnamese and thousands of former Viet Minh fighters joining the ranks. NLF members became known as the Viet Cong and quickly spread across the country. This guerilla force was aided by the NVA. Guerilla and insurgency violence grew into widespread attacks in the South in the early 1960s.

South Vietnam was clearly the weaker sibling. Their troubles came from without and within. Communist insurgents operated throughout the south fomenting anti-government dissension and attacking governmental institutions. Internal political discord kept the South's partisan waters roiled, resulting in instability and political intrigue that plagued the country throughout its existence.

The United States threw its support behind Ngo Dinh Diem as the leader of the new country of South Vietnam. Diem was a French educated Catholic from a politically powerful family with many years of governmental experience. America supported Diem because, according to Secretary of State Dulles, "We knew of no one better." During his tenure Diem unfortunately split South Vietnam's influential religious culture by appearing pro-Catholic and anti-Buddhist. Buddhist anti-government sentiments were cemented in May 1963 when government troops fired on a Buddhist demonstration in the culturally important city of Hue, killing eight people. Diem served as president from 1955 until he and his brother Nhu were assassinated in a coup d'état in November 1963. The overthrow was masterminded by the South Vietnamese military and supported, perhaps even orchestrated (according to some historians), by the CIA. Whether or not America was complicit in the murder and overthrow of Diem, it sealed the deal; we were on a one-way dead-end course in South Vietnam with no real plan of action or exit strategy. America based her actions on one primary, but ill-defined goal: stem the spread of communism.

* * *

After departure of the French in 1956, ongoing hostilities in South Vietnam in the late 1950s and early 1960s could be politically and militarily viewed from three perspectives. The first was that the guerilla conflict was in actuality a civil war between pro- and anti-Diem groups in the South, with various religious and political tendrils. One could also view the hostilities as a war of reunification initiated by the North against the South. Ho Chi Minh, General Giap, and other leaders in the North were never going to settle for a divided country. The fact that by 1960 they were already aiding guerillas in the south to overthrow the government certainly supports this viewpoint. A third perspective was that the nascent war was part of the conspiracy by the Soviet Union and China to conquer weak third world countries and install communist regimes in them. Whichever of the three viewpoints political leaders and generals in Washington based their decisions on would dictate the way for America's future for the next twenty years.

From the very beginning of America's earliest involvement, it was always based on the fear of post–World War II communist takeovers, the belief that one weak country after another would inexorably fall to communist revolutionaries. Thus was born the *domino theory* of American military involvement following World War II.

All of the viewpoints about the situation in South Vietnam were accurate. Yes, there were civil war aspects to the violence, and yes, North Vietnam was trying to forcibly reunify Vietnam into one country;

the fact that the reunified country would be a communist bloc country, controlled by Russian and Chinese hardcore communist doctrine, was the key issue. If North Vietnam had intended to unify all of Vietnam under a western-style democracy, it would not have captured Washington's attention.

President Kennedy deployed additional special forces troops in an advisory role to the South Vietnamese military. There were about 20,000 American troops assisting the South Vietnamese Army by the time Kennedy was assassinated in 1963. Carrying most of America's combat load in South Vietnam at that very early date was the Army's Twenty-Fifth Infantry Division. They were stationed in the Mekong Delta region, the scene of much of the early fighting between Saigon and Hanoi-supported guerillas. In an effort to deprive food and cover for insurgents, the US military began Operation Ranch Hand in 1962. Lasting nine years, the operation involved aerial spraying of powerful herbicides in enemy strongholds and near American bases.

Lyndon Johnson, long a firm anti-communism senator before he became vice president, continued the same communism containment policy when he assumed the presidency following Kennedy's assassination.

After the 1963 coup, the South Vietnamese military establishment ruled, whether behind the scenes or directly. Instability was the common theme for years to come. After the Diem coup, a military junta ruled for only two months before it was itself kicked out by General Nguyen Khanh. Khanh's corruption and incompetence resulted in his resignation just months later. Incredibly, after just weeks during which one government after another failed, Khahn was back in office late in 1964. In February 1965 the chaos in South Vietnam took another unfortunate leap when two generals, Nguyen Cao Ky and Nguyen Van Thieu, supplanted Khan. Ky, a native of North Vietnam and a Buddhist, was head of the country's air force. Thieu hailed from the south and led a South Vietnamese Army infantry division. By June 1965 a coalition of ten generals, known as the National Leadership Committee, led by Ky and Thieu, ruled the country. Even as American troops were now dying on South Vietnamese soil to aid that country, the government in Saigon continued in disarray. Infighting, disarray, favoritism, and incompetence ruled the day.

As the face of the ruling junta, Ky was named prime minister from 1965 to 1967, when an election was held. Charismatic and outspoken, Ky was a natural person for the public position of prime minister. Behind the scenes things were not well. Ky and Thieu neither liked nor trusted one another, and their rivalry was widely known and disruptive to normal governance. Open elections were scheduled for September 1967. In June a large group of generals met for several days to determine who the candidates for president and vice president would be. They agreed on Thieu and Ky. Because of the war that was now raging, everyone understood that the military was to be the real power in the government, operating behind the scenes.

On September 3, 1967 South Vietnamese voters went to the polls to elect the president and vice president, as well as a legislative house that had little power or influence. Thieu and Ky were by no means the only candidates; there were numerous others from the many disorganized political organizations. There were so many candidates that even though Thieu and Ky won only 35 percent of the vote, it was enough to carry them to victory since all other candidates got far less. Once again America put all its eggs in this new Thieu/Ky basket because they were all we had. The Thieu and Ky administration, a front for the military regime that ruled the country, failed to bring reform and legitimacy to the government. Buddhist protests continued, morale and effectiveness in the military were low, peasants were unhappy, corruption was unchecked, and the war was going poorly. The die had been cast.

* * *

It stretches credibility to think that a problem thrust onto the world stage before most of the eventual combatants were born would continue to stew until it was our turn to face it as young adults. But as they're wont to do, years passed and the Vietnam problem festered and grew, like a cancer that knew no end to its ability to usurp lives.

The first time that future warfighters read about the 1963 coup d'état and the assassination of Diem, it meant nothing. There were gruesome photos printed in the glossy news magazines of the day, but that there was a coup in South Vietnam was well outside the things that the Vietnam War generation cared about. Like teens all across America, we didn't give a damn about Southeast Asia. Our lives were full. We had no time, energy, or desire to invest too much thought into problems that were thousands of miles away in a culture that may as well have been from another planet.

If we gave it much thought at all, we assumed that President Kennedy would find a way to handle this and other problems on the world stage. He took care of the Cuban missile crisis, after all. That threat was much closer to home and seemed much more real than political intrigues and monk immolations in Southeast Asia.

American youth practiced enough nuclear bomb drills in school to at least understand that nuclear weapons were serious stuff. The photographs and film footage we saw of Nagasaki and Hiroshima were enough to convince even self-absorbed middle-schoolers that this was serious. We could easily imagine what would happen if such weapons were dropped on American cities. Teachers and adults in my community said that if we ever went to war with Russia, our city would be an early target for elimination because of its heavy manufacturing and automobile industries. Many parents of my schoolmates worked in those factories. Accordingly, we were much more concerned about the Russian nuclear threat than Vietnam, Laos, or other countries in Southeast Asia whose exotic names we saw in print but knew nothing about. In the early 1960s the whole Indochina problem, as it was called before it was known simply as *Vietnam*, didn't seem like much of a threat, it was just something out there that we all assumed somebody would take care of.

The situation in Vietnam did not get better and, in fact, quickly went from bad to worse. The divide that was to follow the conflict for the next decade began in 1964, a watershed year for American involvement in Vietnam. The American military went to war in Vietnam and at home the American people began their campaign against the war. In May, twelve young men publicly burned their draft cards in New York City, and anti-war protests occurred in several cities across the nation that same month. American society was awakening to the reality of war and it wasn't pleased with what it saw.

The dangerous, slippery slope in Southeast Asia experienced a fatal plunge of no return with the so-called Gulf of Tonkin Incident in August 1964. Nothing happens in a vacuum, including this history-changing event. Advisors from the United States trained and directed South Vietnamese sailors to bomb radar stations, bridges, and other targets along the North Vietnamese coastline. As part of this activity, US warships, including the intelligence gathering destroyer *USS Maddox,* conducted electronic surveillance in the region and informed South Vietnam officials of findings. In the early hours of July 31, 1964, South Vietnamese boats shelled two North Vietnamese islands in the Gulf. After this attack, the *Maddox* sailed to the area. On August 2, the *Maddox* encountered three Russian-built torpedo boats that intended to force *Maddox* to leave the area. The *Maddox* fired first, issuing what the military described as warning shots. The three torpedo boats continued approaching and began firing at the *Maddox* with machine guns and torpedoes. F-8 Crusader jets from a nearby aircraft carrier assisted the *USS Maddox.* One North Vietnamese torpedo boat was badly damaged, but the *Maddox* was essentially undamaged, being hit by only one bullet.

The following day, the US destroyer *Turner Joy* was sent to reinforce the *Maddox,* and US-backed raids took place against two additional North Vietnamese defense positions. On August 4 the *Maddox* and *Turner Joy,* allegedly in waters claimed by North Vietnam, reported that they had been attacked by North Vietnamese warships firing twenty-two torpedoes at them. In response to this claim, President Johnson ordered air strikes against North Vietnamese boat bases and an oil storage depot.

Congress responded quickly to what was described as an unprovoked and unjustified attack against an American ship on the high seas. Despite the fact that two bloody wars had been fought by the United States in the past quarter century, it seemed that policy makers and public officials were itching for a fight against the communist bogeyman. Today the Joint Chiefs of Staff recommend a policy of proportional response to incidents, such as what occurred in the Gulf of Tonkin on those fateful summer days ("proportional, worth the cost, consistent with the law of war, and militarily and politically supportable"). Calm heads try to prevail to prevent a small incident from cascading into full blown war.

While war wasn't formally declared by Congress, they punted by passing the Gulf of Tonkin Resolution. This joint resolution of Congress (H.J. RES 1145), dated August 7, 1964, served as the legal basis for the military policies of President Lyndon Johnson and later President Nixon in Southeast Asia and in the fighting between North and South Vietnam. At the time of its authorization, the resolution provided authority for Johnson to do whatever he deemed best, to wit: "Congress approves and supports the determination of the president, as commander in chief, to take all necessary measures to repeal any armed attack against the forces of the United States and to prevent any further aggression." The House voted unanimously and only two senators opposed the resolution, thus it passed with broad support. Johnson's response was to send more soldiers, ships, and planes into the scrum, escalating it from a limited military advisory and assistance mission to full scale warfare.

With the subsequent release of intelligence documents, the Pentagon Papers, and fifty years of investigation, it eventually became quite likely that the second Gulf of Tonkin incident that was reported on August 4 never actually happened.

As public resistance to the war heightened, the Gulf of Tonkin Resolution was repealed by Congress in January 1971.

* * *

In February 1965 Johnson ordered the commencement of Operation Rolling Thunder, a bombing campaign against North Vietnam that was initially intended to last two months. It ended up lasting three years. On March 8, 1965, 3,500 Marines from the Ninth Marine Expeditionary Brigade landed on the beach in Da Nang to protect the vital US air base. In response to these rapid military escalations, the first major antiwar protest, initiated by a student group called Students for a Democratic Society, occurred on April 17, 1965 in Washington DC. Called the March on Washington to End the War in Vietnam, it was the largest peace protest up to that point in American history. Up to 25,000 college students and others marched on the nation's capital to show their concern and displeasure at the looming war. It was the first of many. The deep divide in American society regarding the war had begun and would only get much worse.

In May 1965 the Army's 173rd Airborne Brigade arrived in South Vietnam, followed two months later by the First Infantry Division and the 101st Airborne. The First Cavalry Division/Airmobile and the Eighteenth Engineering Brigade arrived in September. By the end of 1965 there were 184,300 American troops in South Vietnam, as well as Naval and Air Force assets in offshore waters and nearby air bases in regional countries. President Johnson originally deployed troops to provide protection for American bases and facilities. Duties quickly changed from protective to offensive after guerillas attacked key bases.

The war also became a multi-nation affair in 1965, with American allies sending troops to South Vietnam. South Korea, Australia, Thailand, New Zealand, and the Philippines all provided military assistance. South Korea in particular was an important ally in the effort, with as many as 50,000 soldiers assigned at the peak of their involvement in 1968.

Though support was always lukewarm at best, in the mid-1960s many Americans still believed that we were on the right side in this war. Whether we should have become involved in the first place could be argued, but the legality and justness of the South Vietnamese cause seemed clear. A sovereign country we were allied with was being invaded by a communist neighbor with the singular goal of domination and indoctrination, with urging and material support from the Marxist giants of Russia and China, America's avowed enemies.

North Vietnam had one of the largest land armies in the world, behind only the Soviet Union, China, and, of course, the US. Economically they were a poor and undeveloped country that could never sustain such a large military by themselves. Nobody was threatening their borders. Why did they need such a huge force? The answer was coming into focus.

South Vietnam didn't have a chance for survival unless we fought on their behalf. Popular magazines of the time wrote of the atrocities committed by the Viet Cong and their communist backers and detailed the exodus of Christian Vietnamese from the North due to persecution and imprisonment. Clearly, it seemed, we were on the side of good and right. And didn't we surely have a moral responsibility to help them in their struggle? Wouldn't failure to act be akin to a strong, healthy young man standing by and doing nothing when he saw a thug beating and robbing a defenseless person?

Any hope for a political resolution to end the war was not to be. Instead things spiraled downward. The Vietnam problem grew, and more people died, and more soldiers were needed so that the faceless enemy could be defeated. But with every increase in troop numbers, more American soldiers died, and the ranks of the anonymous enemy seemed unfazed.

It was the Battle of Ia Drang in the fall of 1965 that served as a hard slap in the face for the average American. The death of 237 soldiers and many more wounded in two separate related battles forced Americans to view this faraway war differently. The home front was forced to understand that this was not just a police action, as Washington politicians tried to label it, or a war being waged solely by the South Vietnamese Army. American soldiers were fighting and dying. Battlefield reports made it clear that it was a war in which American soldiers were going to die in large numbers.

The military conscription system in effect at the time meant that every young male was eligible to be drafted into the Army after his eighteenth birthday. A few people we knew, boys who graduated from our high schools just a year or two earlier, were going there to fight.

Reports on the nightly news about large battles and Americans dying in Vietnam became a routine part of American life. But with each passing month, with each broadcast on the six o'clock news of the weekly count of dead and wounded Americans, coupled with the lack of credible reports about territory won and held, the number of Americans willing to sacrifice their sons in *Johnson's War* grew smaller. It was clear to all Americans that this war was different. It lacked the noble cause and desperate struggle for survival that marked other major conflicts America had found itself in. By the end of 1967 over 485,000 Americans were deployed in South Vietnam. Despite the great increase in troop numbers, the dropping of bombs at a rate never witnessed before, and the expenditure of billions of dollars, there was no light at the end of the deadly tunnel.

How did it all happen? How had this small problem on the distant side of the world that was going to be taken care of by diplomacy and highly skilled military advisors grown into this unquenchable fire that seemed to consume American society and affect millions of individual lives? How could fundamental questions of right and wrong, of what's correct and incorrect, of what's good and bad, of what's patriotic and unpatriotic, have changed so suddenly? Just how the hell did we get into this very real war that we all knew even then was unlike any other? These were hard questions that Americans, who had for years ignored developments in Vietnam, began asking.

# CHAPTER 2

# OUR CONFLICTED
# GENERATION

A history of the Vietnam War could appropriately just focus on decision makers and war veterans, but a comprehensive and accurate history must report the story of the war's impact on the entire generation that was affected by it. Vietnam, after all, was a war that none of us wanted. We inherited it because of the decisions of others, and our generation, the Vietnam generation, had to deal with it. The seeds of this war, after all, were planted following World War II, before most of the Vietnam generation was born.

While no generation is a homogenous collection of individuals marching in lockstep, many peer groups are unified by similar circumstances or dedication to a singular cause. A classic example is the World War II generation. This so-called greatest generation was molded in the difficulties of the Great Depression and WWII. Forces and events beyond their control worked to bring members of that generation together in a mutually important common cause.

Sometimes, however, a generation is irreparably divided by powerful events. The Civil War generation in America was one such divided age. The Vietnam generation was the next. These wars separated Americans along fault lines of tectonic proportions. In both instances, the nation was deeply divided, and society torn asunder politically, socially, and emotionally.

As was the case with the Civil War, the Vietnam War required Americans, especially young Americans, to choose a side. It forced citizens to decide where they stood relative to the faraway conflict and our country's policy regarding it. Issues surrounding the war tested the resolve and values of good and patriotic Americans as much as any event in the country's long and storied history. The war required us to arrive at our own definition of patriotism and of what constituted right and wrong. For most Americans the dividing line was support or opposition to the war. Whatever actions they might take in response to the war depended first and foremost on which side of this line one fell.

This Vietnam generation was comprised of idealistic men and women forged in the fires of controversy that surrounded the war, if not in the flames of war itself. All of the young men and women who grew up with the war were affected by it. Millions of youth and their families shared similar experiences as they moved through life prior to, during, and following the Vietnam War. The lives of every member of the Vietnam generation were changed. It mattered not if their war experiences were limited to campus protests, lives were forever changed in an attempt to avoid the military draft, or as a member of the United States armed forces. For those coming of age during the Vietnam era the war was an impossible-to-ignore 800-pound gorilla in the room that affected lives with a totality that is hard to imagine decades later.

Attitudes about the war were strongly influenced by age, gender, and political ideology. Young men between the ages of eighteen and twenty-five, and therefore eligible for the draft, had the most at stake. For them Vietnam was an actual or potential reality, not just a political debate or societal phenomenon. Even with an eighteen-year-old male's attitude of invincibility, it was becoming worrisome. It abruptly hit us that this was real, and it could affect us individually. We could end up there! How would we respond? Could we handle it? What were our options?

By 1967 almost everyone knew of somebody who fought or died in the war. It was no longer an obscure place or far-off problem. It was real, and many of us had to come to terms with it. As the scope and intensity of the war grew, steps to stay out of the Army took on a new urgency for many of the nation's youth. Ways to avoid being caught up in it became common topics of conversation within families and in classrooms. Unthinkable actions became reasonable, and even acceptable, by many. Moving to Canada, going underground, even desertion—these were new means to avoid the draft or avoid service in Vietnam. Getting into college to avoid the draft was one of the primary reasons teachers urged hard work and study for good grades. Those who received bad grades or got in trouble with the law wouldn't get into college and would be drafted and sent to Vietnam; this became the oft-repeated mantra of teachers, parents, and counselors.

Youth subject to military conscription were forced to make decisions and take actions because of their liability for the mandatory draft. The decision-making process was complex and the consequences of their decision, great. Almost all of us trod difficult pathways in a search for the definition of right and wrong relative to America's involvement in this faraway land. It was a time of gray shadings with little cast in black and white. Many tried to simply ignore the war, hoping it wouldn't interfere with their lives. But 800-pound gorillas are not to be ignored. None of us wanted the war, but it ended up defining us and forced each of us to determine which side of the line we were on. Once philosophically situated we then had to decide what our next step was. Decisions made at the time based on existing circumstances continue to affect the lives of the Vietnam generation decades later.

Young men were urged to find a lawful means of avoiding the draft and military service. Some were able to avoid the war by purposely taking advantage of various draft deferments or exemptions that allowed them to avoid military service. For most that meant a college deferment. Some close to college graduation stayed to earn advanced degrees rather than become eligible for the draft. Religious vocations and other exemptions or deferments were explored. More than a few men got married, hoping that a wife and children would keep them out of harm's way, though the marriage exemption was done away with in 1965.

Some refused to accept the war and rallied against it with all that they had, even forsaking the country of their birth if necessary. One did not casually oppose federal law regarding mandatory military conscription. If potential draftees strongly opposed involvement in the war, they had stark choices to make that had wide-reaching and long-lasting ramifications.

A third group was the millions of young men who had no deferments or circumstances that shielded them from military service during the long Vietnam era. They were either drafted or voluntarily enlisted into the military. If being drafted into the Army appeared a reality, the war caused draftees to consider options of enlisting into military branches that minimized the likelihood of a Vietnam deployment or at least lessened potential for a combat assignment.

Society was changed by this puzzling and unconventional Asian war. Difficult questions were debated in college dorm rooms, living rooms, restaurant booths, and offices across the country. What obligation did we have to go thousands of miles away to fight in a war involving two foreign countries with whom we had no long-term relationship and in which we were not being threatened? Did we have a moral responsibility to go, or did we have a moral responsibility to stay out of the fight? Was it altruism or imperialism? These were tough questions for kids who were more concerned about grades, girls, and cars than international diplomacy and war.

The military was a respected institution all across America in the post-World War II years. Almost everyone had a relative that served during the last good war and twenty years later sons and nephews still talked about what were by then no doubt exaggerated heroic deeds of those men. But dramatic changes in attitudes toward military service were underway. The spirit of military service hadn't died altogether, but clearly a critical mass of American youth made the decision that this war was not worth the potential costs.

In my blue-collar community, college was a possibility for a few, not a likelihood for the majority. In a sense, that made my decision easier. My friends and I were mostly of a similar mind about military service. It should not be assumed that support for the military equated to support for the war. That was not the case in many families. But despite that fact, friends enlisted or at least did not try to avoid the draft. Family pride and carrying on the tradition of service had much to do with it. In my family, all four of my mother's brothers and her sister served in the military during World War II. An uncle on my father's side was a doctor in that war. Taking steps to intentionally avoid military service wasn't going to happen.

Many young Americans did not feel that college was the correct course of action, regardless of the protection it provided from the draft. Such was the case for me and several close friends. Midway through my sophomore year I left school, fully aware of the consequences that came with the decision. If an otherwise healthy young man wasn't in college, they were eligible for the draft. That was a fact of life for our generation.

In the midst of 1967's Summer of Love, when singer Scott McKenzie sang about young Americans heading to a love-in in San Francisco and with worsening news from Vietnam, many of us chose a path of military service. For a wide variety of reasons, countless young men became voluntary recruits in the armed forces. For me it meant a trip to the local Marine Corps recruiter where I signed my name on the proverbial bottom line.

Young enlistees didn't dwell on the possible consequences of our decision, though we were fully aware of what our actions might mean. Daily news accounts on the television and in newspapers made the stark reality of the war clear. We enlisted anyway because we believed that our country needed us.

* * *

On a personal level, the confidence and conviction I had that going to battle on behalf of South Vietnam was a good and noble thing took a powerful hit a few days after enlistment. For a year I had labored as a roustabout for a small oilfield driller and producer. I worked almost daily with the foreman, Doug. We got along well, despite the difference of more than twenty years of age and our political beliefs. He was a large, gruff, conservative World War II veteran and Protestant, and I was a Catholic from a family of several generations of blue-collar Democrats. He called me a minnow-muncher, I called him a heretic, and we got along just fine.

Doug hired me during a card game at a party I happened to go to at the end of my freshman year of college. I had never met him before that party and happened to end up as his Euchre card-game partner. I had just turned nineteen, was in peak physical condition, and used to hard work from growing up on a large farm. As fate would have it, he was looking for a strong and willing laborer to work his tail off in the oilfields. After we played cards for a while, downing three or four beers in the hot Sunday afternoon sun, he asked in a rather dismissive tone if I knew how to work hard.

His condescending attitude really pissed me off. I replied, "I've worked hard my entire life on the farm and can sure as hell work harder than you!"

"You think so, huh?" was his response. "Then meet me tomorrow morning at six thirty."

I did, not feeling at all well after too many beers and too little sleep. We spent the day working hard and sweating in the sun and I ended up working my proverbial tail off with Doug for a year.

A few days after enlisting in the corps I broke the news to Doug that I was to leave for boot camp soon. I didn't expect cheers but certainly hadn't anticipated what happened. He looked at me with a distressed look on his face unlike any I had ever seen him make as he struggled for words. Finally, he blurted out "You goddamned fool, you should have gone to Canada instead!"

I was dumfounded to say the least, and at a loss for words. He walked away without looking back. We hardly spoke after that. He was truly angry and worried and was disappointed in my decision. It was this sort of lack of clear public sentiment and support that caused confusion and a lack of clarity as to mission for a great many young men. The non-supportive sentiment exhibited by others followed soldiers from the point of their military enlistment, during assignment in Vietnam, and for years following their return home. Mr. and Mrs. America, it seemed in large part, did not support our involvement in the military at that time, even though Uncle Sam was quite adamant about our participation.

This illustrated a dilemma unique to the Vietnam generation. In the two World Wars enlistment was equated with patriotism and was expected unless there was an overwhelming reason why a person couldn't enlist. In the Vietnam War, enlistment was equated by many Americans as foolishness or even stupidity, or worse, a lack of moral character because it implied that one was willing to kill for an illegitimate reason. The *baby killer* epithet, frequently heard by returning Vietnam vets at airports, left no doubt as to how a lot of Americans felt about the illegitimacy of the war. The moral culpability of those who participated was also made clear.

These thoughts and doubts that were planted in the back of our minds, and their subtle psychological impacts, became part of a large dark cloud that had moved from the horizon to directly overhead for thousands of patriotic young Americans.

* * *

There were three powerful forces at play a half-century ago affecting the Vietnam generation that no longer exist, making comparisons between then and now difficult. The first of those factors was the military draft that affected all young men. The reality of potentially being forced into the military during wartime, notwithstanding other plans, was a powerful influence. The second condition in play was significant public opposition to the war and against those guilty by association by serving in the military. Support for the military establishment had plummeted during the decade of the 1960s. Another powerful background circumstance that greatly affected life and politics fifty years ago was prevailing concern about the seemingly inexorable spread of communism and the expanding international influence of the Soviet Union and Red China. Unlike today, these two powerful empires weren't trading partners; they were clear and present enemies of America. Our international policy decisions during that era were greatly influenced by the exceedingly heated tensions and ideological competition that existed at the time.

Much has changed socially and politically since the 1960s. The all-volunteer military that exists today, strong support of military personnel and the armed forces in general by the public, and the end of the Cold War create a very different reality and mindset. Viewing the Vietnam War from the perspective of twenty-first century realities make it almost impossible for young people today to fully appreciate the temperament of the 1960s and 1970s.

* * *

If a person were to judge the Vietnam generation based on video and news accounts of that era, they might come to a faulty conclusion. Anti-war protests, uncivil discourse, burning of draft cards, civil disobedience, violence, and animosity toward the government and institutions could create a picture of arrogance, disrespect, and lack of patriotism. That would be a faulty conclusion in large part. Members of our generation were ready and willing to bear any burden, pay any price and ask what we could do for our country, as President Kennedy challenged us to do. We were ready to carry our burden when the time came. And we did. Many just did not want our legacy to be yet another war in a faraway land based on questionable motives. Our generation had what many considered to be more important social and domestic goals that were difficult to achieve in parallel with war.

Far from being self-focused and unpatriotic, the Vietnam generation spawned a period of social activism. Societal ills were being addressed after decades of neglect. It was our generation that had the courage to recognize that it was time to change long-held assumptions when it came to issues such as the environment, women's rights, civil rights, poverty, and other major domestic ills. We were determined to be different, more socially aware, wiser, less interested in material things and money. We coalesced under the influences of different forces than earlier Americans and our troubles and goals were dissimilar in many ways to theirs. We were the generation, after all, that came of age under the threat of nuclear annihilation. Our reminiscences of childhood were not primarily of an innocent and peaceful time. Our memories were of nuclear attack drills in school, being assured by unconvinced adults that hiding under our desks would keep us safe when nuclear missiles were launched against our towns.

We saw numerous problems in our communities that needed the nation's focus. Americans that came of age during that period have memories of discrimination, segregation, poverty, riots, racism, and destruction of the environment. Far from apathetic, most young Americans desired to make their country a better place by focusing our attention and resources on correction of the many ills affecting America and the world. War would only take attention and resources away from important social issues of the day.

Most generations face unique challenges that determine their role in history. What made our generation difficult to navigate is that, though we wanted to focus on other things and didn't want war, we had it anyway. Our ancestors had their wars and we had ours; war seemed the only constant. Unlike earlier wars, the simmering Vietnam conflict didn't unite our generation or our country behind a common cause. It divided us along lines that left little room for flexibility or empathetic understanding of the other. This ever-present and complex issue we simply called *Vietnam* in the end defined our generation.

All these years later most of our generation still has reminders of the Vietnam War era. For some these reminders are perhaps bittersweet memories of their tumultuous youth, part of their college experience and an introduction to protest and civil disobedience, hoping to bring an early end to what they saw as an unwise and perhaps even illegal war. For combatants the pull of memories is much stronger. Many combat veterans carry the physical scars and aches that each day remind them of the circumstances and places they received their painful memento. Frontline infantrymen who bore the brunt of that brutal guerilla war have emotional scars to live with and memories that they'd very much like to forget but never will.

Veterans have their hard-earned military ribbons and medals to remind them of a youth spent in a faraway land doing things that had once been unimaginable. They have artifacts brought home both as trophies of sorts and as souvenirs, a modern-day form of plunder gathered on the battlefield. The keepsakes bring back immediate feelings and memories that, though unpleasant, are also too much of one's life to discard. To throw away one of these medals or artifacts would be like removing a part of the body. These objects are at the same time a source of great pride and of dark anxiety.

In tens of thousands of homes, Vietnam is remembered because of a son or other relative who went away as a young man and never returned. They exist today forever young in faded photographs that are poignantly remembered by the holder of the photo or used to explain to young family members who the soldier was and where and why he died.

For almost everyone who was old enough to know what was happening during the war, memories include the weekly announcement on nightly six o'clock news shows of how many young men were killed that week. These newscasts kept the waters stirred because they frequently graphically displayed the societal bifurcation that was being played out every day. On the same news show a viewer saw film of antiwar protests and a few minutes later, from the safety of their recliner, watched video footage of actual battles that occurred just hours before in Vietnam.

* * *

One of the trademarks of this distinctive generation was the music. More than any other war, Vietnam had an accompanying soundtrack. Music was inextricably connected with the war, both pro and con. Music was part of every war America was involved in, from the War of Independence to World War II. But it was different this time. Wartime music in the past was predominantly patriotic and supportive. It buttressed the war effort and let the troops know that their countrymen were behind them. This wasn't the case during the Vietnam War. There were clearly more songs in opposition to the war than in rallying support for the war effort and the troops. This didn't bode well for those hoping for a unified populace.

One can follow the course of the war by reading the lyrics of popular songs. As the 1960s began, popular music was largely about happy days and good times—cars, teenage love and youthful angst, surfing, partying, and dancing to the latest trends. By mid-decade the tone was changing. There was music that spoke to concerns of the nation, especially of the young. Lyrics warned of wars and of killing and of hatreds and of what was wrong. On the flip side, other songs began rallying public support of the military through patriotic messages and of duty.

Early songs of warning, such as Barry McGuire's "Eve of Destruction" and "For What it's Worth" by Buffalo Springfield, spoke to young people who were about to enter the world at large. The line "You're old enough to kill but not to vote" in McGuire's tune struck a responsive chord with eighteen-year-olds now eligible for the draft. Songwriter Phil Ochs' "I Ain't Marching Anymore" and Pete Seeger's "Bring 'em Home" were raising national consciousness and concerns about the rapidly widening war by the mid-1960s.

As high schoolers we sang along as these songs played on the car radio. Coming as they did on the heels of the Cuban Missile Crisis, President Kennedy's assassination, and the early steps of irreversible involvement into the quagmire in Vietnam, we understood that these weren't the fun lyrics of typical adolescent music. They had a message and a warning, and we listened. We all felt a growing dread, a feeling that our future wasn't as bright as it used to be.

The music evolved as the war grew and lyrics took on a clear anti-war tone, not just a precautionary message. Soon the likes of Credence Clearwater Revival or CCR, Bob Dylan, Steppenwolf, Jimi Hendrix, The Doors, John Lennon, and many others joined in the musical anti-war/pro-peace sentiments. Originally most songs were fairly generic in their antiwar or peace themes. As the number of dead Americans increased, and the likelihood for a quick end to the hostilities lessened, lyrics became more pointed. Edwin Starr's "War: What is it Good For? (Absolutely Nothing)" and The Association's "Requiem for the Masses" put the issue of death and destruction front and center. Subtleties were dropped and antiwar messages based on the brutal realities of war became more direct. Music also began to reflect the very real divide that existed in American culture. CCR's "Fortunate Son" made clear the different worlds of the haves and have nots as related to the military draft and compulsory service. Fortunate sons, offspring of the wealthy or well-connected, could wave the flag without the unpleasant consequences of having to fight for the flag. The less fortunate carried that burden.

On a parallel, but opposite course, was music that supported the war—or at least the concept of military service and honor. SSgt. Barry Sadler's "Ballad of the Green Beret" in 1966 was popular and linked the ideals of patriotism to military duty. Even Senator Dirksen from Illinois recorded a patriotic song in 1967 called "Gallant Men." It celebrated the concept of fighting and, if necessary, dying for one's country. Merle Haggard's "Okie From Muskogee" and "The Fightin' Side of Me" were typical of primarily country music songs that reverberated from radios and eight-track tape players in pickup trucks all across America in support of the government's decisions and policies toward the war. These songs also directly or subtly questioned the patriotism and values of young antiwar protestors.

These dueling musical lyrics had the effect of further dividing the nation. The youthful antiwar portion of the population sang the anthems of peace with gusto. The older blue-collar portion of the population,

President Nixon's supportive *silent majority* and *hardhat* factions, found solace in the patriotic lyrics of songs such as Sadler's "Green Berets."

There is no question that the music of the era strongly influenced attitudes about the war. The antiwar message clearly seemed the more powerful force in the end, and that helped shape public opinion against the war.

The Vietnam soundtrack didn't end with the war's end. The same phenomenon occurred in the years after the war, with several artists writing songs about the plight of the Vietnam veteran. The majority of songs focused on the desperate predicament of veterans and the lack of support or empathy by their country and countrymen. Lyrics described the difficulties they experienced trying to rejoin mainstream American society. Bruce Springsteen, the Charlie Daniels Band, Billy Joel and many other artists wouldn't allow America to simply forget. They sang of unemployment, an uncaring society, mental health problems, memories that wouldn't go away, and about vets just giving up the fight. Springsteen's "Born in the USA", Charlie Daniels' "Still in Saigon," and Joel's "Goodnight Saigon" were powerful anthems of the post-war period. But just like American society not understanding the plight of her veterans, many in society didn't understand the messages in these songs. They mistakenly took "Born in the USA" as a patriotic rally-round-the-flag tune rather than comprehending the message of what it's like to be on the outside looking in. Anyone who listened closely to the lyrics of Joel's "Goodnight Saigon" might gain a glimpse into the ethos of grunts, willing to go down together rather than violate the sacred code of being there for the other.

For all of us in the Vietnam generation powerful memories are nearly as fresh in our minds as when they were formed. All it takes is the right song, picture, or person to awaken them and they all come flooding back in an inexorable and overpowering wave of emotions.

# CHAPTER 3

# THE MAKING
# OF MARINES

Boot camp was all that Marine recruits were warned it would be, but about which in reality we had absolutely no clue. Oh sure, we were warned. We were told stories by former marines and GIs about what we were about to experience. But we assumed that half of it was hype to enhance the teller's own status and that what remained of boot camp reality we could handle with barely breaking a sweat. We were wrong.

Recruits from the easternmost United States were sent to the Marine Corps Recruit Depot at Parris Island in the stifling South Carolina swamps for boot camp. Would-be marines from the western two-thirds of the country went to MCRD at San Diego in the Southern California desert heat. Along with families and business passengers, myself and a dozen other young enlistees took a commercial flight from Detroit to Los Angeles. Upon arrival at Los Angeles International Airport we were led by a surly and strangely silent sergeant to a green US Marine Corps bus parked in the sun. We loaded onto the bus and the sergeant climbed behind the wheel to transport us the remaining two hours to our new home. Assuming that normal civilian norms were still applicable, we immediately opened windows in the hot bus.

The sergeant jumped out of his seat and roared, "Who the fuck said you could open the windows? Shut them and sit the fuck down and don't say a goddamn word until we get to the base. If the Corps wants you to say something or do anything you'll be told. Until then, just shut the fuck up and don't move from your seat!"

Well, okay. The stage had been set. From the moment we arrived at MCRD to the day we finally graduated, it was a world unlike any other. The Corps' method of breaking down self-serving individuals and re-forming them into loyal, hard-fighting team members isn't easy to take but it is effective.

It began immediately upon getting off the bus, at which point we were ordered to stand on footprints painted in yellow on the hot asphalt. We met our drill instructors: two sergeants and a staff sergeant who was the head drill instructor (DI), quite obviously positioned right next to God himself. As we stood at attention on our footprint markers, we were given a quick introduction to the new facts of life at MCRD. It's fair to say that we were all in a state of shock and thinking *Oh, shit!* to ourselves.

Following that indoctrination, we marched to the best of our ability to a nearby building that served as the first stop on our voyage into the unknown. Two things happened immediately to strip away any sense of the individuality we brought with us. Each recruit was stripped of their civilian clothes, which were shipped home. There would be no need for civvies for many long weeks. Next, hair was cut as quickly and closely to the scalp as possible with electric razors. There is probably no more effective way of taking away a young man's individuality than by shaving his head. Standing in line in our underwear, various sergeants, clerks, medical staff, and others involved in the entry process harangued us with endless shouted orders.

We received numerous shots, administered by corpsmen much more concerned about speed than patient comfort. Measurements were roughly taken by a supply sergeant tired of seeing nearly naked recruits, and utility uniforms that were to be our clothing for the coming months were thrown at us by the sergeant's helper. Miscellaneous other gear, ranging from boots to rifles, was also issued during the day long process. The yelling and belittling remarks didn't pause for a second.

From the supply building we marched to hot Quonset huts that were to be our homes. We were shown exactly how everything was to be arranged and how beds were to be made, with a blanket and sheet so tightly spread that a quarter would bounce when dropped on the bed. These requirements weren't idle threats. During the course of boot camp, while we were partaking in the many activities that filled our days, DIs inspected the Quonset huts to ensure that everything was correct. Woe betide to the recruit whose footlocker contents weren't exactly arranged or whose bed wasn't perfectly made, bouncing quarter and all. His bedding and gear would be found spread around the grounds outside the building and he would spend his precious break time putting everything back in proper order.

Adjusting to the vernacular used in boot camp came quickly. We were no longer individuals with names, we were "You fucking maggots" or "You worthless pond scum". Recruits were informed of the slightest error by the drill instructor shouting and spitting an inch from one's face "Outfuckingstanding, fool! Now get down and give me twenty!" (push-ups). There were many other warm and fuzzy expressive terms and phrases that were part of everyday one-way conversations at MCRD, most of which fortunately never took root in civilian life.

There was, of course, reason behind the madness. Several key lessons had to be taught quickly and permanently. Military organizations long ago figured out effective means to accomplish this educational process. One of the most important lessons was that, in the military, if one person screws up in his or her task, everyone pays the consequence. This concept was a basic fundamental exercise throughout training. If one recruit did something wrong, every recruit in the platoon was penalized. A misstep by one person caused the entire platoon to run a mile or to march on the hot asphalt grinder for another hour under the broiling sun, going through close order drill procedures for the twentieth time. This approach not only taught the primary underlying lesson, but also served as a mechanism by which the team helped an individual do better. A screw-up who routinely caused problems for the platoon was strongly encouraged to do better by his peers, with consequences of his own if he didn't. It was a lesson hard learned but vital in a team event such as combat or most other military functions.

Another message that was on display throughout was the concept of chain of command and unquestioned response to commands. It wasn't up to an individual soldier or marine to ponder an order and take time to decide whether a particular command should be carried out. A military team had to respond immediately and properly. The *immediate* part of the equation was taught in boot camp. The *properly* factor was taught in months of specialized training that followed basic training.

One of the hardest lessons to learn was that the mission is about the unit—the team— not the individual. Soldiers and marines had to lose the self-focus and self-importance we're all born with and think about what's best for the unit and the mission. We had to learn to put ourselves below the needs and actions of the whole, even if it placed the individual in grave danger.

Raising a person's breaking point was another prime objective. That, and instilling a sense of discipline that went hand-in-hand with a raised breaking point. One of my more unpleasant memories of boot camp was being on the receiving end of a teachable moment in which these principles were demonstrated. A significant part of boot camp involved precision close-order drill maneuvers. Countless hours were spent on the hot asphalt lot, called *the Grinder*, practicing these drills. In addition to precision marching steps and coordinated unit movements, precise use of the rifle was paramount. We practiced rifle drills endlessly. They had to be exact and fast, in perfect unison with other movements and with forty-five other recruits. It was all difficult to master.

One day the head drill instructor noticed that my rifle was *canted* on my shoulder. The term meant that it wasn't perfectly vertical. He stopped in front of me and, without warning, slammed the rifle into the side of my head. It hurt like hell. I could feel drops of blood dripping down the side of my neck from broken skin on my ear. The split second he did this my left hand automatically closed into a fist and unfortunately instinctively moved a couple inches.

That was exactly what he wanted. He got in my face and screamed "You want to hit me? You fucking puke, you want to fucking hit me? Go ahead, you sorry son of a bitch, hit me!" He was screaming an inch from my face, trying his best to provoke me.

I sure as hell wanted to hit him. I wanted to kick the hell out of him and leave him lying on the hot asphalt. But I controlled myself. My sense of discipline took over. "No, *sir!*" I lied, in response to his several taunts. This sort of incident was used on everyone. The root event was different, but the taunting and attempts to get the recruit to succumb to their baser temptations were constant. The corps knew we were ultimately going to encounter incidents much worse than whatever we might experience in boot camp and we had to learn to not cave to our baser instincts.

Practicing self-control wasn't just being smart enough to learn a hard-earned lesson. It also had a self-serving aspect. We knew what would happen if we did hit a drill instructor. Such action meant being sent to the Corrective Custody Platoon. In that slice of hell offenders spent days in the hot sun busting big rocks into small ones and sundry other miserable activities. One avoided the CC platoon at all costs.

\* \* \*

I had an unexpected fundamental decision to make early in boot camp that could have changed my future dramatically. Based on the results of a series of aptitude tests we took a few days after arrival, I was called into the command hut of the chief drill instructor one day along with one other recruit. We had no idea what we had done wrong, but we knew we were in deep shit. There was no other reason why anyone was ordered into the staff sergeant's hut. He informed us—obviously based on subterfuge and cheating on our part, in his words—that we *two lowly worms* had scored high on the tests and qualified for acceptance in the Marine Corps' Officer Candidate School. We had to decide then and there whether we would accept this unique opportunity. After a couple minutes of thought, I declined. The DI was beyond indignant; he was angry, very angry. He commenced tearing into me for turning down the Corps after they extended such an incredible opportunity to an unworthy lowlife such as me. I was convinced that the head DI had a grudge against me for the next two months for my arrogance. He knew me personally after that, and that's never a good thing.

The Corps needed line officers as badly as it needed PFCs, due to battlefield casualties, and clearly DIs were under pressure to *encourage* qualifying candidates to pursue the OCS path.

Going to OCS was an incredible opportunity. It would have meant a longer enlistment, however, which was unthinkable at the time. Throughout my life I have occasionally thought about where I'd be and what I'd be doing had I said yes to OCS. Odds are that I'd be dead, as the life span of second lieutenant combat platoon leaders in Vietnam was short indeed. Had I survived the war, skills learned in OCS would have been of great value in my adult life and I would have proudly carried the honor of being a graduate of that fine institution.

* * *

In addition to psychological training, there was of course a great deal of emphasis on physical fitness. We exercised constantly in every manner. We ran, we did pushups and pullups, and we carried heavy weights. There was intense training in hand-to-hand combat. One of the most memorable was with pugil sticks. It was no-holds-barred. If a recruit didn't hit someone hard enough, the DI took the stick and showed him how it was done, with the guilty recruit the victim. Time was spent crawling in the mud below barbed wire and carrying recruits on our backs as if they were wounded. There were many classes on military history, the Uniform Code of Military Justice, and similar topics. The classroom work was like time off. We paid attention because there were regular tests and the old corps instructors did not grade on a curve. At the end of every day we were dead tired and needed no help falling asleep.

\* \* \*

Much time was spent with our assigned M-14 rifle. We disassembled and reassembled them every day and rubbed linseed oil into the wood stock and forearm daily. They had to shine. We had to take them apart and put them back together blindfolded. Perhaps the very first lesson we learned about our rifles was that they're not called *guns*. Pity the poor recruit who called his rifle a *gun*. He was made to stand in front of everyone, drop his pants, grab his crotch with one hand and hold his rifle with the other and yell as loudly as he could: "This is my rifle; this is my gun. This is for shooting; this is for fun."

\* \* \*

There was a head DI and two assistants. A drill instructor was with us twenty-four seven. Generally, once per day we got a break. The DI proclaimed that "the smoking lamp is lit. Smoke 'em if you got 'em." Some recruits lit cigarettes, some just relaxed, and others took the opportunity to write a quick letter home, if feasible. It was generally during this short midafternoon break that we all took our salt tablet. In the days before fortified sports drinks it was thought that salt tabs were the correct way to replenish electrolytes lost to sweat and exertion. Every parent, coach, and drill instructors believed in this folk wisdom during that time period and we dutifully took our salt pills, not knowing they were likely doing more harm than good.

Boot camp included an intense week at the rifle range at Camp Pendleton, located about forty miles to the north. In some ways that week was the most painful of the entire process, as we were forced into positions that locked body and rifle into one steady single entity. Called *snapping in*, it was body alignment and rifle steadiness that resulted in the ability to hit a bullseye 500 meters away. Passing the final marksmanship test at the end of firearms training wasn't optional. Fail and you do it all over again in a new platoon. There were three levels of competence available at the final *shoot for score* day. They were marksman, sharpshooter and expert. I earned the sharpshooter badge, missing the coveted expert award by just three points.

In the last few days of boot camp, each recruit learned their Military Occupational Specialty (MOS). The 0300 MOS group included all infantry classes, including rifleman, machine gunner, recon, sniper, and other disciplines connected with ground frontline combat. Fate declared that I was an 0311–rifleman, those select few that in Vietnam earned the honorable title of grunt. I wasn't surprised. Obviously, more recruits were assigned the 0300 specialty than any other, given the basic mission of the Marine Corps. Other recruits were assigned to other functions, ranging from artillery to truck driver. It was a heightened level of attention to detail that we 0300s carried from that moment forward.

There are few things in life for which I wouldn't take a million dollars for the experience but that I also would not do again for twice that amount. Boot camp and infantry training certainly fall in that category. It was tough, but I also knew it was the gateway into the Corps and that entry into this elite group should not be easy, given the task we were going to be expected to do. A person can accept verbal derision and physical abuse if one knows it's for a cause and an end goal that they support, and they know there is an end to it at some point. I don't know if boot camp in peacetime is less severe, but in 1967 MCRD was an intense place.

* * *

During my boot camp and subsequent training assignments, soldiers and marines in Vietnam were fighting some of the fiercest battles yet in the war. And conditions were clearly getting worse, not better. There was no light at the end of the tunnel as Americans were assured, unless that light was in reality an onrushing out-of-control train. Casualties were heavy and replacements were badly needed. We were those replacements, and we knew it. And to make sure we didn't forget, our drill instructors reminded us of that fact daily in the strongest means possible. They emphasized their point by singling out those that they publicly declared would be dead in six months because of their ineptitude, stupidity, or arrogance. In the back of all of our minds was the thought *I volunteered for this?*

With the successful completion of boot camp came the moment we all worked so hard for: the day we graduated. We were no longer recruits (or pond scum, pukes, fucking maggots, girls, worthless bastards, or other terms of endearment); we had made the grade and officially earned the title of US Marine.

After completion of boot camp at MCRD our next stop in training took us to Camp Pendleton. This huge Marine Corps base is the Corps' largest on the west coast. Its 125,000 acres include a broad mix of landscapes, from coastal swamps and beaches to mountains. It is well suited for virtually every type of combat training, from amphibious assaults onto the beach to helicopter assaults and all forms of ground combat training.

Perhaps the biggest surprise during the Camp Pendleton training from November through early February was how cold Southern California mountains were at night. We spent countless nights on various infantry training episodes and the memory that is most deeply ingrained is the cold. We had no cold weather gear and after sweating in the warm afternoon sun, the nights were long and miserable, regardless of how active we were.

We were frequently warned at Pendleton to be sure to check our boots each time we put them on for scorpions, which crawled into unattended footwear, especially at night if we took them off. They too felt the cold and sought warmth in our boots. We checked our boots every time we put them on. This practice became especially important in Vietnam.

* * *

Throughout the summer and fall of 1967 and into January of 1968 the news was of nothing but escalating battlefield deaths as a result of confronting a fanatically motivated enemy. We saw marines at Camp Pendleton just returned from Vietnam and many were involved in training new recruits. They were deadly serious and though they might have been still under twenty-five years of age, they acted and spoke as someone much wiser. Many had completed two tours of duty; they were not speaking theoretically. The training they provided was from real-life events and we listened attentively.

Military commanders in Vietnam had put out an urgent call for replacements in late 1967 and President Johnson increased the number of troops on the ground. What this meant to those in the military's training system is that schedules were tightened. We were hustled almost frantically through the process, with little time to rest or reflect.

Training got more specific as to the task marines were to carry out. Infantry training was grueling, and the reality of this nasty business quickly sank in. Fundamentally, we were trained on how to kill the enemy and avoid being killed ourselves. Sometimes it was on a large scale and we practiced frontal assaults, hammer and anvil tactics, flanking moves, and large and small unit ambushes. Other times it was one-on-one with bayonets, a garrote, or our bare hands. At this point there was no question about our future. Those of us in infantry training units were going to South Vietnam to fight skilled local insurgents and division-sized forces of crack, well-equipped North Vietnamese regulars.

* * *

After a short leave over Christmas, it was back to work with a stronger focus than ever. The final training was called *staging*. This specialized form of combat exercise was oriented to conditions and practices we were going to encounter in Vietnam. It was all deadly serious. We learned to fire virtually every weapon in the Corps' arsenal, how to navigate via map and compass, nighttime orientation and maneuvers, and endless small unit combat war games.

Training in stealth was a high priority. The focus was on small groups being able to move quietly through the jungle to surprise and quickly overwhelm the enemy or to gather intelligence. We spent little time training for traditional large force battles or tactics used in World War II island campaigns. There was nothing conventional about combat in Vietnam. This stealth training was of extreme value once in-country. We also received a great deal of training in the critical matter of mines and booby traps of every type. These devious devices ranged from a variety of ingeniously rigged explosive devices to punji stakes, sharpened bamboo stakes buried in pits and designed to inflict great bodily harm. As thorough as all the specific training about warfare in Vietnam was, it never came close to the reality on the ground in that faraway hostile place, as we were to find out in a few weeks.

On January 30 the Viet Cong and North Vietnamese Army began the countrywide Tet Offensive in South Vietnam. This offensive was in flagrant violation of a ceasefire to mark the Lunar New Year, an important Asian holiday. It caught American and South Vietnamese forces with their guard down. At least 85,000 NVA troops, freshly moved into South Vietnam, supported by thousands of local Viet Cong guerillas, attacked provincial capitals and bases across the country. January 31 was the bloodiest single day of the war, with 246 Americans killed. I sarcastically thought about my wonderful luck: *Just as I'm about to head to Vietnam, the worst battle of the war erupts.* As it turned out there was good reason to be pessimistic. The year 1968 alone saw almost as many American military deaths as the total for the war up to that point. Late 1967 through mid-1969 was the bloodiest period of the war. Unfortunately, my February 1968 through March 1969 deployment included almost all of the highest monthly killed-in-action tallies of the war. During my thirteen-month tour of duty, over 17,000 Americans were killed—more than the total killed in all the wars after Vietnam. A great many more, of course, were wounded.

* * *

Though the communists were soundly defeated in their several-weeks-long offensive, the fact that they could even carry it off in the first place was a major psychological victory for them. It was a psychological defeat for the American public, who were told for years that there was hope at the end of this dark tunnel. Americans wrongly believed that we were fighting a ragtag army of guerillas that couldn't possibly stand up against the mighty American ground and airpower deployed to Vietnam. What they didn't understand was that we were fighting a proxy war in which the enemy was as well trained, equipped, and dedicated to the cause as any we'd ever faced. The Viet Cong fighter in farmer's clothes might have been what was portrayed in magazines, but the truth was very different. We were fighting an army as capable as ours. Another mistaken assumption made by the American public was that American troop strength far outweighed what the enemy sent into battle. Numbers alone didn't tell the entire story. American troop strength would eventually grow to over a half million. The number of VC and NVA on the ground in South Vietnam was estimated to be 420,000 near the time of Tet. The advantage seemed to be ours. It must be kept in mind, however, that nearly three quarters of American troops in-country were non-combat personnel in rear bases. A much smaller number was on the line fighting the highly disciplined and fanatically dedicated communist forces. While we had the advantage of air superiority, the enemy in large part controlled the ground. In war, control of real estate is what matters.

Support for the war had been slipping for two years in America. Despite a brief period of rallying around the flag during and immediately after Tet, public support soon began to slide again. In the minds of many Americans, the Tet Offensive extinguished any feeling of optimism. This sense of failure and gloom was deepened on February 27 by comments made by Walter Cronkite, America's most trusted newsman. Upon returning from a trip to Vietnam, Cronkite gave a pessimistic appraisal of the war. For the first time he rejected official optimism by officials in Washington. He said that he was now "more certain than ever that the bloody experience of Vietnam is to end in a stalemate." Cronkite didn't cause a swing in public opposition to the war. Large scale opposition to the war was already deeply rooted in middle America. Journalists actually lagged behind average Americans in attitudes toward the war. Cronkite's statement of pessimism was evidence that he finally caught up with much of the rest of the country.

\* \* \*

On February 12, General Westmoreland, commander of United States forces in South Vietnam, requested authorization for the troop limit in Vietnam to be increased once again. President Johnson authorized the addition of 10,500 more soldiers and marines to South Vietnam. Thus, it was that in the midst of the communists' Tet Offensive the Twenty-Seventh Marine Regiment was thrown together at Camp Pendleton for immediate deployment to Vietnam to help counter the offensive. This regiment, Regimental Landing Team 27, was my new home. It was a unit that fought proudly in the South Pacific in World War II but had been decommissioned for many years. It was reformed in the early days of this war but was a stateside unit whose structure was used only in training activities. The regiment was meant to remain in Vietnam for only a few months. The intent was to bolster in-country forces so that the communist offensive could be decisively defeated. We were to become part of the III Marine Amphibious Force, responsible for much of the military responsibilities in the I-Corps, the northernmost part of South Vietnam.

Hundreds of both new and experienced marines were gathered together from many different units and training specialties. The Third Battalion of the Twenty-Seventh Regiment, referred to as 3/27, received more non-infantry specialists than it had riflemen in its ranks. Many of the combat marines, myself included, were boots (fresh out of training). The Marine Corps has a motto that *Every Marine is a Rifleman*. Cooks and clerks had basic infantry training and could be thrown into the fight if required. This claim was soon to be put to the ultimate test.

Given the speed with which the regiment was formed, there was little time to train together or to coalesce as a unit prior to departure for Vietnam and being thrown into some of the worst combat of the war. Unlike similarly formed units during World War II there'd be no slow voyage across the Pacific on ships during which men could get to know one another. There would be no stopover in Hawaii for training. Once we departed, we'd be in the war zone within twenty-four hours.

During the five days of unit formation, life was hectic and demanding. From dawn to dusk we trained and took care of the usual paperwork and medical issues. We lined up for endless shots, some of which, like the Gamma Globulin inoculation, were quite unpleasant. We signed forms, made sure our military life insurance information was correct, and spent long hours at the range practicing with both the M-14 and new M-16 rifles. Veteran combat marines tried to cram as much knowledge and wisdom into our brains as they could. We were also issued uniforms and gear designed for the environment and combat conditions in Vietnam. While in boot camp and training we wore full leather boots, the foot gear worn in Vietnam was quite different. The soles had steel plates to stop sharpened spikes from penetrating into the foot. They also had nylon webbing to enhance air circulation and allow feet to dry out quicker. Utility uniforms were designed with several large pockets to allow carrying the maximum amount of ammo and other gear.

The Third Battalion began life as a nearly fully complemented table of organization (TO) unit. Marine Corps infantry regiments were made up of three battalions, each battalion normally containing approximately 1,100 marines. A battalion had four rifle companies and a headquarters company, which included staff, support, and weapons personnel. Each company had a letter designation. The first battalion of a regiment had companies A, B, C, and D. The second battalion consisted of companies E, F, G, and H and the third battalion companies were titled I, K, L, and M. At full TO strength, a platoon usually had forty-five men.

I was a proud new member of the third squad of Kilo Company, Third Battalion of the Twenty-Seventh Marine Regiment, First Marine Division. Reflecting the Corps' motto, Kilo Company had a mix of MOS classifications. Fortunately, our sergeant squad leader was a second deployment rifleman, but there were also two surveyors, a mortarman, an equipment operator, a truck driver, a supply clerk, and a mechanic. Three of us were boot grunts.

Rumors began flying that our destination was not Vietnam at all, but rather Korea. On January 23 North Korea attacked and seized a US intelligence ship, the *USS Pueblo*. Scuttlebutt became rampant that our real mission was to attack North Korea to free the *Pueblo* and her eighty-three captured crew members (one of which was killed in the North Korean attack). And of course, other rumors had us heading to the thick of the fight in Vietnam in response to the ongoing Tet Offensive. Either option was fraught with danger and none of us had any belief that the coming days and weeks were going to be pleasant.

Incredibly, just five days later the Third Battalion was gathered together for the first time in a large hangar at El Toro Marine Air Station, near Irvine, CA.

On that day, February 17, 1968, President Lyndon Johnson came through the hangar and shook hands with many of us just prior to our loading onto a giant four-engine Lockheed C-141 Starlifter military cargo plane. The look of profound sadness on the president's face as he shook my hand and wished me the best spoke volumes. He knew that he was sending many of us to our deaths and it obviously was an almost unbearable weight for him to carry. It wasn't much more than a month later that he announced that he would not run, nor accept the nomination for the presidency in the 1968 elections.

Johnson gave a speech about the war, about keeping the South Vietnamese free, about stopping communist aggression and the importance of our being there. All-in-all it was a somber event. Suddenly this was real. We were heading off to war! Our feelings were a mixed and confused blend of excitement and fear. We were going to war; it doesn't get any more exciting than that! We were going to war; it doesn't get any more fearful than that. We wondered what lay in store for us. How would we handle the next thirteen months? Which of us, we silently wondered, would die in a few weeks or who was likely to be seriously injured and never the same again? We resigned ourselves to whatever the future held and headed out the door to the waiting plane.

CHAPTER 4

# OUT OF THE FRYING PAN, INTO THE INFERNO

About one hundred of us loaded onto the huge cargo plane with full packs and rifles. Our seabags, stuffed with personal belongings, were piled high in the rear of the cargo space. We weren't allowed to contact anyone to let them know we were shipping out. Once on the plane, many of us wrote letters that we hoped could be mailed home once we arrived in Da Nang. The news would come as a significant shock to families across the country. We all assumed we'd be sent to Vietnam, but we and our families thought it would occur on a more routine basis with some advance notice. In the plane we sat on the floor in long rows, packs on and rifles at our sides. We were unable to move about or even stand for more than a few seconds because of the crowding.

We landed twice for fuel. The first was in Hawaii, but we weren't allowed to get off the plane. The second stop was at Clark Air Force Base in the Philippines. The plane was at Clark for an hour or so and we were able to go into the terminal building to get something to eat. Many of us mailed letters home from Clark. The hot, humid conditions were a premonition of what lay ahead of us in Vietnam. We were sweating just from walking the short distance from the plane to the terminal. After takeoff, again it was a few more hours of discomfort on the steel floor of the plane breathing stale air and silently pondering what the future held for us. We were well aware of everything that had occurred in Vietnam in the last couple of weeks and of the number of casualties that our cohorts had suffered.

From the Philippines we flew directly to Da Nang, landing at the large US military air base. We weren't aware of it at the time, though perhaps senior corps commanders were, but we had just made history. After just a forty-eight-hour deployment notice and creation of the regiment, we were the first regimental unit to fly from the US mainland directly into combat.

We landed at night and were quickly hustled out the back of the plane down its large ramp, carrying everything that we owned. The seabag contents were meaningless now and were headed for long term storage. We had no use for civilian clothes and other possessions. What mattered was what we wore and carried on our back and in our arms—combat gear. Ammunition was packed on the plane with us and we hurriedly carried off heavy boxes of ordnance. Ammunition for our rifles was distributed. Being issued live ammo and loading our rifles had a strong psychological impact. After months of training, the purpose of that training and the mental preparedness we all did on our own was suddenly all around us in the dark, humid environs of Da Nang.

Conditions in Da Nang made it immediately obvious that we were a long way from home. We could hear artillery fired nearby and the smell of burnt gunpowder was strong. Bright lights illuminated the base, showing walls of sandbags and steel pilings sheltering planes and helicopters from enemy rocket and artillery attack. Military trucks scurried about. We stood motionless and stared out into the strange scene that presented itself.

The air seemed thick, heavy and foreboding. It was also hot and muggy, despite the fact that it was the middle of the night in mid-

February. The dramatic temperature change from the mountains of Camp Pendleton was going to take some getting used to.

After we were all off the plane and had our gear in hand, we quickly moved to a waiting group of open military transport trucks. As the sun was rising, the convoy of deuce-and-a-half trucks drove through the narrow streets of Da Nang, already filled with people going about their business. Beyond the city, we traveled through squalid outlying villages and ultimately down a deserted dirt road to a small forward base south of Da Nang near a place called Cau Ha in Quang Nam Province. We were assigned to a historically troublesome region near the coast. One knew without being told that we were now someplace where a person didn't want to go without a sizeable military force.

Beyond the influence of Da Nang there was little in the way of infrastructure. We were truly in the boondocks. Given the look of the villages we drove through and the appearance of the local residents, it may as well have been 1868 instead of 1968. Riding in open trucks through those narrow streets and distressed villages was an eye-opening experience. Suddenly we saw what this war was all about. This wasn't like going to other foreign countries and seeing reasonably happy, middle-class citizenry that exhibited an unspoken confidence in the future. We were viewing the other side of life—South Vietnamese peasants that looked small, poor, and hungry. And utterly noncommittal. We had no way of knowing if hatred or suppressed happiness was under the blank faces that stared back at us. Kids, like kids everywhere, were much more animated. Most smiled in what seemed like a friendly manner and shouted, "Joe Number One," while holding their hands out for food. If they didn't get what they wanted their yells changed to "Joe Number Ten!" (number one being good, number ten meaning that the person or thing is very bad).

South Vietnam was divided into four military operational regions by the US command, designated by Roman numerals I–IV. The northern-most part of Vietnam was called *I Corps*, pronounced "eye corps" in military jargon. The marines had major responsibility for combat operations in I Corps. The region included the Demilitarized Zone, Khe Sanh, the A Shau Valley, Con Thien, Quang Tri, The Rockpile, Hue, Da Nang, Go Noi Island, and other strategic centers. It also contained countless jungled hilltops, small villages, coastal lowlands, and enemy-held territory, where thousands of young Americans were killed or forever maimed.

The rear base for 3/27 was just beyond what was called *the rocket belt*, the point at which the enemy had to be in order for their rockets to reach Da Nang and its various military installations. Since Da Nang was located on the shore of the South China Sea, the rocket belt consisted of a semi-circle from north of the city to the south. Marine units were assigned to run aggressive patrols beyond the entire semi-circle boundary area to seek out the enemy and prevent attacks. The nearby NVA and VC had three Soviet-made rockets in their arsenal. They were 107mm, 122mm and 140mm in size and had a range of six to twelve kilometers. The rockets didn't require motorized vehicles to transport, nor did they need sophisticated electronic guidance systems. They could be set up by a two-man team in about an hour. This meant that our presence in the hotly contested launch perimeter had to be nearly constant.

Beyond the base, the countryside was sparsely settled and gave no pretenses of civilization, comfort, or safety. It was largely a free-fire zone, in that the North Vietnamese Army and local Viet Cong (VC) roamed quite freely. The military parlance for VC was *Victor Charlie*. Not surprising, our generic name for the VC was *Charlie*; a derogatory term for the VC was *gook*.

The tactical area of responsibility for 3/27 was a twenty-five-square mile expanse of overgrown fields, small woodlots, swamps, and remote villages, with adjacent small rice plots. Much of the area was depopulated as the result of decades of conflict. What had once no doubt been bountiful farmland, particularly for the growing of rice, was now covered with thick, thorny, ten-foot-high brush, tall weeds such as the hated elephant grass, and occasional lines of trees that once marked edges of fields. Elephant grass was commonplace and was among the most despised vegetation. It grew in dense stands to eight or ten feet in height and, in addition to providing cover for attackers, its razor-sharp edges caused painful cuts. Small dikes that were once part of the rice growing operations now provided a tempting, but deadly, means to traverse the region above the water line.

Marines who fought and died in this area prior to our arrival gave names to certain areas within our tactical zone. We quickly got to know and understand the rationale behind those names. The worst was a hated place we called *Booby Trap Alley*. Whenever we went in there, we came back with several fewer men at the end of the day. Another area was called *Dodge City*. One more had the name *Riviera*. It was especially memorable in a bad way, as it was a swampy area not far from the South China Sea. The sand, swamps, snakes, bugs, and vegetation that was sadistically designed solely to poke and tear skin, made patrols there difficult to say the least. It was also a region that Charlie controlled, and we entered at our own great risk. There was a leper colony in the Riviera. We never entered the compound itself, but the VC used it as a place to hide and to stash weapons and supplies.

We gave the title *Indian Country* to the entire region. It meant no disrespect to Native Americans, rather it was used to describe the Wild West nature of the area and the absolute lawlessness and mercilessness of it all. Indian Country was largely a free fire zone. This was an important consideration. It meant that the only people likely to be found in the area were presumed to be enemy combatants—no other friendlies or civilians. Noncombatants had long before been evacuated or, at a minimum, warned that the military command of both the United States and the government of South Vietnam declared that the region was a free fire zone due to the preponderance and free movement of VC and NVA fighters. The legal designation meant that US, ARVN, and coalition soldiers could fire at will without approval from higher command and without first going to extra lengths to ensure that the targets were in fact enemy combatants. Unless a person was obviously a civilian, such as a woman with a child, it was assumed that anyone spotted in the area was VC or NVA.

Our assigned patrol area was flat, with mountains visible ten or fifteen miles to the west. There were sizable hills farther south and north as well, but our assigned area was low and swampy to a large degree with one major road, Route 1, and some dirt trails. An abandoned railroad paralleled Route 1 near the coast. Most of the foot trails followed old rice paddy dikes and along riverbanks. These paths were mined and were to be avoided to the maximum extent possible. This meant going through the swamps, overgrown forested areas, and scrubland on patrols whenever possible. The locals often used the trails; somehow, they knew when they were safe to use and where not to step.

It was usually hot, muggy, and uncomfortable. Loamy soil made for difficult walking. It rained often, though not constantly, like later during the monsoon season. Someone from Louisiana or Florida might have found the land and weather familiar, but most of us certainly did not.

The nearby mountains were similar to those in the eastern United States, being tree-covered and providing the perfect hiding places for large numbers of combatants. There were still a few small, active rice paddies and villages where adequate protection was provided, but these remote villages were always subject to intimidation by local Viet Cong tax collectors and recruiters.

A regiment of South Korean Marines had a zone of responsibility immediately south of us.

In-country our priorities immediately changed. Things that were once important no longer were. Things that we had previously given little thought to were now of extreme importance. Our assigned rifle moved to the top of our priority list. The single most important piece of equipment for a rifleman was, of course, his rifle. We valued it above all else. After all, one's own life and the lives of those around us depended on the dependability of their rifle.

Due to a shortage of new M-16 rifles, we were issued the older and heavier M-14 prior to leaving California. We used them for the first three weeks in country, then were issued M-16s. We trained with the M-16 in advanced infantry training and qualified with it at the range, so were familiar with its use. The M-16 and its light 5.56mm bullet and small case initially seemed insufficient for the task at hand. Even in training we heard complaints about the dependability of the M-16 in the rugged conditions found in Vietnam. Some Marines loved it, some wanted nothing to do with it.

The M-14 with its 7.62 mm NATO cartridge was used in boot camp and also used for marksmanship qualification. It's the rifle used in close-order drills and by precision marching units. The M-14 gave the impression of reliability. It felt real, made of wood and steel, not plastic. We referred to M-16s as Mattel toy guns. For those of us who grew up with traditional shotguns and rifles, the M-16's plastic stock and light weight made it look and feel cheap and undependable.

The version of the M-16 that the US Marine Corps used was an older one. The Army had the newer M-16A1 model that had been improved to correct some deficiencies that showed up when first exposed to the reality of Vietnam-style combat. There were continuing complaints about even the new and improved M-16's ability to function in the extreme environment. Its moving parts sometimes jammed due to even small amounts of dirt in the action, a situation that was the norm regardless of efforts at keeping the rifle clean inside and out. Mud and dirt were constant realities. In addition to dirt causing jamming of the forward moving bolt when inserting a new cartridge, the rifle had a problem with spent cartridges becoming jammed in the breech and not extracting. When this happened, it was a potentially serious problem, as sometimes the spent case had to be pushed out by jamming a rod down the rifle barrel. These weren't daily issues, but in combat, lives depended on problems such as these never happening. Complaints about the early M-16 sparked a Congressional investigation in 1967. Among other shortcomings regarding the new rifle, the subcommittee rebuked the Army for failure to provide adequate rifle cleaning gear to troops, including metal rods to dislodge stuck casings.

The length and weight of the older M-14 made it a poor choice for use in Vietnam. The light weight of the M-16 and its ammo was an important consideration. When fighting through the tropical groundcover and difficult terrain in-country, the weight of a rifle and a couple hundred rounds of ammo was critical.

The M-14 was unsuitable for the conditions we were in because it was longer and four pounds heavier. It also offered less fire power. The M-14 ammunition clips we used held ten rounds, while standard issue M-16 magazines could hold twenty bullets. We normally only put eighteen in the clips, however, as the spring which fed the bullets upward gradually weakened if pushed all the way down with twenty bullets in the clip. To make matters worse, the aluminum retaining lips at the top of the magazine, which lined bullets up for proper loading into the chamber, were easily bent. Once these guides bent, the bullets were not properly aligned, causing a jam when the bolt tried to force the next round into the chamber. For the sake of rapid reloading, we taped two clips together with the open ends facing opposite directions, so we could quickly remove an empty clip, flip it over, and insert the loaded clip.

Due to its high velocity, as opposed to mass, the M-16 bullet caused severe damage when it hit a human target. But regardless of personal feelings toward one rifle or the other, the M-16 was the rifle infantrymen carried for the remainder of the war. Though the M-16 had the ability to be fired in fully automatic mode, that rarely occurred. Fire discipline was critical and emptying a clip in a second or two benefitted no one, except perhaps directors of television shows and movies.

The military issued small bottles of lubricant for use when cleaning the M-16. This liquid oily material often made the jamming problem worse by attracting grit. Many soldiers and Marine infantrymen depended on a commercial product called *Dri-Slide*, mailed in packages from home. It was sprayed on and quickly dried. It did an excellent job of lubricating and waterproofing moving parts without causing an oily coating that attracted dirt. In the end, the M-16 proved up to the job but required close attention to cleanliness and maintenance.

There was frustration because the enemy's rifle, the Kalashnikov AK-47, was more reliable than our M-16s. The design of its moving parts was such that it seldom jammed, no matter how severe the conditions. The AK-47 was perhaps the perfect military weapon. Created by famous Russian firearms expert Mikhail Kalashnikov, it had been produced since 1947. It was relatively lightweight, compact and had a magazine that held thirty rounds. The rifle could be quickly and easily fieldstripped for cleaning. It fired a 7.62 mm cartridge also, though with a shorter case and lighter bullet. It had a distinctive and much more threatening sound than the high-pitched resonance of the M-16 when fired.

* * *

Rifles aside, the technical difference between the Vietnam War and today's military is incredible. Technologically, with the exception of helicopters, we were more comparable to World War II conditions than to wars fought after the year 2000. There was no GPS system and no hand-held units to guide us in the wilderness. We all received a significant amount of navigation and orientation training as part of our basic stateside schooling. There were no trail cameras that fed live photos of enemy troop movements via satellite to combat units. Instead we posted two- or three-man listening posts near trails suspected of use by the VC or NVA. No drones flew reconnaissance missions or fired rockets at high value targets. Intelligence was gathered by long range reconnaissance patrols (LRRPs).

There was no satellite communication for two-way radios used by infantry units in the field. No cell phones, social media, text messaging, or email was available to communicate with loved ones thousands of miles away. Our families were in the dark, the occasional letter being the only contact. Letters written two weeks previously being received described what had been, not what was.

Other advances such as infrared viewers mounted on our helmets to see through the blackness or GPS-guided bombs and artillery were dreams of the future or prototypes in the lab. Early versions of the *starlight* scope were better than nothing, but the quality was poor. At nearly twenty pounds for the scope and case, the units were too heavy and cumbersome for regular use by infantry patrols. They saw use for perimeter defense at large rear bases, or forward combat outposts.

We had topographical maps, and it was up to us to figure out where on the map we were. We usually did this by triangulating three identifiable points. We determined where we were going by literally counting footsteps. Usually the third or fourth man back in a column, who was called the navigator, was responsible to keep track of the distance and direction we traveled so we knew how many clicks (kilometers) we traveled and in what direction. This man carried the compass and was usually adjacent to the unit leader, who carried the map. There were many times when low clouds made it impossible to see distant landmarks, resulting in our not being able to determine exact positions. Such times were always tense and dangerous. Knowing one's precise location is one of the most fundamentally important pieces of information that a military unit must possess. This information is used when calling for artillery support, medivac choppers, close range gunship support, and in coordinating movements with other units in the area.

\* \* \*

We hit the ground running in Vietnam, immediately commencing offensive action in the form of patrols into enemy territory. As a result, the period from February 20, 1968 to early June was hellish. We were seldom at our base, running extended patrols for days at a time through hostile territory and taking many casualties. Late February coincided with what some called the Second Tet, a follow up offensive to the original campaign over the Tet holiday. The second campaign wasn't as large or dramatic, but unfortunately for us, consisted of a widespread series of attacks across the countryside rather than urban areas.

A primary objective of the patrols we ran on a near daily basis throughout our tactical area of responsibility was called *search and destroy.* We knew that there were enemy troops in the area but did not know their exact locations. We knew they had weapon caches and supply depots. Our intent was to locate and engage the enemy, kill as many as possible, and to locate and destroy support facilities and supplies. In a war based on attrition, it was hoped that eventually we'd kill enough of the enemy to eliminate their ability to function effectively. The enemy wanted to kill and maim enough Americans to cause a lack of support for the war on the American home front.

A second objective was more political in nature. We wanted to prove that the communists did not own or control the region. The American military badly wanted to demonstrate that we could go wherever we wished. We ran daily patrols into dangerous areas to prove this intention.

Rural villagers were truly caught in one of the lower levels of hell. I developed great pity for local peasants. They lived a hard and dangerous life trying to eke out a living with their tiny rice paddies, a couple of pigs, and a few chickens. At night these families shared their meager grass and bamboo huts with their livestock to help ensure the safety of those animals. Civilians who lived in free fire zones were highly encouraged, sometimes required, to leave. Those that did not leave lived a life of fear and danger. Local VC forced noncombatants to work for them or to supply food and shelter. United States and ARVN troops unfortunately often killed them. It was assumed—since they were in areas ruled by the communists, they looked essentially the same as local VC guerillas, and we had received fire from persons in that area or encountered mines—that they were the enemy. Rural villagers were at the mercy of the Viet Cong in all but the most northern part of South Vietnam, where the NVA was the primary occupying force. The VC killed intellectuals (teachers, doctors, government officials) and other civilians if they thought they were cooperating with the US or the South Vietnamese government. They also forced them to pay a tax in the form of rice and other supplies. Young Vietnamese were often coerced to join the local VC cadre. Whenever we saw somebody out in contested areas it always raised concerns. Was that person a friend or enemy? Or was he or she neither—were they someone who simply wanted to live their life while stuck in this horrible setting?

Normally there was nothing in their eyes or stoic facial expressions and their obsequious manner to suggest their true intentions and thoughts. Sometimes, however, we could read faces and when we saw a face filled with hatred on what appeared to be a civilian, we had little doubt as to that person's activities come nightfall.

Throughout the country, it seemed that every small rural village had two or three people, usually women, that were the ones that came out as we approached and yelled "No VC, No VC." They were desperate to convince us that there were no Viet Cong in the village nor any VC weapons or supplies. Sometimes there weren't; oftentimes there were.

The first phrase of Vietnamese that one learned in-country was *dung lai*, which meant "stop" or "halt." It was shouted frequently when someone looked or acted suspiciously and we wanted to check them out. If they ran, it was up to us to ascertain in about a half-second whether they were a guerilla fighter or a frightened civilian. With weeks or months of gruesome memories fresh in our mind, assuming the latter was difficult. On some occasions we had a small number of South Vietnamese troops with us who acted as interpreters, but usually there was no such help. The second phrase we picked up was *di di* and *di di mau*. This meant a couple of things depending on its use. *Di di* was used to tell someone to "go away" or "get out of here", as when a local was pestering you to buy a hot bottle of soda. *Di di mau* meant "go away now, quickly." With a loud and serious tone of voice, saying *di di mau* to a Vietnamese civilian meant "Get the hell out of here, now!" Probably the most commonly used word was the French word *beaucoup*. It was mispronounced as *buku* and was heard constantly and in every context that could be imagined, in general to indicate *many* or *large*.

Charlie operated mostly at night. Stealth was their game and sneak attacks and ambushes the aces up their sleeve. They loved to create chaos and inflict as much damage and fear as possible, with the least amount of weaponry used for the greatest effect. Surprise attacks on positions at night, ambushes along trails that we were forced onto because of dense terrain surrounding them, and most of all, use of snipers, mines, and booby traps were their primary tactics. They were successful in their efforts to instill the terror of never knowing what we would encounter, where, or when. Charlie was at the same time ruthless and extremely cunning. They used every advantage they had as locals and exploited all of our weaknesses that were inherent as foreigners in a strange land.

Often it was the women that served as snipers and who laid the mines and booby traps. In the sterile language of military reports, these anti-personnel explosives were called *surprise firing devices*. An accurate, if seriously watered-down description. *Booby traps* was a generic term that meant any deadly anti-personnel device. Today they're referred to as *IEDs*. Because they were directed at foot soldiers in Vietnam, they did not have to be powerful enough to destroy armor.

They ranged from buried mines to explosive devices concocted from grenades or C-4 plastic explosives. Unexploded bombs or artillery rounds rigged to explode by means of a trip wire, or detonated electronically by a waiting enemy soldier, were common. In the more southerly part of the country concealed pits, called *punji pits*, were dug in trails in the bottom of which were sharpened bamboo stakes that impaled the falling victim. Other impaling devices were triggered to swing into a person walking along a trail. Explosive devices were hidden anyplace or attached to anything that the enemy thought would kill or maim Americans. Abandoned rifles or articles left on the battlefield had explosives attached to detonate when picked up. Dead bodies were booby trapped. These devices were ubiquitous and deadly. They were probably the most frightening single element in the war, and that's saying something.

Women served as snipers and booby trap technicians because they attracted less attention than did an eighteen- to fifty-year-old male. One day our squad from Kilo Company was guarding Liberty Bridge, south of Da Nang. It was a critically important bridge and was a regular target of attacks and demolition attempts. We observed a woman, dressed in the same manner as virtually all rural residents, not far from the bridge on the riverside trail that we and local farmers both occasionally utilized. She was acting out of place, bent over where there was no reason to be. We observed that she was doing something with her hands. We all thought at the same time that she was in fact burying a mine. Seconds later, as we were watching, she blew up. The mine she was planting inadvertently exploded. A few of us went to investigate and confirmed that she was dead, horribly injured. Her body was turned over to local civilian officials.

* * *

High numbers of casualties quickly affected our unit's capabilities. At the beginning we were near full staffing with three fifteen-man squads per company—a sergeant as squad leader and corporals for the fireteam leaders. The fireteam is the fundamental unit of the US Marine Corps, with three teams per squad. Each squad had a radioman, and each platoon had a Navy medic, called a *corpsman*. Corpsmen sometimes carried a .45 caliber pistol but not a rifle. Corpsmen have always held a special place in the hearts of marines. Their bravery and life-saving skills are legendary. It was normal for them to travel in the middle of the group for safety.

Upon deployment we also had weapons squads for machine guns and mortars. Initially the platoon commander was a first lieutenant, with a captain as company commander. After the first few weeks we rarely had a first lieutenant as platoon commander; it was always a new *second louie*, and turnover was high due to casualties.

Just six weeks after our deployment, at the end of March, our squad had four men left and each of us had been wounded at least once, though not seriously enough to be sent to a hospital or shipped out-of-country. I was in the third squad of the third platoon of K Company and the young corporal engineer who got caught up in the rapid deployment as our fireteam leader was soon promoted to leader of our seriously depleted squad. Most of the company had been killed or wounded by mines, booby traps, and ambushes. Many of the more senior and experienced marines that were brought into the company in California had been killed or seriously injured. Ambushes and snipers in the thick cover were deadly and we seldom saw who was inflicting the harm. The communists always dragged their dead away, so we rarely knew how many casualties we were inflicting on them. In the rocket belt region, we primarily had running battles with the Viet Cong, and local VC sympathizers were largely responsible for the mines. There was a large number of NVA as well, but they were involved in major attacks rather than hit and run skirmishes or the placement of mines.

* * *

We were always tired and sore. We ran patrols constantly, catching a few minutes or an hour or two of sleep whenever possible. The ability to actually get some restful sleep was one of the most precious commodities in the bush. Every minute of rest was priceless and well-guarded. When out of the base area, which was often, each person had to be constantly on high alert, as there were no safe areas where one could let his guard down. There was also no refuge or respite from other unpleasant realities of the tropical jungle environment.

Bugs of every variety were the bane of infantrymen in Vietnam. Mosquitoes in particular were terrible, day and night. There was no refuge from them. One of the most important pieces of gear we were issued was a green towel. We kept the towel wrapped around our head and neck when trying to get some sleep to keep the biting bugs at least off our face. Ticks were commonplace and represented an annoyance, often escalating to serious health problems. They were also hard to remove. Ticks and leeches and other vermin had an uncanny ability to make their way to the most vulnerable places on your body—warm dark areas that were hidden from view. Removing a tick from one's genitals, underarms, or other sensitive areas was painful and difficult. Infection frequently followed removal. I once had a tick bite on the side of my face that swelled badly. With what medication the corpsman could provide applied every day it still took a couple of weeks for the infected area to heal.

The military issued a heavy-duty mosquito repellant that helped but it didn't keep them all away and some critters seemed to like its taste. Usually there were dozens of mosquitoes buzzing around one's face. Sweat and rain quickly washed off the repellant and mosquitoes and other bugs weren't deterred in their attempts to get blood.

Different things bothered different marines, but for me the worst pest were leeches. They were everywhere and they were terrible. They attached themselves to every part of your body and you couldn't feel them until they were so full of blood that their weight made them obvious. Getting them off was difficult. It wasn't possible to simply pull them off. Use of lit cigarettes was one of the more effective ways to remove ticks, leeches, and similar bugs or parasites. When exposed to the heat from a cigarette the attacking bug would release its grip and back away. If one tried to simply pull a tick or similar bug off the skin the head or other parts of the bug remained under the skin where it could cause serious infections. To this day the sight of a leech makes me sick to my stomach.

Snakes were also a nuisance and danger. There were several venomous snakes that we crossed paths with. We gave them names such as three-step Charlie, meaning that after being bit a person could take about three steps before dying. A snake we called the bamboo viper was also especially dangerous. These small-banded snakes were aggressive and attacked anyone who bothered them. Of course, they were annoyed by our simple act of walking through their habitat. Fortunately, snake bites, though a constant threat were not common.

Much of the area south and southwest of Da Nang was low, with swamps being common. In more peaceful times the higher, more valuable lands were cultivated for rice production and therefore burial grounds were seemingly limited to the lowlands. The Vietnamese for generations built mounded graves for burials in the areas not suitable for farming. Often these mounds were the only things higher than the swampy water surrounding them. They were a foot or so above the water and about 5 or 6 feet in diameter and dome shaped. Sometimes these graves were the only dry places to sit for a few minutes or at times even lie down to get a little sleep. When in the field, which was most of the time, sleep was never a solid block of time. It was short periods of ten minutes or a half hour here and there as conditions allowed. When circumstances did allow, getting some badly needed shut-eye time was critical. Of course, at any time only a few of the patrol members could nap—everyone else was on high alert. Using grave mounds as a place to lay down came at a price because all other living things, such as snakes and bugs, also chose those little islands for their dry refuges. Sleep was often interrupted by crawling or creeping creatures on your body.

As might be expected, malaria was also a serious problem, especially if one failed to take the daily malaria pills we were all issued. A very small number of men deliberately didn't take them, actually hoping to get sick and be shipped out of country, but that was rare. And even if they did get sick, at the most, a person would just be sent to the rear for a few days for treatment and then returned to field duty. I always took my pills, but once, when quite, sick a corpsman told me that my symptoms meant I probably had malaria. Being sick in the bush just added to the overall unpleasantness of this situation. We received a number of inoculations prior to leaving for Vietnam and received boosters once there to ward off a variety of diseases. One of the more unpleasant shots was called GG, or gamma globulin—administered for enhanced disease resistance. Almost always, the shots were given by the company corpsman in the field.

\* \* \*

The process of getting ready for a patrol was called *saddling up*. It involved several key steps. First was putting one's flak jacket on, with pockets filled with grenades. Then the filled backpack was put on, containing individual C ration meals and all the other necessities of the day, including many spare magazines of ammunition. The style of combat that was the reality in Vietnam required carrying a great deal of supplies on daily or weekly excursions into enemy country. There was no clear supply line connecting most forward troops to the rear, and resupply by chopper could be hours or days late. In the meantime, a squad or platoon could be knee-deep in shit without ammo or food. An aching memory of overloaded backpacks was the painful infections that often arose from shoulder straps cutting into one's skin.

Bandoliers of ammunition and a belt of extra machine gun ammo were hung around each marine's neck. A heavy-duty Ka-Bar knife was attached on the belt and at least two canteens filled with water were hooked onto the belt as well. Sundry other items, such as a light anti-armament weapon (LAAW), which was like a small, portable bazooka or rocket was slung over a shoulder. Smaller and lighter items, such as communications and signaling gear, perhaps a shelter half (a tarp that is used to create a small tent without sides), were carried in plastic sandbags tied onto our pack or belt.

Various other tools of the trade were attached on the outside of our packs. These might include more ammo, smoke grenades for signaling, a poncho and the ubiquitous and vital e-tool. This device was a small, foldable shovel officially called an entrenching tool. It was primarily used to dig fighting holes, though it found many other uses as well. We carried everything needed for several days of existence and combat in enemy territory. The full weight of these clumsy loads was often in the forty-pound range. The weight and mass of the gear we carried made traversing swamps and sandy or muddy locales very unpleasant.

Some marines carried a pistol, while a small number also carried shotguns, in addition to their rifle. Since ammunition for such weapons was hard to come by, the practice was not widespread. Tunnel rats, those marines and soldiers who entered enemy tunnels and bunkers, carried a .45-caliber pistol and sometimes a sawed-off shotgun.

When the person in charge yelled "Saddle up!" we quickly prepared for action against a deadly enemy. The last step before heading into the jungle was loading our rifles. The process of locking and loading one's rifle when heading out on a patrol—inserting a loaded magazine and then racking a bullet into the chamber—was a powerful psychological exercise. Everyone knew that we weren't going to the firing range or going deer hunting; we were hunting for human beings, who at the same time were hunting for us. Those bullets in our rifle were meant to kill people. That's a powerful reality that is impossible to truly explain.

\* \* \*

C ration meals, known as *meals, combat, individual* in military bureaucratese, were central to our life as frontline grunts. When a case of individual boxes was opened, we always tried to quickly get what we liked, and when unsuccessful, meals were often traded. There were some that nobody liked (ham and lima beans, universally known as ham and motherfuckers) and some that everyone wanted, like the ones with little tins of peaches or pound cake. Whenever I got those, I'd save the desserts until I had both a tin of peaches and a tin of pound cake; they were a special treat eaten together. A box of C rations included a small pack of matches, a pack of 4 cigarettes, a main meal (a can of hot dogs and beans or whatever), some crackers or bread in a tin and small tin of jelly, a packet of coffee or cocoa, toilet paper, a plastic spork to eat with, and a dessert. Besides greasy ham there was a Spam-like ground meat meal, canned spaghetti, a potato-based gruel, a beef stew, and beans and hot dog chunks. Our canteen had a metal sleeve that also served as a cup. It was used to heat water for coffee. Unfortunately, coffee lost much of its attraction when made with heavily chlorinated dirty water.

The tin cans were opened with small can openers that we kept on our dog tag chains. Officially these small but vital items were labeled as P-38s by the military supply folks, but we called them *John Waynes*. Legend has it that the devices earned that name from World War II, when actor John Wayne was filmed using one to open rations as part of a training film. Everyone knew what was meant if we asked to borrow someone's John Wayne. The device has a small hole so it could be threaded onto the dog tag chain that we all wore around our necks.

C-rats were often eaten cold. This was due to either being in a hurry, not wanting to risk building even small fires that could be seen, or it being so wet it was impossible to start a fire. Cold rations had a lot of congealed fat that, while providing necessary calories, also made them difficult to eat. C-4 plastic explosive, when torn into small pieces (like a wad of chewing gum) burns with a small, hot flame and was an excellent heat source for warming rations. We always tried to get some C-4 from the demolition engineers we'd occasionally encounter. Another option was trioxane ration heating tablets. These thumb-sized tablets were a chemical mixture of trioxane and hexamine, compressed into solid form and wrapped in foil. They were removed from their protective wrapper and lit with a match when used. These *heat tabs*, as they were referred to, were excellent items for heating C ration cans or to boil water in the canteen cup for coffee. Unfortunately, the demand for these tablets was high and they always seemed to be in short supply. The C rations we were issued had dates of manufacture stamped on them. Incredibly, most of the meals we ate were manufactured during the period 1945–1960! Fresh C rations were not on our dining menu.

Typical C ration meal contents. This meal represented more recent production than those used in Vietnam. Note the lack of a four-pack container of cigarettes.

Photo by author.

\* \* \*

Marines were issued the old WWII style flak jackets—heavy and uncomfortable, with plates of thick fiberglass or metal. We seldom took them off when beyond perimeter lines, and they were hot and heavy and difficult to lie down with. We were quite jealous of the Army soldiers, who were issued much newer and better equipment—including new Kevlar-style flak jackets. Those vests could be rolled up and used as a pillow when stopped for a break and were much more comfortable to wear.

\* \* \*

We took casualties on a near-daily basis, often several in a day. It was especially frightening because the wounds were frequently major, many caused by various explosive devices, which often meant lost body parts. We had a wake-up call on our first day on patrol, February 21. At the first rest break one of the men sat down next to a tree to use it as a backrest. He ended up sitting directly on a mine purposely placed in that spot for that reason. What it did to his body was indescribable. Disemboweled and shattered bones protruding everywhere. He was so badly injured that there was virtually nothing the corpsman could do to help him, other than inject multiple shots of painkillers. The squad leader immediately radioed for a medivac chopper. With great care and difficulty, we carried the grievously wounded marine through the brush to a small open area, around which we established a security perimeter. Fortunately, the enemy hadn't set up an ambush at the medivac landing zone.

The marine was still alive when loaded onto the medivac helicopter. We continually assured him that everything would be alright. "You lucky bastard," we said, "You're going home! The next people you see are going to be beautiful nurses to take care of you. You'll be fine," we said over and over. "You've got a ticket home." These well-intended lies were told countless times during the war.

He later died in the hospital, becoming our unit's first KIA three days after arriving in the country. This young Marine died before his letter informing family members of his deployment arrived at his home.

Having been in-country for only a couple days, that was our first experience seeing what happens to the human body when it's torn apart by explosives. The human body does not break apart neatly. The sight of protruding, jagged, broken, and splintered bones, bright red, mangled flesh, and the look and smell of guts on the ground is beyond the ability of words to describe. Inhuman screams of agony accompany the ungodly visual scene.

In everyday conversations one sometimes hears someone say "I can never unsee that" when referring to witnessing a bad or embarrassing event that they wish they hadn't seen. This same concept is commonplace in combat. There were countless circumstances that grunts wished they hadn't seen but which they will never be able to erase. The visual reality of that young marine sitting on a mine was the first of a great many permanently etched ugly memories.

We joked about so-called *million-dollar injuries*. Those were wounds that were serious enough, but not crippling, so as to require a person to be taken to a hospital at a rear base, such as Da Nang, for immediate surgery and then to a stateside hospital for long-term care. That person's tour of duty was done. Of course, the trick was to have the injury not result in loss of limbs or other permanent, life-changing damage.

Since Vietnam, whenever I see a movie in which exploding bombs or artillery are depicted and see entire human bodies flying through the air, I think how utterly inaccurate that depiction is. Intact fully dressed bodies don't fly through the air. Bloody mangled parts and pieces of bodies do. It's then up to the survivors to pick up the torso and various mangled parts and carry them until evacuation is possible. We often carried a poncho and shelter half for use when setting up a remote base camp. These items were also utilized to carry body parts as needed.

* * *

*Dustoff* or medivac helicopters were things of legend in Vietnam. During the war, more than 500,000 medivac incidents carried injured or sick soldiers to aid stations or hospitals in the rear. Often the elapsed time from injury to arrival at a medical facility was an hour or less. The most commonly thought of dustoff chopper was Bell Helicopter's UH-1 Iroquois model, called a Huey, with a large red cross painted on the nose. When first produced by Bell in 1959, this unit was designated the HU-1, gaining the obvious Huey nickname. It carried that tag even after 1962 when the model number for some reason was changed from HU to UH-1. The Huey was the first turbine-powered helicopter built for the US military. Over 16,000 were made, and about 7,000 of them saw service in Vietnam.

These unarmed birds were the most visible and are what normally arrived when a medivac for just one or two wounded men was requested. Often, however, medivac choppers were large, double rotor CH-47 Chinook or CH-46 Sea Knight cargo and troop carriers or CH-53 Sea Stallion heavy lift choppers that, after dropping off supplies and new troops, carried dead and wounded back to the rear. In battles in which there were a large number of casualties, the Chinook or Sea Knight choppers were usually what was used.

Hueys dedicated and marked as ambulance medivac units were generally unarmed, while other birds had one or two door gunners. Hueys served double duty in Vietnam. Besides being the primary dustoff chopper they were also the most common gunship, choppers designed for close-in combat and ground support. In 1967 the Army upgraded its gunship fleet to the better, faster and more heavily armed Bell AH-1 Cobra. With the Cobra, the Army also instituted the hunter-killer team concept by teaming a Cobra with a small and nimble Hughes OH-6A scout chopper. The scout sought out bunkers or enemy troops and the Cobra, flying close behind, attacked the positions with rockets and electrically operated machine guns. It was a deadly combo. The Marine Corps obtained a few Cobras late in the war, but for the most part kept using the Huey gunship for aerial support missions.

Any Vietnam veteran will tell you that decades later it is impossible to not look up whenever a helicopter flies nearby. The sound of those powerful rotors swimming through the air brings back vivid memories. All these years later, the smell of wet earth, burnt gunpowder, sweat, and blood are part of memories sparked by the sound of a chopper.

Marines help wounded fighter to an evacuation zone. Official USMC photograph.

That initial eye-opening incident of the unsuspecting marine sitting on an explosive device was our master's class in awareness of mines and booby traps. For months in training instructors tried to instill a fear and knowledge about such weapons, but until we saw it happen up close and without any warning or signs of danger, we couldn't truly comprehend the reality. The VC were very sophisticated in the design, placement, and detonation of their explosives.

We learned very quickly, which was vital, because it all went downhill after that first incident. It was to be the first of a great many, commencing immediately. The terror of not knowing when one was going to trip a booby trap or step on a mine never left for a moment. To this day, I have to force myself to not look at the ground in front of me as I'm walking.

* * *

I was appointed to walk point on patrols, especially squad-sized outings, on a regular basis. I assumed this assignment was because so many members of our squad were from non-infantry MOS disciplines, and because of my rural farm and hunting background, which was known to the squad leader and officers. From the time that I was a boy on the farm I walked the woods and fields to locate wildlife and learn about the natural world. Noticing tracks of animals became second nature, as did noting natural features such as vegetation and soil conditions. By the time I joined the marines, my woodsman skills were quite advanced. This ability was quickly exploited once in Vietnam.

Walking point was intense. It required constant vigilance, as it was the job of the man at the head of a column to locate mines and ambushes prior to walking into them. It was obviously in his interest to spot them, as he was the one most in danger if they existed. Indicators of mines or ambushes were very subtle and since locating these two dangers required different approaches, the two tasks conflicted. Spotting hidden explosive devices required close attention paid to scanning the ground for signs of buried mines or the presence of trip wires. Spotting potential ambushes and snipers mandated intense attention paid to the surrounding landscape, not looking down. Performing both duties required slow and careful movement and never losing focus for a moment. A lesser appreciated joy of walking point was being the person who walked into the ubiquitous spider webs that covered the tropical countryside. They seemed to be everywhere and through some inexplicable ecological reality, most were at face level.

Being able to read the natural environment was a critical skill for a point man, as was possession of a certain sixth sense about conditions and circumstances that were omens of danger. It's hard to explain those conditions and circumstances. They might be slight openings following thick jungle—a place where an ambush was feasible. Or it could be where the lay of the land naturally led and we therefore unwittingly followed—those sorts of places always being potential mine or ambush sites. There was never anything as obvious as freshly dug dirt to suggest a mine or bunkers to portend an ambush. Extreme caution was practiced when using a trail on which we didn't come across farmers or any signs of civilian activity. If the footpath was used primarily by us, it would absolutely be mined, the only question was where.

Finding hidden explosives was as important as spotting potential ambush sites. One learned quickly to spot evidence of hidden explosive devices. It was typically small signs, such as leaves that weren't laying right or other subtle indications that something wasn't right. The Viet Cong were very skilled at concealing their explosive devices.

One of the most insidious types of booby traps were rigged Willie Peter (white phosphorus) artillery rounds. This material caused horrible burns to the body and water made the chemical even more reactive. These rounds were normally used as markers or spotter rounds because they created a large white plume of smoke. This marker allowed artillery-forward observers to properly adjust range and windage for accuracy once firing for effect commenced.

The VC obtained a great deal of our munitions. They had insiders that worked at the bases who stole munitions. Materials were taken from ambushed convoys on occasion. The enemy rigged thousands of HE (high explosive) and WP artillery rounds and other types of explosives strategically located throughout the countryside in anticipation of American units operating in the area.

Another deadly American weapon that was used against us was the claymore mine, a slightly convex above-ground mine that stood on a small pedestal and sprayed a great deal of deadly shrapnel outward when detonated. They were commonly used as perimeter security devices. Many were stolen and utilized by the enemy in ambushes, or when they tried to infiltrate our lines. A particularly noxious trick of the enemy was to sneak into our wires and turn claymore mines around, so they faced inward. During an attack when the clacker, the firing device, was pushed, the grapeshot was directed at American troops rather than at the advancing foe. To ensure that an absentminded troop didn't place claymores in the wrong direction, the front business side had the words "Front—Toward Enemy" embossed in the metal.

* * *

Part of our daily weaponry hung around our neck or slung from a shoulder was the M-72 light anti-armor weapon, a 66mm self-contained rocket utilized against armor or bunkers. An unanticipated problem with this weapon was that the fiberglass carcass, or empty shell, for the LAAW was the perfect size to booby-trap with live grenades with their pins already pulled, but the spoons still in place that prevented detonation. When a trip wire was moved, the grenades fell out of the case, the spoons flew, and the grenades exploded. We had to be sure to smash the carcass each time we fired one.

It's important to understand that the purpose of the enemy's explosives devices wasn't to kill; the intent was to seriously injure and to terrorize. The negative impact on our ability to function as a military unit was affected more by a wounded man than if he were killed. Also, we were always on foot. The VC and NVA did not need large and powerful explosive devices like the ones needed to destroy an armored troop carrier. Their job was much simpler, as ubiquitous grenades and mortar or artillery rounds, rigged to explode when tripped, were extremely effective anti-personnel devices. The Viet Cong and NVA in a sense had the best of both worlds when it came to anti-personnel explosive devices. They were well supplied by North Vietnam and her powerful allies, Russia and China. But they also often used our own stolen devices against us.

A lesson learned early in Vietnam is that you step exactly where the person ahead steps. There was an incident in which we were under fire and moving rapidly along a trail. At point, I saw a small branch that was across the trail at an unnatural angle. It just didn't look right so I ran around it as did the next three men. The fourth one didn't, and he tripped a booby trap, seriously wounding himself and causing us to have to stop while under fire in the open.

Often the mines were in areas that also provided tactical value for the VC and NVA, that is, somewhat open areas where an ambush could also be sprung after the mine detonated. One of the more sinister, but effective, tricks the enemy used was to ambush a unit of infantrymen after an explosion created confusion and caused soldiers to bunch together. This deadly tactic was frequently used. It was difficult to not be able to immediately respond to an injured marine, but an ambush had to be assumed and precautions had to be taken first. It was likely that the VC or NVA were there waiting for us to gather around the wounded man, at which point they'd execute their attack.

It was less effective for enemy forces to ambush a long, strung out column of men, especially in thick vegetation, than to attack when we were grouped together. The question they faced, of course, was do they take out the first two or three men or should they hit us in the middle or end of the column? If they could cause us to bunch up, it gave them a great advantage. One of the most frequently shouted commands in the war was to "spread out!" To avoid any confusion in translation, the exact commands were clearer, as in "Spread out you goddamned fools, do you all want to get killed?" It was critical that, even in thick vegetation, soldiers not get too close together. Successful enemy ambushes depended on column density for effectiveness. Staying spread apart as much as possible lowered the chance of multiple casualties. In thick vegetation, staying separated from one another was much easier said than done. Whenever I see a war movie and notice troops clustered together, I want to shout to the screen to have them spread apart.

It was also a frequent trick to inflict casualties at one point and then set up the main ambush at the nearest location where a medivac helicopter could land to take away the wounded or dead. Choppers and all the people milling around them when loading casualties made inviting targets. Unless one has had the opportunity to be near a large double-rotor helicopter with the turbine and blades spinning just short of lift off (which was the norm, for a quick emergency getaway) it isn't possible to appreciate the incredible noise associated with them. A North

Vietnamese officer could scream orders to a squad of soldiers preparing an ambush thirty yards away and we wouldn't have heard them.

Despite impressions to the contrary, the VC and NVA regulars weren't ghosts. They also needed certain physical conditions to carry out their actions. Their advantages lay in the fact that they knew the landscape extremely well, spoke the local language, and in that they carried much less gear. Their home or base area was likely nearby, and they could easily and regularly communicate with local residents about where we patrolled and our routes. The enemy didn't want to move through extremely thick jungle or deep swamps any more than we did. They naturally sought out areas that were covered in forest or jungle to avoid being seen, but that were open enough to move through without the need of machetes. They also used trails when possible, knowing the area better they just didn't use the same obvious trails we did. When leading a patrol, the point man watched for landscape that was somewhat open, allowing firing lanes and large trees that provided cover for enemy forces. Tree lines adjacent to open areas often harbored enemy forces or snipers. There was less concern when traversing extremely thick cover with no trails. NVA and VC bullets couldn't magically pass through tree trunks any more than ours could. Regardless of the ground cover, patrols progressed slowly, about one kilometer per hour at best in typical conditions. Extreme diligence was necessary at all times to watch for the ubiquitous booby traps, snipers, and ambushes.

I ended up walking point for most of the first seven months in-country. There were several times when I spotted an ambush and was able to take offensive action. It's impossible to describe the feelings when an ambush is sprung. Some men will never know there was an ambush because they were killed immediately. Patrols are conducted in silence and with intense concentration in a landscape that is eerily quiet. When this silent focus is broken by numerous rifles suddenly exploding in noise at the same instant and at close range, a person's senses are stunned. Usually a deadly second passes before the body can react. The sound is amplified and scattered by echoes reverberating off trees and hillsides, further adding to the confusion. One has to make himself as small a target as possible, return fire, and find whatever cover is available in a fraction of a second. Being the person that triggers awaiting ambushes is decidedly unpleasant duty.

* * *

Friendly fire casualties were a problem in Vietnam's combat environment. Mistakes often happened on the battlefield for a variety of reasons. Decisions must be made in seconds or minutes based on limited knowledge of all the pertinent details, with deadly consequences. Emotions run high, no matter how experienced the decision-maker is and those emotions affect decisions. When the shit is hitting the fan, it's hard to be cool and calculating, especially when the shit is bullets and mortars. Bad decisions, based either on lack of information, false information, or fear, cause serious problems and death. It's all part of the *fog of war* reality which assures that unfortunate or stupid things will happen. Friendly fire casualties have long been a terrible fact of life. There were a number of incidents in which Americans were killed by friendly fire in Vietnam because of the fog of war or because a person's cognitive process was affected by the dire situation. An incident that occurred in another unit while 3/27 was in Vietnam saw several Americans killed when an artillery spotter gave the wrong coordinates. He gave his unit's coordinates, rather than the NVA's. When under great stress the mind doesn't always work well.

My squad was once involved in a potentially deadly fog of war accident. It occurred while sweeping through a wooded area, taking fire from unseen NVA. An armed observation plane, called an OV-10 Bronco, was flying low to find the NVA. The pilot mistook our squad for the enemy and commenced firing 20mm cannons at us. It was very frightening for several minutes having dozens or hundreds of these rounds explode just a few feet away while we hid behind trees or rocks. By incredibly good luck there were no casualties in that friendly fire incident. It was just another example of easily made mistakes complicated by being in a jungle setting and the very close proximity of enemy and American units. Try as one might, there will always be serious problems with communications and coordination of various units, especially when there are different radio frequencies for all the diverse units and when planes flying hundreds of miles per hour are involved.

We took great pains to know the whereabouts of friendly units and what they were doing. We could not depend on radio contact solely because the NVA and VC had acquired many of our radios from the battlefield or through agents working at our bases. They became skilled at impersonating American units on the radio. We had to be vigilant about contacts or calls of which we weren't certain. Within the company the radiomen knew each other and could recognize voices but when we were operating with other units this wasn't the case.

* * *

Slowly the days and nights passed, one feeling and sounding much like another. There was no light at the end of this tunnel and certainly no feeling that we would survive the experience to talk about it later in life. Days merged into weeks and time dragged on slowly, with each day a challenge to our physical and mental resolve. In a letter sent to my brother in late March I noted that of the forty-five men in our platoon when we arrived, there were nine of us left.

One late afternoon on a typical day in the field, our platoon came upon an abandoned farmhouse that was surrounded by a masonry wall. The bullet-pocked building was made out of a masonry type of material and long-vacant. It must have been a nice place to live long before this, probably prior to World War II. We wanted to use the house and yard for a secure night stop but first, like always, had to check it out for enemy soldiers and booby traps. This was a routine action at every physical facility we approached or area where we wanted to stop.

One other man and I were sent forward to search the house and grounds. We carefully searched the building and surrounding yard and found nothing. We then went toward a nearby tree line to check for snipers, ambushes, or anything that seemed out of the ordinary. We hadn't gone very far, walking through shallow water, when all hell broke loose. The entire tree line opened fire on us at close range. Many bullets screamed next to my head and I could feel the force of the bullets as they passed inches away from my body. Miraculously there was an old rice paddy dike a few feet away. I dove for the dike and dropped face down into the mud on the safe side. The dike was only about a foot high. My partner, who was perhaps fifteen yards away, did the same.

Unfortunately, my M-16 was under me in the water and mud. "Well this is outfuckingstanding!" I said aloud for my ears only. I saw no viable alternative whereby our situation could end well with us standing up and walking away. I knew that the prospects for my partner and me were gloomy indeed in that stinking mud; the day we all dreaded seemed to have arrived for us.

I could hear and feel bullets slamming into the small earthen dike as I slowly squirmed around to face the sky rather than the mud. Cautiously putting my head and rifle over the lifesaving barrier, I began firing at shadows and smoke puffs from the ambushers' rifles. Dirt blown loose by incoming bullets peppered my arms and face. These were almost certainly local guerillas, as better-trained NVA soldiers would not have missed from that distance. As could have been predicted, my rifle jammed with mud after a minute or two and I had to try to clear it lying on my back in the shallow water. About that time the enemy must have figured they had killed me, so they aimed their fire a bit higher. The remainder of the platoon was within their range as well, directly behind us. They began exchanging fire. I could hear and feel scores of bullets just inches over my face; I was caught in the middle of crossfire.

At the time I had no idea as to the fate of my partner. In all the excitement I didn't know if he had been shot or was able to return fire. It turned out he was okay and was also trying to shoot from behind the same small dike about fifteen yards away. He too was in the crossfire.

Because we were on the same side of the dike as the rest of our unit the greatest danger was now the shots being fired by fellow marines, as their bullets were passing by extremely close. Friendly fire was our greatest threat. I screamed at the top of my voice several times for them to stop firing but to no avail. It's clear that we were assumed dead by our comrades as well as by the enemy. I shouted, "*Stop shooting*," and when that didn't work shouted, "*Stop the goddamned shooting!*" which was no more effective, my voice drowned out by distance and gunfire. I was actually getting quite angry. Neither of us dared raise our head or attempt to signal our unit because any movement placed us in their line of fire.

Eventually the ambushers broke off the engagement and the rest of the platoon stopped firing. They carefully made their way toward us and were shocked to see us both alive. After we had a chance to gather ourselves together and for me to clear the mud from my rifle's operating mechanism, we continued to the wooded area to search out the ambushers. We found several blood trails, but the attackers had simply vanished into the forest. VC and NVA, like marines, never left their dead or wounded behind. After a battle all that normally remained were blood trails. Because it was dusk and the jungle was dark with shadow, we didn't pursue them. That would have been folly in the thick woods at dark. It's likely they had well-hidden tunnels or bunkers nearby.

All too common Vietnam combat condition.
Photo from Wiki-Commons. Photographer unknown.

This incident was typical of many skirmishes. The enemy was well concealed in a tree line and we were in the open. We carefully aimed at muzzle flashes or smoke but rarely had a human form in our sights. Sometimes we simply sprayed bullets at the tree line in order to gain a few seconds during which we could find some sort of cover. Less often but even more unnerving, were the close-up or what we called eye-to-eye skirmishes. They were usually brief, but intense. If one survived the initial surprise ambush, the subsequent firefight involved quickly, but carefully, aiming at the enemy soldier who was looking at you and also taking aim to fire. Whoever fired first lived for the next encounter.

We ended up spending several nights at that compound, as it was strategically located and provided a relatively safe base from which to run patrols and seek out the enemy. It was also near a river, so it gave us a chance to clean up a bit. The house, though severely damaged, and the short masonry wall surrounding the courtyard provided relatively safe cover should it be needed. We occasionally ran across these abandoned homesteads in the Vietnam countryside. The vast majority of locals lived in grass and wood huts clustered in small villages. These homes, which stood by themselves in the countryside, must have been owned by someone of considerable wealth relative to the majority of residents. They often had a pagoda in the yard for religious ceremonies. These small pagodas were a common sight throughout the country. A haunting feature of pagodas near long-abandoned rural homes is that they often had evidence of freshly burned incense in them, regardless of their remote location in enemy territory.

A memory of that particular period of time in the rural compound is the capture of two VC women near the river one day. It was a strange and yet potentially deadly encounter. They were dressed like hookers and offered *boom boom* (sex). One didn't have to be very bright to understand that something was wrong. It seemed quite clear that they were in fact a couple of the infamous *angels of death* that were so feared. The angels were enemy women who enticed troops to their death. They were undoubtedly part of the same cadre of Viet Cong that ambushed my partner and me a few days earlier. They were sent by chopper to the rear for interrogation. Their accomplices were almost certainly close by, but we did not find them.

During the first three months in-country we were always dirty and wore the same fatigues week after week. Washing up involved wading into one of the shallow, stagnant rivers we came across. The water was muddy and didn't do much to clean us off. *Jungle rot* was a common and potentially serious ailment that occurred because our feet were almost always wet and dirty. I developed a serious case of this affliction that took many years and much prescribed medication to finally heal years after returning home. One of the most frequently requested items in care packages from home was foot powder. It was nearly impossible to obtain in-country but was important for health and comfort purposes. Its use was far more widespread than only for application on one's feet.

There were often several days in a row that boots were never removed or taken off just momentarily to remove a burr or similar irritant. When in a relatively safe area boots were taken off for short periods to dry out as much as possible. The lesson taught in infantry training about always checking boots prior to putting them on was religiously followed in-country. There was no telling what sort of critter might crawl into them when unattended.

One of the realities that separated grunts from rear echelon troops is a practice that no doubt seems strange to the unknowing. Grunts didn't wear underwear. Because we were always wet and dirty, tight-fitting underwear, which of course would have been always wet and dirty as well, caused serious health problems.

* * *

After being in-country a couple months, I received a promotion to E-3, or lance corporal. It wasn't much, but it resulted in a few more bucks to send home each month. Troops in Vietnam received the standard wage for their level, plus overseas and combat pay. Base pay had increased very little since the Korean War, averaging around ninety dollars per month, plus another thirty dollars or so for the added overseas and combat benefits for lower-level enlisted personnel. Grunts had minimal need for money in Vietnam. Unlike rear-base personnel, who had many places at which they could spend money, front line soldiers had extremely few. Many infantrymen had 80 or 90 percent of their monthly pay sent directly home and received only a small amount of their pay each month for personal in-country use. Pay was in the form of military scrip, officially known as Military Payment Certificates (MPCs), not American dollars. Scrip had the value of actual currency, however, and the Vietnamese gladly accepted it. There was a profitable black market for MPCs in the larger cities of Vietnam.

* * *

In addition to point man duties I was also designated as the backup radioman. This meant that when the regular squad or platoon radioman, (usually a young grunt, as it was not a specialized technical position), was wounded or killed, it was my duty to immediately take the radio and carry it. I was in the third squad of the third platoon of Kilo Company. The radio designation for my squad's radio was Kilo Three Charlie. *Three* to designate the third platoon of Kilo Company and *Charlie* to designate the third squad of the third platoon. Kilo-6 was the platoon leader and 3-Charlie-6 was the squad leader's radio designation.

As a result of backup radioman duties, I still have a small notebook that contains code information needed for various radio communications. There were many different frequencies radio operators had to know in the event we needed to talk to pilots, choppers, tank units, artillery units, other ground units, the ARVN, or other units.

Keeping track of radio frequencies for specific communications was critical. For instance, medivac missions used frequencies that were coded as button vermillion at 35.50 megahertz and button yellow at 43.50 megahertz. A medivac request had nine required items: 1) the priority of the medivac; 2) the unit involved; 3) coordinates of the pickup site; 4) number of persons needing evacuation, both wounded and killed; 5) Whether airborne assistance in the form of jets or gunships was required; 6) whether the landing zone, (LZ) was secure; 7) the best direction of approach for the chopper; 8) how the LZ was to be marked (what color smoke, flare, or other signals. This was critical as the enemy used false signals to trick choppers into an ambush); and 9) the radio frequency to be used once near the LZ.

Field units were required to give spot reports and casualty reports to battalion headquarters on a regular basis. These were basic information updates such as location, combat actions, number of casualties, number of enemy casualties and captures, equipment losses and replacements needed, basic supply needs, and more.

Radio communication was complicated by the fact that normal, everyday language and terms couldn't be used, as radio messages were monitored by the VC and NVA. Everything was in code, though not an especially sophisticated one. Trying to be too clever with codes resulted in breakdowns in vital communications. A system called *Shackle* was the basis of much radio communication. In this arrangement, ten-letter words with ten different letters, were utilized, and each letter equated to a number, zero through nine. Two Shackle code words used were *roundtable* and *copulating*. In roundtable, R meant *one*, O meant *two*, U meant *three* and so on. Having a pen and paper handy to make the translations from letters to numbers was crucial.

There was a list of pre-assigned code words, which were occasionally changed. Specific frequencies for each unit we were likely to communicate with were also given code names. Everything we did, from the basics such as ordering more bullets to intelligence reports, had a code.

Specific or actual times were never used over the radio. Delineating times used a method called *tango time*. This was a previously agreed-upon time, such as 11:00 a.m., from which the scheduling of actions was based. For instance, on the radio the operator said "Tango time plus three" for an action to take place at 1400 hours.

I always kept my notebook safely wrapped in plastic in my backpack, so as to always have it available. As a part-time radioman, I didn't memorize everything. This information and memories of how important these things were in their proper time and place, is hard to let go. The passage of time has made something that once literally had life and death implications little more than an interesting curiosity.

* * *

One of the more difficult emotional aspects of deployment in Vietnam was preparing to go into locations where we knew we would encounter strong resistance. As we hiked into these regions, we knew what awaited us. We anticipated the screams of men badly maimed by a mine or the sound of the jungle exploding in gunfire in an ambush. The smell of burned flesh and gunpowder mixed together was a scent we all knew. Fears were very real, and we could taste the anxiety as we saddled up and headed out, knowing the inevitable was just minutes or hours away. Each time we ventured out we all silently hoped and prayed that today wasn't our day, or if it was, that death came quickly, with minimal suffering.

A densely wooded area we called *Booby Trap Alley* was only a few square miles in size but was one of the more feared pieces of land in the Da Nang area. It was near our base camp and was a hotbed of VC activity. Thus, we spent a lot of time in there and paid dearly for it. It was an overgrown area of thick vegetation, including many thorny bushes and clinging vines. It was almost impossible to negotiate through the brush and we were often forced to use machetes to hack our way through or take a chance and follow faint trails. Because of the conditions, we often had to resort to using the paths. The enemy was always waiting for us on these trails with mines, ambushes, and snipers. Almost always we were out in small group size, platoon and squad patrols being by far the most common, with roughly ten to thirty men.

In late March our platoon swept through Booby Trap Alley once again. It was another effort to locate and destroy VC and to let them know that we would not be restricted in our movements. This particular day was worse than most.

We suffered several casualties from hit and run ambushes and booby traps. About mid-morning the radioman was injured, so I placed the radio on my back, like a backpack. Shortly thereafter, the corpsman and I separated from the main portion of the platoon to make our way to another wounded man. We were carefully following a faint trail in the dense cover when we came to an old overgrown wire fence on the top of a small dike, maybe forty-eight inches high overall and covered with thick brush.

When we got to the fence I repeatedly tried to crawl through a small hole, but the radio kept getting snagged on the wire and I couldn't get through. I started to take the radio off and drag it through behind me when Doc (we called all corpsmen *Doc*) said he'd go through first and clear the tangled wire out of the way. He got through, but immediately on the opposite side of the fence he activated a mine. Being just a couple of feet apart, the concussion knocked me down and unconscious for several seconds. When I came to moments later, Doc's severed leg, with the boot still on, was lying on my chest. He was separated by the dike and fence remnants, moaning in pain. I received minor shrapnel wounds to my arm but nothing disabling or life-threatening.

Fortunately, the radio on my back wasn't damaged and I began calling for help. At the same time, the rest of the platoon was taking fire and was pinned down, so assistance was not available. Doc was in bad shape, but still alive, and I helped him the best I could, suppressing the bleeding with gauze from his medic's bag and using a piece of cloth as a tourniquet. He was conscious enough to give himself a morphine shot. I was on high alert at the spot where he lay wounded, fully expecting an attack from nearby enemy fighters. It was a common practice for the enemy to attack in these vulnerable circumstances. Occasional explosions, either grenades used in close combat or additional mines, occurred around us, as did sporadic rifle fire. The platoon commander was eventually made aware of our situation by radio contact and several marines made it to our location after ten or fifteen minutes. By good fortune, the fighting remained a hundred yards or more away and we successfully got Doc out of his perilous situation.

The fighting eventually subsided, and we were able to evacuate the dead and wounded back to a safe area where they were choppered out on a medivac. Doc was still alive but clearly in serious condition due to blood loss and other injuries. Carrying him and his leg through the thick brush was difficult and a painful experience for him. There was just no way to be gentle given the conditions. We heard some time later from another marine who was at the same hospital as Doc that he survived.

* * *

It might seem obvious in retrospect, but one of the things that becomes apparent in combat is how heavy and cumbersome dead bodies are and how difficult it is to carry them—especially through swamps, thick cover, or in hilly situations. Even worse are the wounded. Comrades desperately want to be as gentle as possible to minimize pain and further damage to the wounded man's body, but it's just not possible. It's heartbreaking while it's happening.

The radio saved my life, or at least my body, that day in the Alley. Had the primary radioman not been wounded and therefore I didn't have the radio on my back, I would have been the first one through the fence and tripped the mine myself. Additionally, the small dike protected me from the flying shrapnel for the most part, showing just how hit and miss combat survival is. Combat is very much luck or fate oriented. Sometimes a bullet misses by an inch, sometimes it hits its mark. Sometimes a person misses stepping on a mine by an inch other times it feels the footstep and does its foul deed. It's all very impersonal. The best a person can do is to learn quickly and act in a manner that lessens the odds. They're never eliminated, and one can't account for fate or just plain bad luck.

This very typical battle in Booby Trap Alley was representative of many skirmishes. The enemy wasn't trying to drive us out of the country and take sole possession of the piece of land; they wanted to bloody us up and cause morale problems. Conversely, we weren't trying to drive the VC or NVA out; we knew that was an impossibility. We wanted to make sure they knew we could and would go wherever we wanted to, to demonstrate that they didn't actually possess it. The war was so unlike earlier wars in which the underlying objective was to seize land and hold it.

On the front lines of the Vietnam War there were no days off and there were no holidays, as we were to learn the hard way a few days after the incident in Booby Trap Alley. Easter Sunday was anything but a day of peace and beauty, such as we normally associate with this holy day. It began in a manner that should have suggested a peaceful day, but it wasn't to be. A beautiful dawn with blue skies and pleasant temperatures greeted us. A helicopter brought in a chaplain and articles needed for a religious service. Most marines present participated in the service, standing or kneeling with flak jackets on and rifles nearby. The rough, unchurchlike surroundings didn't detract from the ceremony. Hymns were sung, prayers said, and the priest who made the special trip to spend the morning with us spoke of rebirth and better days ahead. The sound of helicopter rotors nearby and a Puff the Magic Dragon airplane laying down streams of bullets a couple miles away made for a surreal setting. Nearby, marines that couldn't stay for the service headed out on patrol. Our platoon's turn was to come soon.

Following the service, it was time to get back to the task at hand. The war wouldn't be won with Hail Marys. We saddled up and headed into the unknown. There was no holiday dinner at grandma's house that day, rather there were encounters with an enemy that only wanted to see us dead, no matter the day. An Easter day that began with such hope and the promise of better days ahead ended with a dozen men wounded and two killed by mines and ambushes.

# CHAPTER 5

# A COLLISION OF
# DEADLY FORCES

I n May, the North Vietnamese Army and regional Viet Cong guerillas launched another countrywide offensive. The attacks included ground assaults against American and ARVN bases and bombardment with artillery and rockets. Intelligence previously confirmed massive influxes of NVA troops into enemy safe areas near large cities. These troops were fresh and well equipped with the latest Russian and Chinese firepower. Several American offensive operations were initiated to overcome enemy assaults and to launch counterattacks against major NVA bases.

Battalions from three Marine regiments, the Fifth, Seventh, and Twenty-Seventh, conducted Operation Allen Brook in an area called *Go Noi Island* as part of this counteroffensive. Go Noi Island is a low-lying, several thousand-acre piece of enemy-held land fifteen miles south of Da Nang in the broad swampy basin of the Thu Bon River. This well-known stronghold, with its difficult terrain, was part of the deadly region that we called *Dodge City*. Located due west of the town of Hoi An, it was a strategic base for North Vietnamese soldiers and VC. The locale consisted of thick brush, tall elephant grass, swamps, and sandy soil, which made walking difficult, and many tree lines that once marked the edges of cultivated fields.

Route 1, the trans-Vietnam highway connecting the Chinese border on the north and the Mekong Delta to the south, ran east of the island and the jungled Que Son Mountains were just southwest. These highlands provided a sheltered sanctuary through which NVA troops made their way across South Vietnam on Route 534 from Laos for battle assignments in the Da Nang and Hoi An region. Go Noi Island was honeycombed with tunnels and reinforced bunkers. It had an underground hospital and a stockpile of weapons and other equipment.

At least a division of additional enemy combatants, 10,000 troops, had amassed there in recent weeks. Military intelligence feared that a major offensive on their part against Da Nang was imminent. We were to attack and neutralize the enemy forces before they could attack the Da Nang air and naval base and other nearby high priority targets.

In the days prior to leaving for Go Noi Island there was little suggestion of what actually lie in store. We lacked credible information and did not appreciate the deadly reality of this enemy base of operations. Major offensive efforts against the North Vietnamese Army were fought throughout 1967 into early 1968 by other Marine units on Go Noi. Enemy combatants soon returned, however, building new facilities, including a hospital and numerous reinforced bunkers. To enhance the invulnerability of their bunkers and underground facilities, the North Vietnamese and Viet Cong had torn up a nearby railroad and used the rails as reinforcing beams and bulwarks. The communists controlled the entire geographic area with a well-entrenched political and military command infrastructure. The local populace maintained a strong Viet Cong orientation, making the island a safe haven for both NVA and VC military units. Go Noi was home to three local Viet Cong units, the R-20 Battalion, V-25 Battalion and T-3 Sapper Battalion, as well as Group 44, the headquarters for the enemy's operations in Quang

Nam Province. The Thirty-sixth and Thirty-eighth Regiments of the 308th North Vietnamese Division were based there, as well as many troops from the NVA's Second Division.

Marine brass might have been aware of the size and capability of the force that awaited our arrival but the average marine in 3/27 certainly wasn't. We also did not know that we were to be dropped in the middle a deadly ambush that had been formed to welcome us upon our arrival.

On May 4, units from the Seventh Marine Regiment began carefully making their way toward the interior from the outside. After a couple days of fairly light resistance, things got worse as they approached the main stronghold. On May 13 one company from 3/27—I Company—was sent in to assist the Seventh Marine units. They were inserted by helicopter on Hill 148, the highest point of land in the region, and began working their way in. On the morning of May 17, I Company was ambushed by a large dug-in force of NVA. They suffered high casualties and were trapped in a perilous situation in the open on a dry riverbed. By the end of that day virtually all of the company's officers and NCOs, sergeants and corporals, were dead or seriously wounded. Of the total Marine casualties on that first day of the battle, I Company sustained fifteen killed and fifty wounded. They were no longer a functional fighting force because of the number of casualties.

Deeds of bravery and of service to fellow marines on that deadly day were commonplace. One of the most compelling involved an eighteen-year-old from Illinois, Robert C. Burke. Burke was a machine gunner with I Company and he undertook a one-man assault on the enemy that saved countless lives, though it ultimately cost him his own. He singlehandedly assaulted several fortified bunkers, eliminating fire and allowing seriously wounded comrades to be removed from danger. He then took out several snipers that were shooting any marine that ventured from cover and continued pouring fire into the NVA force shooting from a nearby tree line. He fired until his machine gun malfunctioned due to extreme heat, the barrel and mechanism melting. He then took an M-16 from a wounded marine and attacked enemy positions, throwing grenades into bunkers. Despite the 110-degree-heat and extreme danger, he fought to the death protecting his comrades, breaking the enemy's attack long enough for survivors to escape and join forces. He was awarded the Congressional Medal of Honor posthumously, at age eighteen—the youngest recipient to be awarded the medal during the Vietnam War.

Burke's courage and his actions under withering fire are a perfect example of the US Marine Corps' insistence that all marines are riflemen. Burke's MOS was as a mechanic, not an infantryman. But like all marines, he received mandatory combat infantry training right after boot camp. He then trained in his Marine mechanic MOS. When the Twenty-Seventh Regiment was pulled together in mid-February, he was one of many brought into the regiment with an MOS other than the 0300 infantry class.

* * *

K Company and L Company were scheduled to join the fray at that point by means of a truck convoy, but with I Company's emergency situation, plans were quickly changed. We were to now go in as soon as possible via helicopter, to a landing area as close to I Company as could be found. This was our first helicopter assault, and we knew that shit was hitting the fan in a big way at our landing zone. With this knowledge in mind, it immediately became apparent that flying over Vietnam in a chopper is seriously deceptive. From the air the countryside is beautiful and peaceful. It's hard to imagine that violent death awaits at the end of the short helicopter ride.

Had we been deposited outside the main battle area things might have been different, but insertion was near the midst of the fighting. This meant a hot LZ. The first three marines off our large CH-53 Sea Stallion chopper were immediately shot or hit with mortar shrapnel as they exited the rear ramp. Those of us who followed quickly loaded them back on the bird, which was immediately converted from a troop carrier to a medivac chopper. Running through a hail of bullets, simultaneously cursing and praying, we ran out to set up a perimeter. There is nothing in this world more frightening than landing in a helicopter in a landing zone under attack as the choppers arrive—a hot LZ. The process of landing and exiting the aircraft is one of extreme vulnerability. Advantage is entirely with the concealed ambushers.

The NVA had clearly fixed their mortars and machine guns on our landing site. The accuracy of their rounds was deadly. Landing became so treacherous that the last troop helicopter was diverted to a location nearby that was out of the immediate fray and where 3/27 brass was setting up a command base. Those marines joined us on foot as quickly they could.

The situation went quickly downhill for our two rescue companies. We were surrounded and taking fire from all sides, with mortars and rocket propelled grenades (RPGs) pounding the landing zone. Machine gun fire made movement almost impossible except by crawling. Landing zones by their nature must be free of trees and other cover, such as boulders, so we had nothing to get behind for safety. We had elephant grass for concealment but nothing for cover and protection from bullets. To add insult to injury, elephant grass has sharp edges that will cut skin like razors. Crawling through it caused its own problems. Despite the great danger all around us, little things like sweat burning in fresh cuts on the skin caused frustration out of proportion to the situation.

Air and artillery support were called for as a last resort. The bombs and artillery were falling almost on top of us, the NVA were that close. It speaks to the accuracy and training of the pilots and artillerymen that they could place ordnance that close and yet not hit us. A few days later we watched a Phantom crash into the ground in front of our position, shot down while conducting a similar low-level bombing run.

We slowly worked our way closer to I Company, carrying dead and wounded with us. We ultimately reached the remnants of the company and were able to combine forces and somewhat secure a fighting area. The marines of I Company were joyful, to say the least, when we finally inched our way to them.

Marines on operation on Go Noi Island. Official USMC photograph.

We fought our way to an area that provided a little more cover in the way of some trees and tried to set up a defensive position. All the supplies we were going to have for several days were in our packs and pockets or hanging around our necks. We were going to have to survive on one meal per day. Ammunition quickly became a serious concern because heavy fighting was rapidly depleting our supply. Hot weather and extreme exertion made the water situation critical.

It was not possible to do the normal aggressive actions such as patrols, as we were essentially trapped. That night, when I was supposed to catch an hour or two of sleep, I was awakened by gunfire from an attack on our position. I looked up and green machine gun tracer bullets were flying directly over my face a scant few inches away. The force and heat of the rounds created a powerful emotional and physical impact. Every fifth bullet in machine gun ammo belts is a tracer, so the gunner can see where the rounds are going; it makes what looks like a line through the air. I prayed that the gunner wouldn't lower his gun barrel by even a fraction of an inch. Had I jumped up when I woke up, I would have been cut in half. After a few seconds the NVA gunner moved his gun a little to the side and the bullets went elsewhere. I immediately crawled into the shallow foxhole hastily dug the evening before. We beat this and other attacks that night back.

The next night a large and determined Chinese soldier snuck into our lines and it took three of us to subdue and capture him before he could kill anyone with the large knife he had in his hand. Since he had no other weapons it seemed clear that his intent was to silently kill as many marines as he could while we were in our foxholes. One of the most frightening commands heard during combat events is the order to *fix bayonets*. For most of the first several days of the operation we kept bayonets attached on our rifles because of the high likelihood of close combat.

\* \* \*

Clouds and ground fog resulted in nights that were pitch black and visibility limited to a few feet at best. Whenever we moved away from our foxhole, we always gave whispered warnings so that nearby marines knew who was moving. We had no protective fence of any sort and it was easy, in fact quite common, for enemy soldiers to walk right into our lines during the course of the operation. Gunfire and curses of "what the fuck!" shouted by marines during the dark nights were evidence of attempts by the enemy to broach what line of defense we had.

Aerial support craft dropped flares that lit up the sky for a minute or two and then blackness descended again, darker than ever due to the sudden switch from glaring artificial brightness to total darkness. A common sight in the night sky was Spooky or Puff the Magic Dragon gunships. These interchangeable nicknames weren't attached to any particular model of airplane filling the role, but rather the presence of these aerial attack planes in the night skies over Vietnam. The aircraft were World War II vintage DC-3s and AC-47s, and newer C-123s and C-130s that were modified and fitted with electronic machine guns called *miniguns*. In 1965 the Douglas AC-47 was the first of the series of planes to be modified by the US Air Force, designed to greatly increase the firepower of close air support aircraft. They could lay down six thousand rounds a minute with accuracy, providing an important layer of support for American troops when under attack.

The ammunition for the miniguns contained red tracer rounds, creating curving red lines from the invisible plane down to the ground. Like many scenes in combat, the view created by Spooky or Puff gunships during nighttime aerial attacks was a dramatic sight to behold. In night fights they also dropped flares that illuminated large areas for two or three minutes. The night was often disrupted by flares. Flares were dropped over the battlefield by these planes during Allen Brook, but their guns were mostly silent because we were actually located too close to the enemy. There was no clear delineation between their location and ours. This demonstrated a deliberate combat tactic frequently used by the NVA. It was their intent to wait to initiate contact until they were very close to American forces. In this manner it was impossible for us to call in support from artillery or attack planes because we were only yards apart. As with many battles, Allen Brook was in large part fought on the enemy's terms, another deliberate strategy of North Vietnamese military strategists. Even when we initiated an action against known NVA bases the fighting was on terms controlled by the enemy. They revealed themselves and attacked only when it was to their advantage. During periods of aerial bombardment they remained hidden underground.

\* \* \*

Every day of the operation was incredibly hot. Daytime temperatures were never below 110 degrees according to corpsman medical thermometers. It was very muggy, as was the norm in this low coastal area near the sea. We were running seriously low on water, food, and ammunition. In fact, our water supply was essentially depleted.

We carried all the dead to one location in the center of our position, trying to keep them in the shade. The two neat, long rows of dead young Americans in body bags, with some of the dead just covered with whatever we could find when we ran out of body bags, was a terrible sight.

The heat and lack of water was a critical problem. I personally witnessed two young marines die of heat stroke. They writhed and moaned in pain, their brains and key organs destroyed by the heat. There was nothing we could do. I knew of four marines that died of heat stroke and dehydration.

I was determined that it wasn't going to happen to me. There was an old bomb crater fifty or so yards from our position that was filled with filthy green scum-covered water. It was worse than a mud puddle in a manure-covered barnyard. I got so desperate at one point that I crawled over to the crater, brushed away the worst of the scum and dirt and filled my canteen with water. I dropped in a couple Iodine tablets and drank it. It was the vilest-tasting, hot and disgusting water one can imagine. As I drank, the smell of rotting corpses was overpowering. Looking around a bit it became clear that the bodies had to be in the water. I moved some floating debris and saw two badly decomposed NVA corpses floating in the water a few feet from where I had filled my canteen. I had no choice; I moved to a spot in the bomb crater a little further away and refilled my canteen.

Extraction of casualties was critical, so we focused on securing a nearby open area on the edge of the fighting, far enough away so that medivac choppers could land. The procession of medivacs over the coming days was a terrible sight. The medical situation was dire, as by the end of the day on May 18 several of the eight corpsmen on the operation with us were dead or wounded.

Medivac choppers were life-savers, and their pilots and crews were amazingly courageous men. It's impossible to know how many soldiers survived despite serious injuries because they were able to be evacuated on a timely basis to a distant hospital. It was common for the enemy to wait until the choppers were just landing to spring ambushes on them and us. The chopper crews knew that but always came in anyway, no matter how dangerous the conditions. The aluminum skin of the choppers didn't slow down a bullet in the least, so their crews had no more protection than we did out in the open and they made bigger and better targets. On one occasion I was standing a few feet away from a chopper that was being loaded, talking to the pilot on the radio—we were looking at each other through the plexiglass of the chopper's cockpit while talking over the radio. Suddenly an ambush was sprung, and bullets ripped through the skin of the chopper from front to back. Several men standing near me were also hit. I saw a tracer round go through the chest of a nearby marine and exit from his back, still burning. He fell dead at my feet. The pilot hastily (as quickly as a huge helicopter can move) got the chopper airborne. I had no way of knowing what happened inside the bird and how many men were hit but fortunately the pilot hadn't been.

At one point during that period a twin rotor CH-46 came in to evacuate some wounded. We loaded it in a hurry. I can see the picture in my mind clearly of the chopper lifting off and at about thirty feet high being hit by an RPG. It exploded in flames and fell, burning bodies jumping or falling out as it descended. War is full of such ugly sights that can never be unseen.

Of the many impressions one is left with as a result of combat, the sound of the human voice under great stress is one of the most powerful. Such communications were always at the same time forceful and emotional. Raw and desperate feelings were obvious. During Operation Allen Brook and in every other battle, large or small, in the war, commanders, ranging from corporals to captains, screamed for attention and immediate action at the top of their voice in order to be heard over the noise. Expletives were used in virtually every sentence or command for added effect. "Gunner, get your fucking gun up here, now!"

"Shoot that goddamned sniper in the tree. He's already killed three fucking marines!"

"Corpsman, up—*now!*"

"Get Six on the fucking radio to find out where the goddamned medivac is!" Language was crude and desperate but no more so than the circumstances. There was no place for calm or highbrow conversations or the niceties of civilization. It was kill or be killed, not a book club gathering. Deadly confusion and disorder reigned, and frantic human beings were trying to make the best of it in order to survive.

Battles also have other unique sounds. Grunts quickly became experts at distinguishing one weapon from another. The notes of the M-16 and AK-47 were different. The NVA heavy machine gun sounded different than the American M-60. A shot that hits its target doesn't sound the same as a shot that misses. The sounds of mortars versus RPGs versus rockets were dissimilar. When it came to incoming artillery rounds and rockets, the whistle gave about two seconds of warning that it was going to land close. One had better react quickly.

* * *

As the days passed our ability to be more aggressive grew and we took the fight to the dug-in enemy. The focal point of the NVA position in our particular zone was a well-fortified tree line. In a final desperate attempt to gain the initiative and remove the NVA from their bunkers, an attack was planned. On the afternoon of May 25 we lined up and made a suicide frontal assault against the heavily defended fortifications.

The specific date stuck in my mind all these years because on a personal level it was one of my worst days there, and it was deadly for the entire unit. For my sister it was to be a much happier day. She was getting married in Seattle in a few hours. After all these years I clearly recall feeling sad and being quite angry at fate because I was going to ruin her wedding day. My sister, of course, wouldn't learn of my fate until several days afterwards. I had no doubt whatsoever but that I was going to die that day, thus ruining the anniversary date for her for the rest of her life. In what still feels like a miracle, I obviously didn't die on her special day. But in subsequent years I came to the conclusion that this date will go down as the single worst day of my life. That's a strong statement to make, but thus far it hasn't been surpassed. I can't imagine the circumstances that might eclipse that day, or any of the days leading up to it.

NVA riflemen with their AK-47s and RPGs were supported by machine gunners and mortar crews. They were in concrete bunkers and trenches; we were on foot in an open field in front of them. We commenced advancing across the field toward the tree line. Early in this advance the platoon radioman was killed. In this instance he might have been the random target of an NVA machine-gunner, the intentional target of a sniper or the anonymous victim of artillery or a mortar; I didn't know, and it didn't matter. But often the man carrying the radio was targeted because of his strategic importance. The persons near him were also targeted because it was assumed they were officers in charge. Carrying the radio was a bit like putting a bullseye on your chest. As backup radioman I removed the radio from the dead man and put it on my back. The PRC-25 radio was about three inches thick, a foot wide and fifteen inches high, with a spare battery hooked to the bottom which provided another two-by-ten-inch area of cover. Again, it saved my life as it also had two months earlier.

We were about midway to the tree line when a mortar or rocket landed directly behind us. It knocked me off my feet and some shrapnel hit me in the neck and in the back, though superficial injuries resulted because of protection afforded by the radio and flak jacket. The radio was completely destroyed. Had I not had it on my back I would have been killed or suffered grievous spinal cord injury without question.

Fighting went on for the rest of the day, with close air and artillery support again called in, including napalm drops so close nearby that our own men were burned. Incredibly, the NVA came out of their deep, reinforced bunkers after the bombardments and continued the fight. The tree line was eventually captured but at a great cost and as the result of incredible bravery. For that day alone at least four Bronze Stars, six Silver Stars, and two Navy Crosses were awarded. But in reality, the numbers could and should have been higher. Heroism and bravery were the order of the day, but most of the selfless valiant deeds were unseen or undocumented.

* * *

There was little to differentiate day one from day ten in this operation. The heat never relented, resulting in many heat-related casualties. The enemy strength kept steady, as fresh NVA reinforcements moved in to support them. On what I think was the third day of the operation, we spent hours policing the battlefield while constantly being shot at by NVA snipers in trees all around us. We piled helmets, bloody flak jackets, and mangled rifles into large piles, monuments to the valor of the young marines on the Go Noi battlefield, most just recently out of high school.

Several of those young men were new arrivals to our unit. Because of the many casualties we experienced over the last couple months 3/27 received replacements prior to Allen Brook to augment the battalion's strength. Being a newly assigned soldier or marine in Vietnam was hard. One was forced to learn a great deal in a short time or die. Though it might seem that being in-country only two or three months barely qualified us to consider ourselves hardened veterans, it in fact did. They were months filled with danger and death. We called new replacements *FNGs*—fucking new guys. It was nothing personal, but inexperience placed them and others in danger. I knew several FNGs that were killed their first week in the field. There were also instances in which others paid the price for unwise action of a new inexperienced rifleman. FNGs were also referred to as boots, a generic term for inexperienced soldiers. Boots were at the bottom of the pecking order. A commonly heard refrain was "Hey boot, get the hell over there and offload that chopper," or "Boot, go burn the fucking shitters!" It was no fun being a new guy, but if you survived the first few weeks in Nam, replacements took your place on the bottom rung.

* * *

The third battalion was extricated from the battlefield on May 29 with the aid of several tanks and relief companies from other Marine units. A comprehensive account of Operation Allen Brook would require a book of its own. The official US Marine Corps version of the operation provides a dry, but factual account for history on behalf of the men who were there.

At some later point I came across a very brief article in a military newspaper about Operation Allen Brook, I suspect it was the *Stars and Stripes* paper. I tore out the story that summarized all that was Operation Allen Brook and weeks of incredible effort, heroism, and danger into one paragraph. It reads: "The 3/27 Marines took over control of Allen Brook and met the heaviest North Vietnamese resistance of the operation while sweeping into Cu Ban Village during the afternoon. As the battalion swept through elephant grass and into a tree line at the edge of the village, they were met by a hail of automatic weapons, rocket, and mortar fire." That was it. That was the story of the operation. What they wrote of was just the first few minutes of days resembling hell. That summary is so sterile it's almost an insult to those that were there. Accounts of battles always fall far short of adequately describing combat actions. The blood, guts, fear, and pain that is the reality of such a scenario is impossible to portray in simple words. In a later letter to a brother, I described the second day of the operation as an almost unending firefight from dawn to dark, with so much smoke in the air it was hard to breathe.

Though costly, Allen Brook was a military success, like every major battle we were involved in. We broke the back of the enemy force and prevented an offensive against high-value targets. Over 900 NVA were killed that we knew of, while we suffered 170 marines and two corpsmen killed and 1,124 marines wounded. Our division was awarded a Presidential Unit Citation "for extraordinary heroism and outstanding performance of duty . . ." The secretary of the navy also presented the Meritorious Unit Commendation to 3/27 for its deeds in Allen Brook: ". . . those qualities of valor and professional skill which were in keeping with the highest traditions of the Marine Corps." It's a hell of a hard way to earn an *atta boy*.

Recognition by military brass for valiant deeds is important, but much more meaningful are words of appreciation and respect by one's peers. For several years I received a Christmas card from an I Company marine who was present on that difficult day. In the card he wrote "Thank You" and "I Company" above his name. That said it all.

* * *

But the infuriating thing about Allen Brook, and every other of the dozen operations I participated in, is that they were essentially for nil. American military policy and strategies weren't about the capture and holding of land controlled by the enemy. The intent was to go in and harass the enemy, kill as many as possible (confirmed by body counts), and send a political message that we can go wherever we want regardless of the cost in blood. After we sent that message for the day or week or month, we left and allowed the VC and NVA to resume their operations in the area and for them to once again control the land that we had fought so hard for. There were many places in Vietnam, including Go Noi Island, where Americans had fought and died on the very same ground several times. Each time we relinquished it back to the enemy. The very next month after Allen Brook saw marines once again going into Go Noi Island on yet another operation to stake our claim.

Though fighting raged across the country throughout 1968, the first five months saw two major combat offensives by the North Vietnamese. The first was the countrywide Tet Offensive begun on January 30. Three months after Tet, from April 29–May 30, another major series of attacks across the country known as the May Offensive occurred. It was even bloodier than the first. The battle for the city of Hue and the siege and daily battles at the Marine base at Khe Sanh are perhaps the two best-known. Marine bravery and heroism at Hue and Khe Sanh deserve to rate with the legendary days of the Corps. Those marines faced tremendous odds from a numerically superior enemy that waged a no-holds-barred fight against the marines and civilians alike.

Atrocities committed by the VC and NVA in Hue were incredible. At least three thousand civilians were rounded up and systematically murdered. Many were left lying in rows in the city, dead bodies on their stomachs with hands tied behind their backs and telltale bullet damage to their heads. Marines who had seen the unthinkable and were hard to shock were stunned at the carnage. Other civilians were dumped in mass graves that were found after marines and the First Cavalry and 101st Airborne Army units freed the city. The NVA and VC targeted their enemies broadly—Christians, governmental officials, teachers, doctors, and anyone that they considered traitors and anti-communist reactionaries. The NVA had between eight and ten battalions in Hue. Capture of the city involved weeks of vicious urban combat with progress measured in feet or yards and house by house. Marine losses in the battle were 142 dead and 1,100 wounded. Army casualties were 74 killed and 509 wounded. South Vietnamese forces lost at least 400 killed and over 2,100 wounded. NVA deaths were placed at 2,500 to as many as 5,000.

For seventy-seven days marines at the besieged Khe Sanh outpost lived through daily bombardments of rockets and artillery at a level that seems inconceivable today. Desperate battles fought by infantry and artillery units of the Third Marine Division are true stories of heroes. Aerial resupply of the base and close air support provided by Marine, Air Force and Army aviation units under some of the most dangerous conditions ever encountered are likewise stories of indomitable courage and an example of comrades willing to give all for their fellow service members.

North Vietnam wanted to establish a *Liberation Government* in northwestern South Vietnam from which they could carry out military and political campaigns in the south. The US base at Khe Sanh was all that stood in their way and they made every effort to destroy it. North Vietnamese General Giap wanted to make Khe Sanh a second Dien Bin Phu, a massive defeat for the Americans that would drive them from Vietnam as it did the French. The similarities were striking. Both bases were in valleys with massive enemy forces controlling all the high land around the base. As at Dien Bin Phu, there was no ground access due to NVA occupation of the region, only air. Giap didn't count on the bravery of the Americans, both on the ground and in the air, at Khe Sanh, however. He didn't take into consideration Operation Niagara—the daring Marine Corps and Air Force effort to keep the base supplied with beans and bullets despite every deadly attempt to stop the resupply flights.

A daily average of 360 incoming rounds of mortars, rockets, and artillery bombarded the men at Khe Sanh. One day an astounding 1,100 rounds were poured into the base. They were completely surrounded by three NVA divisions, about 20,000 men, against a force of about 5,000 Marines under siege. Yet those young men went out beyond the fence and bunkers daily to confront the enemy and make the point that we weren't cowered by their presence or numerical superiority. With the miracles of modern technology, millions of Americans were able to follow the siege of Khe Sanh on television news reports, making it an even more surreal experience for those in the bunkers as well as for viewers watching film of the scene from the comforts of home. The primary strategic reasons to maintain the Khe Sanh base were to send the message to North Vietnam that we were not going to allow them to claim a major portion of western I-Corps as their own and also to block their advances to bases and cities to the east and south. Our being there, at any cost, was meant to accomplish just that—be there—and make it clear to the world that we would not be driven out.

In the far northeast corner of South Vietnam were some of the most valuable and strategically important assets of the war. At the city of Dong Ha, coastal Route 1, the main north/south highway in the country, intersected with Route 9 from the western frontier and Laos less than ten miles south of the DMZ. In addition, the Cua Viet and Bo Dieu Rivers were major water transport routes used by American and South Vietnamese ships. Whoever controlled these two roads and the bridge over the Cua Viet River in Dong Ha largely controlled shipment of supplies in northern I Corps. From April 30–May 3 one of the fiercest battles of the war was fought by American units to hold this vital real estate. On May 2 approximately 600 Marines from Battalion Landing Team 2/4, the *Magnificent Bastards* confronted and defeated an estimated 10,000 NVA troops from the 320th Division in the Battle of Dai Do. BLT 2/4 suffered eighty-one killed and 397 wounded. On May 2, in Dai Do alone, 2/4 lost forty killed and 111 wounded. Three hundred eighty NVA were killed in that one battle. Total American losses from April 30 to May 3 were 233 killed, 821 wounded and one missing from the Third Marine Division. The Navy saw fifteen killed and twenty-two wounded. ARVN losses were listed as forty-two killed and 124 wounded. The NVA suffered an admitted 2,366 killed and an unknown number of wounded. Forty-three NVA were also taken prisoner by American forces, providing valuable intelligence about the rationale and scope of the May Offensive.

In the southern and central regions of South Vietnam, Army and Navy fighting men were bravely combating an invisible enemy in a hostile environment. Conditions varied depending on what part of the country one was assigned. In the Mekong River Delta, a sprawling area of half land and half water, the enemy was deeply entrenched. American soldiers and sailors ventured at great risk into that watery wilderness in boats and by trekking through swamps in an attempt to root the enemy out. Because of their ability to simply disappear into the surrounding landscape and villages, Charlie had a major advantage over American forces that had to expose themselves in river patrol boats or helicopters in order to access land controlled by the VC. Ambushes and mines were commonplace, and the environment of the Delta region was as hostile a place as one will find on this planet.

Soldiers in the Central Highlands fought an unending series of battles against a mixture of VC and NVA regulars whose numbers were constantly replenished by soldiers from North Vietnam streaming down the Ho Chi Minh Trail. Day after day and battle after battle, young Americans paid a high price attempting to keep the wild Cambodia border regions out of North Vietnam's control.

General Giap hoped that the May Offensive would give the North strategic real estate and supply infrastructure gains that would enhance their negotiating stance at the upcoming Paris Peace Talks. As was the case with the first offensive launched in late January, the endless battles fought between the two initiatives and the May Offensive were major defeats for the North Vietnamese. They did not capture or hold any of their objectives and losses were stunning.

*　*　*

The spring of 1968 was also very costly for American and South Vietnamese forces. The week of May 5–11 was the deadliest of the war for Americans, with 616 deaths. The month of May was the bloodiest of the war for American military units overall, with 2,169 soldiers killed. Eight hundred ten of those dead were Marines. The USMC also suffered 3,349 wounded in May. The Corps was taking so many casualties that recruitment could not keep up. As a result, the Marine Corps had to acquire some of its recruits through the military draft system. Levels of Marines in-country were constantly below what was approved and needed for combat effectiveness. By far the deadliest year of the war for Americans, 1968 saw nearly 17,000 killed. Marines suffered 5,063 killed, twenty-six missing in action and 29,320 wounded in action in that bloody year. Per the Marine Corps History and Museums Division, USMC deployment levels reached their peak in 1968 at 83,600 Marines in-country. The Army reached its maximum in-country personnel deployment level in 1969, at 360,500. Many of these deployed personnel were, of course, non-infantry. Infantrymen accounted for close to 80 percent of the casualties, although grunts represented a far lower percentage of in-country soldiers and marines. It was a rough year to be a grunt in Vietnam.

Some additional statistics that surprise the unaware: the average age of soldiers in Vietnam was nineteen to twenty, depending on the source of information. The average age of WWII troops was twenty-five to twenty-six, again, depending on the source. Additionally, for combat troops the average number of days in actual combat in Vietnam was at least 240 days, more for Marines as our deployments were 30 days longer. In WWII average days of combat for South Pacific soldiers was forty days over a four-year period, with lengthy periods between combat for regrouping and training. Author Ronald Spector, in his authoritative Vietnam history book *After Tet: The Bloodiest Year in Vietnam* provides additional surprising statistics. He wrote: "Note that the KIA rate for the Army is higher than the World War II rate during January–March 1968 and only slightly lower during April–June 1968. For the Marines the rate is higher during the entire period January–September 1968. During January–June the Marine casualty rate exceeds even the rate for European Theater in World War II." For grunts in Vietnam the reality of near constant combat and the ever-present threat of injury or death was something that affected every aspect of our psyche and day-to-day life.

The glazed look, the so-called thousand-yard stare on the faces of combat veterans, is real. It comes from battles such as Operation Allen Brook and many others, whether large or small. I vividly remember constantly telling myself at the time to erase those scenes, sounds and things that I did from my mind at all cost, or they would destroy me. Unseeing what was seen and mentally undoing what one had done to stay alive isn't easy to accomplish. Such memories are burned deeply into one's mind. I guess I succeeded. Over the years, however, I've looked down at my hands countless times and wondered how these hands could have done the things they did and how could these eyes have seen the things they saw. It seems that somehow new body parts should have replaced the old upon return to *The World*, as we called life outside the war. Just as the blood and mud is washed off one's body and new untarnished clothes replaced blood-soaked utilities worn in battle.

Most combat in Vietnam was anonymous. It was not documented in newsprint or recorded by television cameras. The participants of those battles were utterly alone. They had no audience and history will never record their deeds. Battles such as Operation Allen Brook were "minor" affairs that rarely got mentioned in major media outlets.

For the fighting men there they were anything but minor. Rather they were days filled with death and heroism, friendship, honor, sacrifice, despair, and pain, but they were largely anonymous as far as the outside world and history were concerned. The full stories of what happened on those days, beyond the raw statistics, will die with the participants.

* * *

When I arrived in Vietnam, I had no idea that being the man who carried the unit radio on my back was in my future. It never occurred to me that I would be designated as the backup radioman. I'm not sure why I was given that assignment, as I had no training for the duty. Sometimes I think it had to have been decided by those higher powers one chooses to consider as God or gods or fate, or whatever one ascribes such inexplicable actions to. Carrying the radio was not pleasant or easy duty. The device was heavy and cumbersome, adding to what was already at least thirty or forty pounds being carried in the heat and mud. It meant being near the center of danger, available for the unit commander to carry out his duties regardless of the situation or dangers. It meant being targeted by snipers because of the radio.

This unforeseen and unasked for duty changed my life forever. Without it I would unquestionably be dead or would have spent my life permanently crippled. Perhaps there is a life lesson here: the many unexpected or unasked for difficulties we encounter in our lives might somehow be the very things that in the end make our lives better.

With the advantage of hindsight, it might seem melodramatic, but even before Operation Allen Brook many of the young men I served with believed without the slightest doubt that we weren't going to make it back home—as did I. At some point we would die, either on a pointless routine patrol turned deadly by explosive devices or snipers, or in a major battle. This was a common feeling among grunts in frontline units. As more time passed and incidents piled up, the certainty of our inevitable demise became clearer. Many of us survived too many incidents that the odds were impossibly high against surviving and we knew that sooner or later our luck was going to run out.

As mental and physical stresses accumulate, depression and anger do as well. Some took out their anger at the military establishment or the Vietnamese, others blamed God for letting them suffer. If He knew we were going to die, why didn't He just get it over with and not allow it to happen after many months in-country. There were just too many point-blank ambushes where others were hit, or times when someone else stepped on a mine, or when a sniper hit the person in front or behind but somehow, for some reason, not the grunt who was left alive to witness and ponder.

In an attempt to increase survival odds grunts tried tactics resorted to by humans for millennia. Talismans, good luck charms, and various rituals were practiced. These ranged from the wearing of rosaries or tokens around one's neck, carrying a picture of a girlfriend or family in a pocket, the ace of spades card attached to the helmet, to a variety of other actions that a grunt thought helpful or personally important. It seemed that everyone tried something. The ace of spades became the symbol of the war, especially among the infantry. It meant several things: the logo for a very special club; a calling card left behind to let the enemy know we had been there, especially when left with dead NVA or VC soldiers or around destroyed enemy equipment or facilities; a sign of brotherhood or unity; and even a symbol of resistance to the military and the war. It was proudly displayed by the infantry in various manners, and Vietnam veterans often display it decades later in solidarity with others that they never knew and will never see, but who shared the experience of combat in Vietnam.

Most survivors of combat wonder *Why me? Why did I live when so many others near me died or were terribly wounded?* Survivors wonder if there is something in particular that we're supposed to do as the result of the gift of life that we received. Was there a quid pro quo attached to being allowed to live? If so, what was or is expected in return for our safe return? What can a person do or give that can possibly equate to having been given life itself?

It might seem incongruent to speak of the act of crying when writing of grunts in a war zone. Despite the physical pain and mental difficulties experienced or witnessed on a near daily basis, tears were rare. At the worst depths of anger and depression and sadness, very few cried. Feelings of anger and even revenge filled the mental voids caused by the death or injury of friends. Psychologists can determine the benefits or costs of such an approach to war, but the war fighters in Vietnam didn't have time to cry or allow depression to hinder the nasty job they'd been sent to do. Instead, anger and even hatred for those who we felt responsible for the pain, injuries, death, and sadness around us grew and occasionally exploded in unacceptable, albeit predictable, ways.

Military discipline and adherence to treaties are critical in war. Civilized moral behavior, as irrational as it might seem in combat, must prevail. The alternative is madness and cruelty and an evil place in which there can be no victory and no peace. Terrible incidents such as the My Lai Massacre occur when stresses exceed the breaking point and military discipline and adherence to rules of war are abandoned. The ever-present reality of never knowing who the enemy was, attacks by civilians, anger grown into hatred of all involved, and a breakdown in discipline led to horrible deeds that should never happen—not even in war.

Deeds of warfighters that cross the lines must be judged in the military world, not the clear-cut rules of a tidy civilian world. Don't for an instant think that other persons wouldn't commit a similar offense in the right circumstance. No nineteen-year-old kid went to Vietnam with the thought that he was now free to do evil things. The reality of the Vietnam War battlefield sometimes brought out the dark side that lurked deep under the surface. Usually it surfaced purely from the strong desire to stay alive. Sometimes it was revenge. Often it was because the breaking point had been reached. Each of us has our breaking point, especially when it is impossible to identify the enemy and there is no place that is truly safe. One was as likely to die at the hands of a grandmotherly *Mama San* or by a smiling ten-year-old boy, as by a highly skilled soldier from the North Vietnamese Army. Rather than condemn those who experienced un-human circumstances that took them past their emotional limits, noncombatants should pray that they personally are never in a situation so terrible that they too break and commit what had heretofore been an unthinkable act. Maintaining military discipline in Vietnam was a challenge for officers. Troops knew that America did not support the war or their presence in Vietnam. Some felt anger about being there under the prevailing circumstances—fighting an unpopular war in a foreign and hostile country that in large part seemed unappreciative of their sacrifices. We all knew that we were at the bottom of the pile. Nothing could be worse. A frequent refrain by combatants in Vietnam in response to possible disciplinary actions was "What the hell they gonna do, shave my head and send me to Nam?"

It was impossible for a placard-carrying peace protester to understand the strain that troops fighting in Vietnam were under. They could never understand why decent young men sometimes snapped and did things they would never have dreamed of doing prior to being sent to Vietnam. And the word *sent* is key. Nobody wanted to be there just for the hell of it. We were there because the American government, on behalf of the American people, sent us there.

In June I put in a transfer request for reassignment to a unit called Graves Registration. Quite obviously a rifleman couldn't just say he didn't want to be a grunt anymore and ask to be assigned to the position of driving USO show girls around. We were 0311s and that's what we would remain until death or discharge. However, rumor had it that Graves Registration—one of the most thankless jobs in the military—was short of help and was seeking transfers into the unit. Graves Registration was responsible for handling dead bodies once they got to the rear. I reasoned that as bad as that job was, at least it was safe and at the end of thirteen months I could go home in one piece. The request was denied. I knew of several others from my company that also applied for the same transfer and I suspect dozens of other grunts did from units across I Corps. Anything, it seemed, was better than what we had.

# CHAPTER 6

# IN THE EYE OF
# THE HURRICANE

O ur battalion was in such bad shape that for the month of June
the brass sent us to the outskirts of Da Nang to guard the air
base. It wasn't completely altruistic, there were reports that yet
another NVA offensive was about to take place with the air base being
their target. It didn't happen, quite likely because of damage inflicted
in the prior weeks during Operation Allen Brook.

Back in the civilized world things were happening that gave a
false sense of hope. On March 31, President Johnson gave a speech
that had broad ramifications. He not only told America that he was
not going to run for another term, he also extended an olive branch
to North Vietnam. He told the world he was ready to "go anywhere,
anytime" to discuss prospects for peace. Johnson stopped the bombing
campaign across most of the north and offered to begin negotiations
for an end to the war (the cessation of bombing in North Vietnam and
her supply lines would seriously negatively affect us later in the year
and in early 1969).

Peace talks between the US and North Vietnam commenced in Paris on May 10 and many of us foolishly, desperately, thought that perhaps the end of this war was getting close at hand. We reasoned, logically enough it seemed at the time, that with the heavy losses the VC and NVA suffered in the last six months it must surely force them to bargain seriously for a peaceful solution. But of course, it wasn't to be. Peace talks quickly became as stalemated as the long war. In reality nothing had changed concerning the war and its prosecution on both sides. North Vietnam was as determined as ever to unite the country under their control, no matter how long it took. The United States was concerned about its reputation and dependability as an ally on the world stage. They did not want to appear weak or undependable. Disarray in the South Vietnamese government continued unabated. Public opposition to the war grew daily on the American home front. Despite battlefield achievements, we seemed no closer to victory or an end to the war.

The North and their backers had correctly read the mind of the American people. They knew the country no longer had the stomach for war and would eventually leave; all the American people and government wanted was a way to exit with at least some honor still intact. And so North Vietnam negotiated in a manner that dragged out for years, and in the meantime many more thousands died.

The assignment to guard the air base was a mental and physical lifesaver. It gave us a chance to recuperate and regroup. While on air base guard duty we also did a lot of Combined Action Platoon (CAP) work. We went with doctors and other specialists to local villages to treat the sick, help build or rebuild homes, and other humanitarian actions. The American military did a lot of this kind of public service work and we didn't get the credit for it that we should have. Notwithstanding what the radical fringe of domestic war protesters alleged, we were not only *not* baby killers, we did a great deal to help the poor and the hungry and the sick. I take pride to this day recalling that we gave freely of our food, money, and labor to help Vietnamese civilians.

Military doctors and nurses donated a great deal of time working at crude clinics providing health services ranging from inoculations to surgery. Very often in these CAP missions we were trying to repair damage perpetrated by the Viet Cong against the people and their homes in remote villages. Rural residents who did not support the VC cause paid a high price.

* * *

During this assignment we got to some of the American facilities in Da Nang a couple times. As is normal in any war, there was a significant difference in the circumstances experienced by frontline combat troops and soldiers in the rear in support units. In Vietnam the rear echelon troops lived quite well, but the grunts did not. There was a serious problem getting needed supplies out to the front lines. Our country's military experience in Vietnam may have been unique because of the ratio of frontline versus rear support personnel. There was an unusually high percentage of troops in the rear doing a variety of tasks and the minority of in-country troops were in combat units. About 60 percent of military personnel assigned to Vietnam were some manner of rear support function and about 40 percent were combat troops of one classification or another (rifleman, artillery, tanks, special forces and advisors, chopper pilots and crews, etc.). A high percentage of the casualties came from troops serving in combat units. When one considers this lopsidedness in the assignment of military personnel in Vietnam, the casualty rate for the infantry can be more fully appreciated.

Some of us went to the USO club one day and had cheeseburgers, fries, and a Coke. I thought it was the most delicious food I ever had. I also saw a couple of friends from home who were based in Da Nang. We talked about the good old days and took pictures, a few of which I still have.

All the photographs I have from my time in Vietnam show rear base settings. The only exception is one taken shortly after arrival with a small instamatic film camera that was soon ruined by water. It's a fuzzy picture of a Phantom jet dropping a bomb near our lines. The rear base pictures were taken on those days when we were in the rear and thus depict a clean and safe setting. The few copies of newsprint items I have from Vietnam were torn from the *Stars and Stripes* or other military newspapers I found in the rear and mailed home.

Photographs taken by grunts while on patrol or on extended combat missions are rare. Combat photos that exist were taken primarily by professional journalists or military photographers. There was no way for infantrymen to carry camera and film in the field for days or weeks at a time, as they were quickly ruined by rain, mud, and water. There were frequent occasions when we waded across swamps with chest deep water. Anything that had to be kept dry we held over our heads and that was basically limited to our rifles. The circumstances while on patrol or in combat situations were such that taking pictures was just out of the question.

My friends and I made it to China Beach, a resort of sorts on the South China Sea. We lay on the sand near the waves in a scene similar to many like it prior to enlistment when we made trips to various beaches to spend days in the sun. This setting was hauntingly reminiscent of home and the nostalgic tug was strong. It only seemed natural that upon leaving we'd jump in a car and head to the local drive-in restaurant for a cold drink and burger. During the many days that involved only the jungle and combat there was nothing to remind one of home, so the feeling was different and the homesickness tug less powerful. On the front lines the pull was one of simply wanting to survive to see home again. There was no illusion of the good old days while on patrol or in combat. But that one day at the USO Club and China Beach was wonderful and memories of better days filled my mind.

The use of drugs followed American servicemen from America to Vietnam. Grunts learned from hard experience, however, that there was no such thing as a safe area or a leisurely walk in the woods. We knew that danger always lurked nearby and that we could come under fire at any time or place. This need for constant vigilance, I believe, kept most soldiers in forward units away from drugs, or at least kept use to a low level and only when relatively safe. There was certainly drug use, but it was not detrimentally excessive or routine.

The more time spent in the rear, where boredom could become a serious problem, the more likely problems such as drug use or breakdown of discipline occurred. We spent very little time in rear base areas and thus boredom was almost never an issue. Drugs were surprisingly widely available and hawked by kids and adults in practically any village we went through in the Da Nang area. There was little doubt but that local profiteers and the VC were running the drug rings. For Charlie drugs were both a source of funds as well as a means to negatively impact American military personnel.

We never knew what was around the corner, but we did know that to stay alive we'd better stay straight and alert. Pot was quite common and on occasion was included in care packages from friends and family, along with personal care items.

Shows for the purpose of entertaining the troops are part of every war. But there were limits on where they could go based on logistics and security. The reality is that only those stationed in safe rear areas got to enjoy seeing the various entertainers and beautiful girls that were part of USO shows. The men that needed that diversion the most were the ones that could not take advantage of it. There was no way whatsoever that entertainment troupes could be taken to remote mountain top landing zones and forward bases which were frequent targets of attack.

When at rear areas for brief periods we had the opportunity to hear AFVN—Armed Forces Radio Vietnam. They played popular music and some war news, but always generic information that had no intelligence use for the enemy, who monitored American media. News from the home front was fairly limited over AFVN, which made sense because we weren't the only people listening.

It was difficult not knowing about current affairs or hearing only the headlines. When we heard about the assassinations of Martin Luther

King and then Bobby Kennedy, and of the race riots that followed Dr. King's assassination, we were greatly dismayed. The murders caused significant morale problems, especially Dr. King's murder and its impact on black soldiers in Vietnam. It was like the world we so desperately wanted to get back to was falling apart.

The North Vietnamese propaganda network took full advantage of the anger and disarray in America. There was a station out of the north that broadcast news about antiwar protests, riots, and political assassinations—in a very negative context, of course. The station also carried broadcasts by Hanoi Hannah, a sexy-sounding woman who taunted Americans and warned of their impending death and defeat, while occasionally playing popular American music. Her information was well documented, and she broadcasted names of individuals in specific units and was somehow well aware of what our operational activities were.

The enemy left many propaganda leaflets for us to find. The number and type of leaflet broadened as troubles back home increased. There were two primary types of leaflets – those directed at all American soldiers and those directed at blacks. Many propaganda leaflets had pictures of anti-war demonstrations on them and messages that our fellow citizens thought of us as nothing more than baby killers. The NVA and VC both printed these with pictures of large demonstrations and protest signs from the States. Many of the signs carried by protestors were directed against American soldiers as much as against government policy. Leaflets aimed directly at black soldiers showed pictures from the civil rights struggles in America and photos of Jim Crow segregation. An especially powerful pamphlet printed by the South Vietnam National Liberation Front showed a dead black soldier lying in swamp water with the caption "The Vietnam war is a hell hole of racism for the Negro GIs over and above the usual hell of war. Your genuine struggle is on your native land. *Go home now and alive!*" I was able to save several of these propaganda leaflets by mailing them home.

Propaganda leaflet used by North Vietnam and the Viet Cong to exploit racial issues in America. Photo by author.

American troops in Vietnam were well aware of the massive antiwar protests occurring across the country by fellow Americans. We knew what the protestors were saying about us and that some fringe elements were actually encouraging the North Vietnamese to prevail. It was painfully obvious that our peers, young men and women of our same ages, were protesting against our service in the military and accusing us of war crimes. It was very hard to take.

Letters from home were vitally important links to reality. Mail call was the most eagerly awaited event of all. It was irregular, with mail being dependent on supply choppers for the most part. All of us made it a point to write as often as feasible and to say as little as possible about actual events to minimize worry by family members (my letters to a brother sometimes being the exception to this rule). There was nothing anyone could do, and it was of no value to our families if they were made to worry. We all did what we could to ensure that our families were not aware of our day-to-day situation. An interesting method of mail from Vietnam was the use of the tops of individual C ration meal boxes as postcards. They were about the size of a standard post card and worked well for quick notes. Postage wasn't required for letters or cards sent from military units in Vietnam.

One byproduct of our time at Da Nang on base security involved getting to know a ten or eleven-year-old Vietnamese boy who hung around the guard shack. This guardhouse and gate was on a dirt road some distance from the actual air base. I spent a lot of time in that shack during the month of June checking people going to the base, mostly to work, and got to know this boy quite well. He spoke broken English and seemed a bright and happy child, despite the chaos around him. He called himself Joe and in long conversations he talked about someday going to America to live, going to school and basically of living a normal life. Joe lived near a small village and was a farm boy. One day he walked his family's water buffalo down the road to the guard shack. It was an amazing sight. Water buffalo were common sights in Vietnam's rice paddies, with a farmer walking behind them plowing the field but seeing this small boy on the top of one, close enough to touch, was very impressive! These animals were dangerous and more than one was shot because it charged a soldier. The US government reimbursed farmers for such casualties of the war. I have a grainy, faded photograph of Joe and have wondered many times whatever became of him. I hope he's living a happy life somewhere.

CHAPTER 7

# DIFFERENT BATTALION
# BUT MORE OF THE SAME

E arly in the summer of 1968 Marine Corps commanders made
several organizational changes, one of which affected 3/27. It
was decided that the Twenty-Seventh Marine Regiment was to
be sent back to the States over the course of the summer, beginning
with the Third Battalion. It was always the intent to send the Twenty-
Seventh Regiment back. Deployment was meant to be a temporary
assignment in response to the Tet Offensive. This move was essentially
in name only. The majority of the enlisted men and lower level officers
were to remain in-country, assigned to other units.

As a result of these organizational realignments I was temporarily
reassigned, along with several others, to Charlie Company, First
Battalion, Twenty-Seventh Marines from late June to early September.
First Battalion was to return to the States at the end of summer, at which
time most men were to be transferred to yet another frontline unit.

With the airfield guard duty ended, our new company was sent
back out to an area southwest of Da Nang, once again along the so-

called Rocket Belt. During that period we had a rear base that we operated out of, but rear only in the sense that there were tents and we slept on cots on the few occasions that we were actually there.

Experiences in Charlie Company were essentially the same as life in Kilo Company. That summer we ran a lot of two- and three-day patrols in a large contested region to the west of 3/27's former tactical area of responsibility. This zone was also heavily impacted by VC and NVA and we were trying to impose a presence by making frequent forays into it. There were also a few more civilians living there. A dirt road led to a village for which we provided protection. Many mornings at daybreak it was our responsibility to walk the road from our base to the village to sweep it for mines. It was at least a couple miles in distance. Only after we completed the sweep and detonated mines could any military trucks travel on it. We found mines many days. A three-man engineering team was with us carrying mine detectors and they detonated the mines in place. We grunts provided the necessary security. A lesson learned on these mine sweeps was that the enemy found if they wrapped their anti-vehicle mines in enough layers of plastic our mine detectors, which were based on detecting the presence of metal, could not spot them.

Those daybreak mine detection sweeps always had a surreal feel for me. In my youth on the farm, I was frequently out and about at dawn to start the day. I have clear memories of walking in the summer fields at sunrise, hearing the birds and feeling the cool clean breezes and temperatures that are reserved only for those who are out at that time of day. Walking down this dangerous road at dawn for several weeks gave me that same feeling—except, of course, everything was very different.

With the roads swept for mines Combined Action Platoons frequently went in this and other nearby rural villages to treat the sick and provide other services. CAP teams were comprised of marines from several disciplines, from medical to construction. We went into villages to help civilians suffering from a variety of problems, including atrocities committed by the VC. Destruction of the hooches and grain storage bunkers used by rural villagers by the Viet Cong were quite common if residents didn't cooperate.

Atrocities by the Viet Cong were real. Residents that were viewed as potential threats to the communist cause were eliminated. We saw the results first-hand and heard credible stories of other crimes. Disembowelment of live men and women, taking or killing children in front of their parents, and various forms of torture. These were the tools of fanatical Viet Cong cadre leaders and propaganda experts to keep rural residents in line.

Intentional offenses against civilians by American units were not common. Officers were strict for the most part in how civilians were treated. One of the offenses for which commanders sometimes took disciplinary action was deliberately damaging property or livestock of civilians. In reality, enforcement of what might be considered as adherence to common humane behavioral standards was more difficult than it would seem. Preventing unnecessary damage to property was hard because civilian property was often used to assist the VC or NVA. On occasion we burned rural hooches after attacks against us originated from near them and where, after brief firefights, we found hidden rifles and supplies for the VC. It was clear that the men captured or killed in these instances were Viet Cong.

Positively identifying the enemy was even more troublesome. There were questionable incidents in which what might have been a civilian was shot because they were running away after shots were fired or otherwise brought attention to themselves in a manner that made them look guilty. Were some innocent civilians impacted? Undoubtedly, yes. And that bothered most of us but in the reality of this guerilla war there was very little to be done about it while at the same time maintaining some semblance of safety.

Considerable effort, often placing us in great danger, was taken to locate local enemy cadres and camps. On a number of occasions small teams, generally five or six marines at the most, operating in maximum stealth mode, reconnoitered rural villages at night. We looked for troop movements, meetings of local VC officials, or other evidence of the presence of enemy combatants or officers in small rural villages.

* * *

The reality of the terrible effects of war on noncombatants is but one of the many reasons that conflict must be avoided in all but the most extreme circumstances. Collateral damage and deaths of innocent men, women, and children will absolutely occur once the uncontrollable wildfire of war has been lit. The inevitable fog of war and the unleashing of extreme passions cannot be fully controlled by even the most sophisticated military structures or treaties defining the rules of warfare.

War is ugly and brutal and brings out both the best and the worst in people. It's asking a lot of a young man under great stress, who has actually lived the brutality of war, to always carefully consider every immediate life and death decision. That thoughtful consideration or evaluation of information can very well cost him, or a comrade, his life. One of the most difficult aspects of Vietnam was that one often didn't know who the enemy was. The farmer walking a nearby trail had just as good a chance of being the person that planted deadly mines that maimed so many Americans as not. Especially in a free fire zone where there were not supposed to be civilians, the decision of whether or not to shoot is a difficult one to say the least. Choose wrong and either more Americans will die, or an innocent Vietnamese will die.

There was no way to identify local guerillas. Without question we frequently walked by or even talked to Viet Cong or their accomplices in the Da Nang area but had no way of knowing it. We knew that the guerillas who planted the mines or worked as snipers were all around us and that they could have been an old woman or a child of ten or twelve. When we witnessed the death and maiming that their dirty work resulted in, as we did on a near daily basis, hatred was the end result. It was easy to learn to distrust and hate on a broad basis because we could trust no one. In fact, staying alive depended on development of deep distrust. Naiveté got a person killed really fast. This daily reality of not being able to identify the enemy and of his taking great advantage of this fact, was difficult to live with. This was not a neat and clean war with traditional front lines. It was a war where every subterfuge, deceit, and trick were used as a weapon against us.

* * *

In early July the whole company moved its base of operations to another location near the village where we did most of our CAP work. We rode, for the first and last time ever while in Vietnam, in and on LVTs (Landing Vehicles, Tracked, also known as Amtracs). These are tracked amphibious landing vehicles, normally employed to move marines onto shore from offshore troop ships. They are also used to transport troops on land, especially across areas where there was no road. They were lightly armored, however, making them susceptible to explosive devices. The vehicle directly in front of the one several of us were sitting on top of hit a mine, killing and wounding several of the marines inside. I purposely chose to sit on top of the unit I was on because I didn't want to be inside should the Amtrac hit one of the many mines that we had found along this road. The possibility of snipers or ambushes seemed preferable to the deadly result of being inside if we hit a mine.

That was the last time we used any manner of ground transport. For all the months prior to this we never used motorized ground transport outside of the immediate Da Nang area. Later in my tour, when stationed in the northern mountains, travel was also by foot, except for rare helicopter-based events.

We also virtually never had armor or tank support. There were only two occasions when one or two tanks were on an operation with us. The first was near the end of Operation Allen Brook in late May, the second was once while in Charlie Company. Ninety-nine percent of the time it was just us, without armor of any kind, walking, regardless of how far or how dangerous it was. On the second occasion we had tank support we were deep in the heart of Indian Country but near an area that still saw some small-scale rice farming. What is still vivid in my mind is the damage done to the fields. In just minutes the tank did great damage to the fragile paddies and the system of dikes that no doubt took generations of farmers to build. As a farm boy, that really bothered me. I could only think about the trouble and work we just caused those unfortunate farmers. The attitudes of locals toward us were important. We were supposed to be winning the hearts and minds of the Vietnamese, not alienating them. When we did things that harmed local residents all we did was increase the numbers of VC in the area. That increased our chances of being on the receiving end of deadly force.

In August the NVA once again amassed in the area near Da Nang and carried out what was called the August Offensive. General Giap called it the Third General Offensive. As in prior months, forward Marine and Army infantry units were the trip wire used to provide advance warning of enemy movements and attempt to thwart the invasion.

On one occasion our squad from 1/27 and a squad of ARVN, fifteen to twenty of us total, turned a bombed-out church into an outpost of last resort for about a week. The building was in the middle of nowhere, although decades before the area had obviously been settled. Our little group was completely cut off from help and surrounded. Though the days were fairly quiet, on two nights we fought fierce battles, face-to-face on a couple of occasions, sometimes too close to use grenades safely. Eye-to-eye combat is the worst. Miraculously no one was killed during these attacks and wounds received by several of our American and South Vietnamese force were not life threatening.

Similar skirmishes were being fought by other marines in the rocket belt all around Da Nang. In the end, after nearly a month of fighting throughout the region, the NVA's August Offensive was thwarted. Though an encounter with a deadly and determined enemy was the primary feature during this event, I also remember it for another reason. We had very few non-lethal possessions that we carried. The non-lethal items we took the trouble to carry were things that were important to our comfort or well-being. High on this list of desired items was the poncho liner. These camouflaged nylon liners were highly coveted and for reasons unknown to grunts in the field were in short supply. They offered some comfort when sleeping on the ground and most importantly they were large enough to wrap around oneself to help deter biting insects. My liner was stolen from my backpack while at that church and I've never forgiven the ARVN soldier that I suspected of taking it.

Many of our more serious battles occurred at night. The VC in particular were active after sunset when they enjoyed the cover of darkness. They knew the local area intimately and could move effortlessly in the woods and fields. As a result, we ran patrols virtually every night from small encampments where our platoon or company was dug in. When operating in an area for a week or more and in a platoon or company-sized unit, we sometimes strung concertina wire (coiled interconnected barbed wire given this name because it expands like the concertina music instrument. It's also called Dannert wire, a World War II designation) around our encampment when possible and dug fighting holes around the perimeter. The wire was heavy and impossible to carry in large amounts by infantrymen alone, so we deployed it only when it could be delivered by chopper or truck. Infiltrators often tried to come through the wire, and they were very skilled at it. Marines on duty around the perimeter shot at movements and sound. We were in free fire zones in these settings. In most of the area it was the norm to shoot at sounds. The only people there were us and them and if we knew it wasn't one of us, it had to be one of them. Sometimes animals were the victims. Often these noises were in fact VC or NVA testing our lines, gathering information or setting mines or booby traps. Other times they were a prelude to a full attack.

The Vietnamese tropical nights were filled with sounds of nature. Humming bugs, small animals scurrying in the weeds, and occasional deer or other large mammals making noise as they stealthily moved near our lines kept us on edge. Lightning bugs, a joy to watch on summer evenings in much of America, often took on a sinister appearance in front of our lines.

The darkness and tricks employed by the VC made nighttime patrols dangerous in every regard. Beyond the perimeter grunts encountered a sly enemy in the dark jungle but we also faced nervous marines with itchy trigger fingers upon returning. Grunts walking point carried a hand-held device that fired a small flare, of various colors, when approaching their perimeter. The enemy also had these devices and they used them to fool sentries. Before leaving on night patrols we discussed the time of return, what direction we should be coming from and what color flare was to be used as the signal. We carried a two-way radio, but contact was with the lieutenant, not individuals on the line. There were times when the VC or NVA fired a flare and shouted in English just outside the wire in an attempt to be allowed access.

I knew that I had been seriously emotionally and negatively affected by the war one night when I shot a deer in the wire and felt more pity about killing the innocent deer than if it was another enemy soldier.

* * *

The US military had a practice of lobbing artillery shells in a somewhat indiscriminate manner that was called harassment and interdiction fire (H&I). Based on some intelligence or suspicion that enemy soldiers might be moving through a particular area, artillery rounds were dropped in the vicinity in hopes that they would kill, slow down, or at least interfere in some way with the actions and movements of the enemy. It's impossible to know how effective this practice was. It was another manifestation of the free fire zone approach. This practice affected us to a considerable degree. When we ran nighttime patrols, we had to carefully coordinate our movements with artillery units firing H&I rounds into our tactical zone of responsibility.

* * *

At one point that summer Charlie Company teamed up with a company of Republic of Korea Marine Corps marines (ROKMC) for a week or two. It was part of Operation Mameluke Thrust, if my memory serves me correctly. The ROKMC had military responsibility for an area immediately south of the region that the Twenty-Seventh Marines were responsible for, an area south of Da Nang along the shore of the China Sea which, like our tactical area of responsibility, was a deadly place to venture.

The ROKMC seemed more aggressive, almost ruthless, seemingly not having to follow the same code of conduct that we did. We ran joint patrols with squads of ROKMC through an area largely controlled by guerillas. The same deadly results due to mines, snipers, and hit-and-run ambushes were encountered. One patrol took us through a small rural village. As was often the case, everyone was on emotional edge because of what we experienced minutes before. In this little medieval village an old woman, what few remaining teeth she had black from a lifetime of chewing betel nut, was hawking a hot bottle of what she alleged was soda. She was persistent because no doubt whatever few coins or military scrip she might receive for it may have been her entire income for that day. After several warnings for her to stay away, likely assuming she was a saboteur, an ROKMC shot her at point-blank range. What was unthinkable and unforgivable in a normal setting felt ordinary. I remember thinking *what has become of us?*

None of us were foolish enough to buy and drink whatever might have been in the bottle. It most certainly would not have been Coca-Cola. We were always cautious about eating or drinking anything given to us by a stranger. Suspicions, based on actual incidents of poisoned food or water, were strong.

Even when with locals believed to be trustworthy it was a difficult notion to eat their food or drink whatever it was they were proffering. Cultural differences were huge, including food and drink. It was difficult to turn down an offer of food from a hungry and poor villager. It was, after all, a very kind gesture on their part, but when the choice was fisheye soup or fermented fish in a container that appeared to have never been washed, it was only the very brave that accepted. Surprisingly, however, Coca-Cola was common in the larger villages and towns. Sometimes even in the most rural villages Coke bottles were commonplace. Not that we ever drank it, very often the bottles did not contain the same liquid as when it left the bottling facility. It was common for the bottle caps to be saved and the bottle re-capped repeatedly by the locals. There was no telling what the bottles actually contained.

Charlie used everything from sex and drugs to food or hard drink to tempt Americans to do things or go places that led to their death or capture or to poison or incapacitate them. We were constantly warned about fraternizing with Vietnamese women. The VC trained prostitutes to lure soldiers into traps where they could be captured or killed. The Angels of Death. Some were cunningly cruel and often worked as small teams. A commonly repeated allegation was that the women sometimes inserted a device with razor blades attached into their vagina. We never knew if this was true but just the thought of it scared the hell out of most young men. Others used weapons ranging from drugs to guns and knives. Even if the women were not VC operatives intentionally trying to harm Americans, the threat of sexually transmitted diseases was real and took its toll.

* * *

The greatest fear of the grunt wasn't being killed or maimed; it was being captured. Great care was taken to avoid capture. For instance, a grunt's rifle virtually never left his hand. Other than the few days in Hawaii on R&R, my rifle was either actually in my hand, strapped on my back, or within inches of my arm twenty-four hours a day for every day of thirteen straight months. Infantrymen slept with an arm on or around it, walked with it in their hand or on their back, and at all other times it was always within reach. To this day I can remember my rifle's serial number (691674). When in thick cover great care was taken by everyone to make sure nobody got separated. No one ever wandered off looking at something or just to take a walk.

The enemy in South Vietnam rarely took prisoners. There is a reason that almost all of the prisoners released in 1973 were officers and pilots held as POWs in North Vietnam; captured infantrymen seldom survived. They were most often executed outright though some were held in primitive conditions without medical attention for interrogation, followed by a certain death. Pilots shot down in North Vietnam had some political value and, due to radio contact and other planes in the area, it was usually known whether a pilot ejected alive. The government in the north cared enough about world opinion that they didn't want to be caught indiscriminately killing captured pilots. Torture was common in the Hanoi Hilton, the infamous prison where pilots were jailed, but North Vietnamese leaders wanted the pilots kept alive for propaganda purposes. The VC and NVA in South Vietnam had no such concerns. There are numerous eyewitness accounts by surviving soldiers describing how the enemy summarily executed Americans that were wounded or ran out of ammunition on the battlefield.

It might seem overly dramatic in retrospect, given the safe distance of time and space, but many grunts kept an M-16 round strapped on their helmet for ultimate personal use if about to be taken prisoner after having expended all their ammunition. I have little doubt but that some were utilized for that purpose. There was good reason for this seemingly over-the-top action. The VC and NVA cared nothing for the niceties of the Geneva Convention on the rules of war. While NVA soldiers typically immediately executed wounded or captured GIs they came across on the battlefield, the VC often tortured first. In the rural areas near Da Nang, in particular where we operated, we were chillingly familiar with the stories of torture. We heard about the foul deeds of a psychopathic VC woman code-named Apache, who delighted in long tortures ending with castration with her razor. She was eventually killed by a Marine sniper.

* * *

In August there was an incident that still sends a chill down my spine. We were at a remote location where we previously built some bunkers and sandbagged foxholes. These far-forward outposts were called

Platoon Patrol Bases (PPBs in the inevitable military alphabet soup jargon). We had been there for several days going on local patrols, when a typhoon hit. It was a hurricane that lasted a full day and night. The wind and rain were incredible, and we had no place to go for cover. We stood in the torrential rain and hurricane force winds for about twenty-four hours, trying to hold on to something to not get blown away. We couldn't go into the bunkers we had dug because they were completely filled with water. It's hard to describe how miserable we were. That wasn't the worst part, however. The second night the storm subsided quite a bit and though it was still windy and stormy, we sent out the normal LP.

Every time we stopped for more than a few minutes we always sent LPs, two- or three-man listening posts, out about 100 yards in front of the lines. The job of the LP was to detect enemy movement nearby. We all did it and it was dangerous and nerve-wracking. Sometimes we had columns of VC or NVA walk just a few feet or yards away. On occasion someone in the LP made a noise or was otherwise discovered. On the second night of the storm this happened. The two-man LP members were captured we could hear them screaming in the wind. We immediately ran out to find them. When we did, they were dead, and we discovered that Charlie had killed them with multiple stab wounds amid signs of torture with knives. The elusive enemy, likely a small unit, was nowhere to be found.

Listening posts highlighted the importance of the seemingly mundane steps taken to stay alive. Even the darkest-skinned African American grunt had to put black camouflaging paste on his face to reduce glare. Pockets and belts were checked to make damn sure nothing moved or rattled. If a person wore a watch with a fluorescent dial it was turned upside down to ensure that the faint light wasn't noticeable. Hand signals were used to silently communicate. If a PRC-25 radio was utilized as part of the listening post, extreme caution was used to ensure its silence.

With the passage of time a lot of events merge together without a distinct timeline to separate them. There were just a lot of routine things that happened. After a while one didn't think about them the same way a civilian back in *the world* would react. These things just happened, and they happened regularly. For instance, there was a day, like so many others like it, when we were walking single file across a deep swamp, with water up to our chest and our rifles held high. As I happened to be looking toward him, the head of the man in front of me basically exploded. A second later the sound of the shot fired by a sniper in trees well over a hundred yards away was heard. There was nowhere to go and nowhere to hide. We returned fire the best we could and slowly finished wading across, clumsily carrying the dead Marine through the deep water as a few more bullets hit nearby. Something that in normal life would have made the front page and sparked a major police investigation was just another normal event in war that didn't warrant any special action. The rest of us just silently thanked the gods of fate that it was him and not us. Snipers were a serious problem. Concealed spiderholes in particular represented a constant menace. They were extremely well camouflaged and unlike a gunman in a tree, snipers using these small underground covered pits could immediately hide after a shot with minimal likelihood of being found. As often as not these snipers were women. Like hidden explosive devices that were a constant terror, snipers were a close second at creating fear, especially in the countryside where the VC were predominant.

We had a problem with agents of the VC sabotaging our hand grenades. The sabotage no doubt occurred in the rear where many local Vietnamese worked at US bases, doing a variety of jobs. They weren't all friends. Grenades have a fuse that lasts about 5 seconds after the spoon flies. This is obviously so that it explodes several seconds and some distance after it's thrown. Across the country there were instances in which the grenades were apparently taken apart and short-fused, as we called it. When thrown, it would explode almost immediately, killing or seriously maiming the person who threw it and anyone near him. A marine from Los Angeles from our platoon threw a grenade into a cave prior to us going in to search it. As soon as it left his hand it exploded, killing him immediately. Several of us were nearby when this happened but because he was in the mouth of the cave the shrapnel didn't hit anyone else. It happened on several other occasions that I heard about.

We went into bunkers, tunnels, or caves whenever we found them. In many ways the NVA and VC prosecuted the war underground. The extent of the tunnel complexes throughout South Vietnam was incredible. They were large enough to house large numbers of troops and supplies, as well as entire hospitals. In the southern part of South Vietnam the VC utilized elaborate tunnel complexes. In the northern part of the country the NVA dug extensive underground complexes that included not only reinforced concrete and steel bunkers but large underground living and hospital facilities. Tunnels, bunkers and spiderholes were present in every part of the country. Entering underground facilities was dangerous and frightening work. We always threw grenades in first, though the tunnels and bunkers were designed so that an explosion near the entrance wouldn't hurt someone hiding further in. We all went into natural or manmade hiding places, but small GIs and marines paid a price for their compact size. They were most often the *tunnel rats* that entered into the dangerous underground world of Vietnam.

Entrance to an underground tunnel. Wiki-Commons photograph.

The NVA and VC were supplied by Russia and China. The term *Chi-Com* was used often and referred to Chinese communist weapons, especially grenades and RPGs. Chi-Com items were not as well made as Russian-made equipment. North Vietnamese Army troops for the most part used the Soviet AK-47, though some carried model 56 Chinese SKS rifles. The SKS was originally a Soviet military rifle but it was quickly replaced by the AK-47. SKS rifles were adopted by communist countries around the world because they were inexpensive and rugged. The Chinese version was a favorite of the Viet Cong. They were fitted with either a blade- or spike-style bayonet. China not only supplied North Vietnam and the Viet Cong with war materiel, they also sent military advisors and frontline combat troops. These soldiers were sometimes encountered on the battlefield along with their NVA and VC allies. Though both China and Russia at the time denied battlefield involvement by their military, both countries did in fact have advisors and infantrymen in combat against American and ARVN forces. China was deeply committed. That country ultimately admitted their extensive involvement in May 1989. According to the semi-official China News Service, they sent a total of 320,000 combat troops and invested at least twenty billion dollars aiding North Vietnam and the Viet Cong over the course of the war. The disclosure was made a month after military officials in the Soviet Union admitted that a contingent of Soviet advisers in Vietnam took part in combat against US forces and helped shoot down American planes. The China News Service report cited *The History of the People's Republic of China*, published by the official State Archives Publishing House, as saying more than 4,000 Chinese soldiers were killed during the war. During both the Korean and Vietnam Wars, Chinese Communist Party chairman Mao Tse Tung, and the People's Republic of China which he founded and led, had a special hatred for America and Americans. Our Marine units did not encounter Russian troops to our knowledge. It appears that they primarily supported North Vietnamese Air Force units.

* * *

Many infantrymen in Vietnam felt that enemies of the US at the time gave more thought to the field-level realities of war. For instance, their equipment was simple but reliable and effective. Their standard mortars were one millimeter wider than ours so they could easily utilize rounds captured from us, but we could not use their rounds. They seemed to understand that it was the foot soldier and the equipment he could carry with him, that won wars, not high-tech equipment that failed when exposed to conditions that were less than perfect. Grunts believed that an over reliance on sensitive high-tech weaponry and computers as opposed to boots on the ground was, and still is, a flaw in the thinking of our top military leadership. Specific highly focused actions can successfully be undertaken remotely with high-tech devices such as drones, but large-scale ground wars cannot be fought successfully from a distance. In the end, ground troops fight and win wars, not computers and ultra-expensive high-tech weaponry.

These same grunts have disdain for military bureaucrats and politicians who talk about conducting war as if battlefields were orderly well-maintained factory floors where everything works exactly as the machinery and computers are designed to. In real war, everything and anything that can possibly go wrong, will. There is nothing orderly about it. Rather there is mud, dust, water, darkness, fear, disorder, missed communications, malfunctioning equipment, an enemy much stronger than intelligence said they should be, jealousies, stupidity, lack of information about what's going on, the manifestation of every human weakness, and much more. Ultimately, success in wars depends on the decisions and actions that each soldier makes as an individual, while still working as a team and within a unit structure. Wars will never be won by computers. They'll always be fought and won by the foot soldier.

# CHAPTER 8

# IN THE ENEMY'S BACKYARD

Amerian troop deployment hit its peak in the summer of 1968 at slightly over 536,000. By the end of summer, the Corps finished its reassignment of marines formerly assigned to the Twenty-Seventh Marine Regiment. The Twenty-Seventh was returned to the states—1/27 to its assigned base in Hawaii and 2/27 and 3/27 to Camp Pendleton. Since most of the former members of the Twenty-Seventh Regiment were transferred to other units in Vietnam, few returned stateside. In early September 1968 those that were remaining in-country learned which units they were being transferred to. Almost all were going to northern I Corps, along the DMZ and near the Laotian border to replenish the ranks of Marine units in that area. I was going to Golf Company of the Second Battalion, Ninth Marine Regiment—*The Band of Brothers*. The Ninth Regiment was the Corps' mountain regiment. Their main rear base was at Dong Ha, a few miles south of the DMZ and several miles inland from the ocean. The Twenty-Seventh Regiment was in the First Marine Division and the Ninth Marine Regiment was part of the Third Marine Division, though this organizational assignment meant little to marines on the ground. The Third Division was commanded by Major General Raymond G. Davis, a veteran of World War II and Korea. General Davis was awarded the Medal of Honor for his courageous actions at the Chosin Reservoir in Korea in 1950. The Ninth Marine Regiment was commanded by Colonel Robert H. Barrow.

On September 7 we flew from Da Nang up to a military airstrip near Dong Ha. This date marked the second time that a significant event in Vietnam occurred on the same day of a family wedding back home; this time it was my brother who got married. Life went on back in *the world*, regardless of the parallel but vastly different reality that existed in Vietnam.

It was raining heavily when we arrived late in the afternoon. For whatever reason, there was no transportation waiting for us and we literally sat and lay on the tarmac, in the rain, the entire night. The next morning trucks arrived and took us to the nearby Ninth Marines' rear base. On the following day a chopper flew the several of us that were being reassigned to G 2/9 out to their temporary mountaintop camp in the far northwest frontier.

\* \* \*

The Annamite Mountains are the defining feature in the northwestern portion of South Vietnam. They were to be my home for the next six months. The Annamites are a rugged and scenic range of forested mountains, much like our Great Smoky range but steeper, with more limestone cliffs and outcroppings. This portion of Vietnam is on the edge of the mountainous terrain, which includes Laos and northern Vietnam, but peaks still reach over six thousand feet above sea level. It was a wild and dangerous region with far more NVA there than Americans. The NVA operated freely in the northwestern corner of South Vietnam and across the border in Laos. We were there to make the point that we weren't just giving them those provinces and to stop or slow their advance on major urban areas and bases further south.

The reassignment of former Twenty-Seventh Regiment marines to this area was based on revised strategic military planning. Following the lengthy and deadly NVA siege of the Khe Sanh combat base in the spring and early summer of 1968 and its closure that summer, the Corps made a fundamental decision that greatly affected all marines in the north.

Khe Sanh and other large bases in the area had been critical to previous American strategy but no longer. The original mission of northern I-Corps bases was to serve as a blocking force to prevent free movement of NVA pouring into South Vietnam across the DMZ and from sanctuaries in Laos, and to hinder their movement south to attack key cities and bases.

In May 1968 General Davis became commanding general of the Third Marine Division. Upon assuming this command, Davis made significant changes as to how marines prosecuted the war in the northern I-Corps provinces of Quang Tri and Thua Thien. He declared that henceforth major forward bases in this frontier region were to be abandoned. These bases were established in 1966 as part of what was known as the Strong Point Optical System (SPOS); also known as The McNamara Line. In addition to American troops, the defensive system utilized thousands of acoustic devices and motion sensors to detect and provide the American military information about North Vietnamese infiltration activities. Pushed by defense secretary McNamara as an anti-infiltration barrier as well as an intelligence gathering system along the DMZ, in reality American bases created prime targets for NVA artillery and rockets from across the Laotian border and the DMZ. The marines were essentially trapped on their bases and faced NVA forces that far outnumbered them whenever making forays from these bases. The siege at the Khe Sanh base manifested the marine predicament in a highly visible and costly manner.

The infiltration barrier's ineffectiveness was also vividly demonstrated by the enemy's January Tet Offensive. The NVA, wishing for a dramatic surprise victory, simply avoided the barrier. Rather than allow the SPOS to detect their infiltration activities and have to fight their way through the line of marine bases, they sent thousands of troops and necessary materiel down the Ho Chi Minh road network through Laos and Cambodia. Once safely south of the northern I-Corps barrier system the NVA moved army units to the main attack points of Hue, Da Nang, Saigon, and other priority targets in the south.

General Davis believed that mobility and the ability to attack the enemy was the key to victory. He no longer wanted marines in bases that were the frequent victim of attack and bombardment with artillery. General Davis told his commanders "We had something like two dozen battalions up there all tied down to these fixed positions, and the situation didn't demand it. The way to get it done was to get out of these fixed positions and get mobility, to go and destroy the enemy on our terms, not sit there and absorb the shot and shell and frequent penetrations that he was able to mount."

According to Naval historians the rationale was as follows: "In a nutshell, Khe Sanh could be abandoned because the Marines now had enough troops and helicopters and enough latitude of action so that they could operate in a mobile mode, dominating the whole region, rather than being tied to the fixed defense of a base in the center of it." This new policy guided Marine operations for the remainder of the war. It also required replenishing the Corps' manpower in the region, which was the reason many former members of the Twenty-Seventh Regiment were assigned to units in the far north.

* * *

With the implementation of this new approach, riflemen operated as a quick response mobile force, via helicopters and on foot. Instead of being sitting ducks awaiting attack in bases surrounded by the NVA, Marines were going to be the attackers. Resupply was to be from the air. Forward bases such as Khe Sanh, Camp Carroll, and others were abandoned. A key facet of this new mobile approach was that where the infantry went, the artillery followed. Instead of having artillery units in large permanent bases, they set up along with infantry units on cleared mountain tops. Helicopters allowed rapid movement of guns from one peak to another as need arose.

With Marine infantry and light artillery no longer restricted to large bases, we took the war to the enemy and eliminated the luxury they enjoyed for years of having free rein to operate. Key to this new aggressive action was a series of mountaintop landing zones. Artillery contingents and companies of marines were dropped onto strategically placed LZs, from which aggressive patrols were run to locate the enemy. One company typically remained at the LZ to protect it, while other marines scoured adjacent areas several square kilometers in size. LZs and supporting light artillery were placed such that these targeted zones of focus were covered with quick response artillery support and infantry backup as needed.

During the fall and winter period, the northwestern mountainous area of Vietnam is commonly cloudy with frequent rain due to the monsoon season. The region is quite cool during the monsoon, especially at night when it was no doubt in the upper forties. With no cool weather clothing marines spent many chilly nights in our soaked summer utilities. We were ultimately issued a green sweatshirt with the Third Marine Division logo to wear and a pair of light nylon gloves, for which we were very grateful.

There was a positive tradeoff to being in that area. There were virtually no local guerillas, only NVA regulars to face and though there were some mined areas, the presence of random booby traps was significantly reduced. That was a wonderful development. I also did not have to serve as backup radioman in 2/9 and my point man duties were lessened.

\* \* \*

Running generally east and west just south of the DMZ is what the French called Route Coloniale 9, commonly called RC9. It traversed a dangerous region from Dong Ha on the east near the coast to the interior of Laos. It was the northernmost east–west road in South Vietnam. Because of its strategic location, a number of American bases were built along it early in the war. Those bases include some famous locations of which legends are made. Dong Ha, Con Thien, Camp Carroll, The Rockpile, LZ Stud, Khe Sanh, Ca Lu, and Lang Vei. These are names burned into the minds of grunts and special forces troops who fought along the bloody road. It was a narrow old asphalt road built by the French in the early part of the twentieth century. LZ Stud was originally established by the First Cavalry Division in early 1968 to support Operation Pegasus and the relief of the Khe Sanh base. Stud was later occupied and expanded by the Ninth Marine Regiment, who renamed it Vandegrift Combat Base after former Marine Corps General and commandant Alexander Vandegrift. After closure of the main bases in the summer of 1968, Vandegrift took on more importance in the movement of men and materiel. It saw some improvements, including a few large tents for supplies and for overnight sleeping and a metal landing strip. An Army artillery unit was also based there with their long range 175mm guns.

Commensurate with the growing importance of Camp Vandegrift was the increasing number of supply convoys from Quang Tri and Dong Ha on Route 9. The base could not be supplied by helicopters alone. These truck convoys were targets of ambushes by the NVA, making the trips hazardous undertakings. We rode security on these convoys on a couple occasions, riding in the back of the trucks or manning the .50 caliber machine gun mounted over the cab. It was serious business because ambushes or sniper events were a constant threat.

At that point in time the road was long abandoned for civilian use and was becoming overgrown, with vegetation growing up between the cracks. Only military traffic used the road. If one could remove oneself mentally from the circumstances of war, the road and scenery in the region west of The Rockpile were stunning. It wound through beautiful countryside, following rivers and valleys through the mountains. The central and eastern portions of the road were partially in the open and less protected by forest canopy. As a result, Route 9 wasn't used much during the daytime by the NVA. It was often used at night for NVA troop movements.

What was referred to as the Rockpile was actually three geologic formations of large limestone outcroppings rising out of the flat plain. They were remarkable geologic features. We called one of the formations Razorback, due to its particularly jagged appearance. Because of their height and the fact they looked out over Route 9, they were of significant strategic importance. On one occasion my squad climbed Hill 440, one of the Rockpile formations, to dislodge NVA from its top. We were forced to use ropes to climb as the sides were nearly vertical. Unlike earlier wars in which most combat involved regimental or larger sized units, this wasn't the case in Vietnam. Very often small units, squads or platoons, totaling less than thirty men, were the point of the spear. Only the largest formal operations consisted of battalion or regiment-sized force.

Hills throughout Vietnam were given numeric designations that depicted their height in meters above sea level.

Rockpile geologic formations near Landing Zone Stud
on a typically foggy day. USMC photo.

From September 8 until I left the field more than six months later, we were on foot for the most part. Except for a few brief stays at Vandegrift in late December and again in mid-January, 2/9 Marines never saw a bed other than the ground, nor a shower other than a local stream. Food was virtually 100 percent C rations. A sizable share of our supplies had to be dropped by parachutes, with helicopters responsible for the rest. Each of us carried several days' worth of provisions. We not only toted many pounds of various munitions plus a backpack filled with the necessities of living and fighting in the wilderness, we often also carried a nylon sandbag filled with additional supplies and ammo tied to our belts. The weight and clumsiness of the gear we carried made for difficult maneuvering in the mountainous terrain.

Visibility was often limited due to fog and low clouds and we sometimes had trouble getting supplies dropped. More than once we couldn't locate a drop. There were periods when for a number of days, we ate one C ration meal per day and at one point ran out of food entirely for a couple days. When one is burning up several thousand calories per day carrying many pounds and traversing rocky jungle-covered hills all day under great stress, food is vital. Sometimes our air-dropped supplies fell into the hands of the NVA. Once in a while we came across bananas growing wild and they supplemented our food supply.

When considering supplies needed in a war zone, the natural reaction is to think of critical items such as food and ammunition. In the mountains we frequently got our water from streams, treating it with halazone tablets. But there were other necessities: spare batteries for the PRC-25 two-way radios, toothbrushes and toothpaste, razors for shaving, replacement clothes and boots, soap, and other items for hygiene. At least twice during the time we spent in the mountains unit commanders authorized the growing of beards because we could not get razors and blades with which to shave. Lack of toothbrushes and toothpaste sometimes was a problem. Food was frequently in short supply.

* * *

In October I received a requested absentee ballot from home for the 1968 general election. I sat in the rain on a remote mountain top and hurriedly completed the ballot because the chopper that brought in the bag of mail was about to depart with casualties. Voting for the first time in those somber conditions, in what proved to be a key presidential election, gave me a strong appreciation for the power of the right and duty to vote. Throughout my adult life whenever I heard an apathetic voter complain about the time or trouble involved in voting, I was very unsympathetic.

* * *

The months we spent in the mountains was divided into two distinct periods. From September to early January we participated in Operation Lancaster II, Scotland II, and Kentucky with other Marine units. The coordinated focus was on the area near the DMZ north of the former Khe Sanh base, south to the Route 9 area. We fought for possession of one hill after another, constantly moving south from the DMZ region. We reoccupied hills that were abandoned earlier after the Khe Sahn siege. Hills 881 North and South were two of these. It was powerfully poignant being on hills so bloodied by other Marines just months earlier. There were thousands of well-equipped fresh NVA troops in the immediate area, outnumbering us significantly.

On a couple occasions we were choppered to distant hilltops, but usually we traveled by foot. We also had forays further south near the Da Krong and A Shau Valley areas. These critically important geographic features, very near and parallel to the border with Laos, formed a natural passageway into the northern portion of South Vietnam for enemy forces and resupply convoys. The entire region was a wild mountainous area controlled by the NVA. The valleys were a key part of the Ho Chi Minh Trail.

During the war, the condition of the Ho Chi Minh Trail network was falsely reported to be little more than foot paths on which people carried supplies south. That was true in the 1950s. By the late 1960s the road network, totaling about 16,000 kilometers, consisted of well-maintained gravel roads about twenty feet wide, capable of carrying modern military trucks and other equipment. A dozen major bases and full-service facilities lined the route providing everything from hospitals to complete storage, repair and maintenance capabilities for equipment and roads. Many of these bases were concealed deep within large caves and underground structures. Tens of thousands of engineers, mechanics, doctors and nurses, security troops, and other necessary support staff manned the bases. Repair crews along the network could often rebuild bridges and repair other bomb damage in hours. To protect the vital network, the roads were protected by antiaircraft artillery and heavy machine gun emplacements at frequent intervals. Due to the heavy jungle and tall trees, it was almost impossible to see NVA facilities from the air and thus enemy trucks, facilities, and troops were well concealed.

North Vietnamese weapons were not only along the transportation network. The NVA had many antiaircraft guns throughout the frontier and DMZ region, as well as artillery and other crew weapons. Just across the border in Laos a mountain called *Co Roc* was strategically used as a base for NVA long-range artillery. Those guns represented a regular threat. Their 122mm, 130mm, and 152mm howitzers pounded the Khe Sanh base for months earlier in the year. Located fifteen kilometers west of Khe Sanh, artillery on Co Roc was just beyond the range of Marine and Army artillery, even the Army's large 175mm guns that were previously at Camp Carroll, east of the Rockpile.

There were memorable nights on mountain tops watching NVA rockets and anti-aircraft artillery being shot up at our planes. It was an amazing, if deadly, fireworks show. The planes must have been high flying B-52s or Phantoms heading into North Vietnam from an air base in Thailand or perhaps operating from aircraft carriers. The rockets and AAA fire originated just a mile or so away from our position at that point in time.

The war in the northwest frontier was clearly different than farther south. It was more typical of large-scale battles rather than hit-and-run tactics used by local guerillas. The area was largely unpopulated except for tribal groups called *Montagnards*. These people were loosely allied with the US and were strongly anti-communist. The NVA brutally persecuted them and essentially tried to eliminate them. We found several of their villages destroyed by the North Vietnamese and in one case dead bodies were still on the ground. The Montagnards were a throwback to a thousand years before. Their lives hadn't changed much and were more like it was 968 rather than 1968.

In one abandoned, burned-out village I found a hand-made wooden bow carved out of a beautiful multi-colored wood with a reddish hue. It was a marvelous piece of craftsmanship. Hoping to save it, I carried it for several days, using it like a walking stick in the rugged terrain. I badly wanted to take it home as a souvenir, but it was unfortunately lost during one of the daily operations in the mountains.

We ran a small number of special assignments during this period. One mission involved being dropped into the DMZ by helicopter to rescue a Long Range Reconnaissance Patrol (LRRP, pronounced *lurps*) that was surrounded and about to be wiped out. As part of the new, more aggressive policy to take the war to the NVA in northern I-Corps, more Army and Marine surveillance teams were deployed. Their dangerous task was to monitor troop movements and gather dependable information regarding location of supply lines and bases. These reconnaissance teams took every measure to remain hidden but sometimes they were found by the NVA. This particular LRRP had been spotted and was in grave danger.

Conditions prevented the large CH-46 Sea Knight choppers from being able to touch down and we had to rappel down rope ladders the last ten feet. The enemy was all around, laying down heavy fire. We fought our way through the mountainous terrain and a forest of dead, mangled trees to the Army unit. Once we joined up with the commandos, the choppers, which had departed to a safer location away from NVA ground fire, came back to extract us in the same manner. We couldn't see the NVA in their brown uniforms among the rocks, trees, bunkers, and caves, but the gunners on the birds could and were exchanging withering fire. After several tenuous and frightening minutes, we were loaded and departed the area back to Vandegrift Combat Base. Four of the enemy killed that day were unmistakably Chinese.

The NVA routinely utilized the demilitarized zone as a crossing and staging area, despite its neutral treaty designation. The DMZ was like a scene from a science fiction movie. Almost every square yard had been bombed, and much of the area was a forest of dead and indescribably mangled trees. When the damage an artillery round or bomb does to a tree is seen up close, there is no mystery as to why the human body doesn't stand a chance against that murderous shrapnel. There were many areas in I Corps that resembled a ravaged no-man's land landscape. As a result of heavy bombing and defoliation with aerial spraying of herbicides, there were large areas with almost nothing green or alive in them.

The widespread use of herbicides was a double-edged sword. In some areas it did help reduce cover and concealment for the enemy, but less than hoped for in the opinion of most grunts. The countryside was just too vast and defoliation too limited to have a real effect in the big picture. We spent a lot of time in sprayed areas. The ability of the enemy to move about and occupy those areas did not seem to have been negatively impacted. Even with extensive spraying of the many infiltration routes, the North Vietnamese Army was able to move men and trucks into the South essentially unhindered. The toxic spray likely had a greater negative impact on American personnel and civilians than on the NVA and VC. The material was designed to be resistant to rain and to be persistent in the environment. The main toxin, dioxin, is a long-lasting chemical that was on the ground where we laid and in the water we used to clean up in and drank on a near daily basis. We brushed against foliage with herbicide adhering to the leaves and it was on food, such as wild bananas, that we occasionally ate. We constantly breathed air that contained the dust of dioxin from the soil or from vegetation.

\* \* \*

In late October I received some great news: I was approved for R&R (Rest and Recuperation in official military terminology, although rank and file troops used the more common I&I jargon: Intoxication and Intercourse). All servicemen in Vietnam were given a five-day (including travel) R&R period, which could be taken outside of the country. Having been in-country for eight months, my chance for R&R came just six weeks after deployment to the north, and a respite from the fighting and bad weather was greatly appreciated. The military provided air transport for those who chose to leave the country, which of course most did. There were several approved destinations: Sydney, Kuala Lumpur (Malaysia), Hong Kong, and Honolulu being some of the more popular choices. Persons going to Honolulu were specifically forbidden to go to the continental US from there. Of the several options, I chose to go to Honolulu. To make this vacation happen I needed to get back to Da Nang however possible. Transportation arrangements were largely up to the individual. Leaving for Hawaii necessarily took me through another part of the Vietnam experience that I and other grunts rarely saw. The rear. Getting to the rear, in this case Da Nang, was complicated. First, I had to find room on a supply or medivac chopper to get out of the mountains. Generally these went to Camp Vandegrift and from there I had to find a chopper to our main rear base. From there I found a military flight down to Da Nang. Once at that air base I hitched rides on military trucks and made it to a friend's unit.

Many troops in large rear bases such as Da Nang enjoyed a near stateside standard of living. Most had quarters with cots, TVs and stereos, three square meals a day, cold beer and soda, USO clubs nearby and basically an eight-hour job each day. Some of the offices and officer quarters in the rear were air conditioned. Some soldiers and officers even paid *hooch girls*, local Vietnamese, to clean their barracks. There was an extreme dichotomy between combat troops and support personnel. Rear echelon soldiers were referred to as REMFs by the grunts, rear echelon mother fuckers. It was nothing personal, grunts certainly understood that war involved a great deal of bureaucratic and critical logistical necessities. But the daily difference between infantrymen enduring combat experiences and a REMF doing his duty in a rear base could not be avoided. Getting replacement gear in the field was inexplicably difficult. We wore clothes that were in bad condition and at times had to wrap tape around our boots because the soles were flapping. Seeing support personnel in new boots and clean uniforms of the latest design while our khaki uniforms were ripped and filthy, created division and anger.

I ate dinner at a mess hall at the Da Nang base the night before I flew to Hawaii. There was a long line of marines in new jungle boots and pressed fatigues, even camouflage utility uniforms, which we didn't have in the field yet. My utilities were dirty and ripped, though I was to be issued a new uniform (and underwear) the next day for my trip to Hawaii. I felt very much out of place.

A young marine standing behind me in the chow line made the comment "Jesus fucking Christ, we're having roast beef and potatoes again?" I just lost it. I slugged him and jumped on him, calling him a sorry son-of-a-bitch and that while he's living the good life with hot food and cold beer other guys just like him were dying and living in misery. A couple of nearby marines pulled me off because I kept hitting him. As he left the mess hall, he turned to me and said I was crazy. Perhaps I was. After all it was a very illogical thing on my part to have done; we were all on the same side. None of us asked to be there. We were all American youths that would much rather have been somewhere, almost anywhere, else. But he wasn't one of *us*, and he just couldn't grasp or relate to the lives of grunts. After that I had no desire to have anything to do with the REMFs; it felt like they were on a different planet. They had their important job to do and we had ours. But the tasks were so different and the gulf between us so wide that it precluded understanding of the others' problems and gripes.

\* \* \*

Hawaii was wonderful. At the airport I rented a Mustang convertible. My first stop was at a store to buy civilian clothes and then rented a motel room, where I cleaned up and changed from a lance corporal to what every soldier on R&R wanted to be for the four days of leave: a lowly PFC—a Proud Fucking Civilian. Being clean and wearing civvies was a fabulous feeling. Walking down the street the first time and feeling totally safe in doing so was both surreal and exhilarating. The temptation to shout something happy and meaningful at the top of my voice was overpowering. I wanted people around me to know how incredible this whole experience was and how fortunate they were to live it every day.

The issue of our divided generation made itself visible in Hawaii, however. With my short hair, dark tan, and overall appearance, there was little doubt about who I was—a soldier on leave from the war in Vietnam. I encountered a large number of my peers, college-aged young men and women holding hands, joking and laughing, enjoying life to the fullest. It was hard to reconcile the two very different lives that we were living.

My experiences in Hawaii were all positive and the memories long-lasting. I heard the Beatles' "Hey Jude" for the first time on a street side café jukebox and loved it. It's still one of my favorite songs. I drove all over the island of Oahu and spent a lot of time lying on Waikiki Beach. I visited Pearl Harbor and took in some shows with hula dancers and other trappings of traditional Hawaiian music, dance, and customs. Not once did the topic of the war come up in conversations with people. Getting back on the plane returning to Vietnam was one of the hardest things I've ever done.

* * *

Once back at the Da Nang air base it was my responsibility to figure out a way to get out to my unit, which was on an unknown mountain top near Khe Sanh. I first got on a military plane going to Dong Ha. Once there, I checked in at a headquarters for the helicopter units to see if any supply or medivac choppers were heading out to G 2/9. I was told that there weren't any flights planned for a couple of days due to weather but that my help was needed in a Huey gunship due to a shortage of door gunners. For two days I was a window gunner on a Huey. We flew missions in support of medivacs to an area near the DMZ, which was fairly hilly. I recall flying very fast at near treetop level to avoid being seen by the NVA until the last minute. Helicopters are susceptible to being brought down even by rifle fire. On one trip we followed a twisting river through a valley. We were low and flying fast, twisting back and forth following the river through the hills. It was quite a ride. We were shot at a couple of times and I returned fire but seriously doubt if I even came close to hitting anything.

I finally got on a chopper that was going out to G Company and returned to the mountains around the first of November. From that point until late March the comforts of civilization were to be just fond hopes and dreams. The Ninth Marines spent the next two months doing more of the same, wandering the mountains and seeking out the enemy on desolate jungle-covered hills and in wild valleys where white water cascaded down steep canyons. In late December we were choppered back to Vandegrift and ran patrols in the nearby mountains. On Christmas Eve, Golf Company set up an ambush on Route 9 west of LZ Stud, but fortunately it was a silent night. On Christmas Day we patrolled along Route 9 west of the Rockpile in the morning and had a holiday meal in the afternoon. Real food in special containers was brought out to us. It was a bit like a picnic, with no shots fired that day. In early January we once again returned to the border area and resumed our aggressive patrols into enemy-held land.

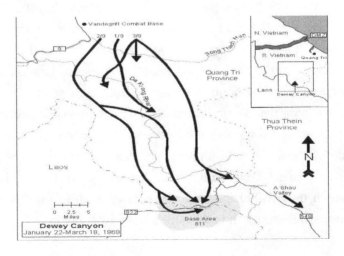

On January 22, American military actions in the northwest frontier region were brought under the unified umbrella of a large and very quickly organized offensive labeled Operation Dewey Canyon. General Davis intended to locate and destroy stockpiled supplies and disrupt the NVA supply system. A key part of our strategy of disrupting NVA supply and troop movements was targeting the Ho Chi Minh Trail. This well-maintained road system started in North Vietnam, skirted the DMZ inside Laos, and continued south along the border to Cambodia. Its official name in North Vietnam was Strategic Supply Route. It had many branches coming into South Vietnam all along the Laos and Cambodia frontier. Two of the main branches entered South Vietnam nearby. Route 9 lay south of the DMZ near the former base at Khe Sanh and route 922 linked the NVA's Base 611 with Route 548 near the strategic landmark of Tiger Mountain. Once in the safe zones of the Da Krong Valley, and the A Shau Valley further south, the NVA were free to use 548 to attack interior cities and bases in South Vietnam. Supply and troop convoys on route 922 were daily occurrences during this time period.

The Da Krong and A Shau Valleys were major strategic centers where the North Vietnamese stored materiel and massed troops prior to offensives. The landscape had a dense jungle cover, with large trees and a thick canopy that was impossible to see through from above. The roads leading into the valley and along its course were almost invisible from above. Conditions provided safe sanctuary for large numbers of NVA soldiers and all necessary support facilities. General Davis had information that the NVA was preparing for yet another large offensive against American and South Vietnamese facilities near Hue and Da Nang. He knew that disrupting the NVA supply chain and destroying their pre-positioned supplies and troop facilities was critical if another Tet-like offensive was to be nipped in the bud. As his rationale for the offensive, General Davis stated: "It makes me sick to sit on this hill and watch those 1,000 trucks go down those roads in Laos, hauling ammunition down south to kill Americans with."

The Second Battalion was joined by the First Battalion, Ninth Marine Regiment, aka *The Walking Dead* and by the Third Battalion of the Ninth Marines. Two/Nine was assigned to the west side of the Da Krong River and valley along the Laotian border. One/Nine and Three/Nine had primary responsibility on the east side of the river and valley. Two/Nine air-assaulted into the northern part of the region to establish Landing Zone Razor on a nearby mountaintop for supply and medivac choppers and placement of light artillery. Once mountain top LZs and company bases were established, offensive operations against the enemy in the nearby mountains began.

Marines from 2/9 establishing a mountaintop landing zone
near the A Shau Valley. USMC photo.

Engagement with the enemy was frequent since the NVA were widespread throughout the district. Working our way through the frontier region wasn't as simple as walking down existing roads or traversing level lowlands in the valleys. That would have been suicide. It meant hiking and fighting through the rugged highlands adjacent to the valleys.

* * *

On January 29, an ARVN unit joined the operation and later in February, the Second Battalion of the Third Marine Regiment arrived as reinforcements. The operation was successful in locating major supply depots, ammunition dumps, artillery pieces, and troop facilities. At two locations well equipped NVA hospitals were located, dug securely into mountain sides. One hospital was abandoned just the day before we found it. At one captured North Vietnamese supply depot a large supply of food items was discovered that we dined on. It was a nice alternative to cold greasy C-rats. We were more than a little pissed when bags of rice stamped with "US Aid" were discovered— food meant for poor Vietnamese villagers stolen by the NVA.

One of the grisliest duties from this period was that twice we were ordered to dig up mass graves to estimate the number of NVA KIAs from recent actions. That was disgusting work for which few words exist. I recall thinking how young the dead North Vietnamese soldiers were. Like their young American enemies, I assumed that they had not wanted to be there either.

In late January a monsoon system settled over the mountains that lasted for more than two weeks. It was a time of danger, difficult conditions, and want, as the weather favored enemy movement and attack while preventing air support and resupply for American forces. Bad weather and day after day of low clouds, rain, and fog made aerial bombing runs in the mountainous terrain nearly impossible. This resulted in an old weapon being brought to bear, the Battleship *New Jersey*. The *New Jersey*'s sixteen-inch guns fired what were in effect projectile bombs on NVA positions and convoys. The mountainous terrain limited the effectiveness of normal bombardment by fighter planes. The use of the *New Jersey* provided an excellent alternative and was a morale booster as we walked in knee-deep mud in the pouring rain. The word on the ground was that each shell cost as much, and weighed as much, as a small car. We could hear the battleship's shells fly overhead on occasion and when we did, we'd joke that "there goes another Volkswagen."

A common trait among marines in Vietnam was dormant heroism. All it took was the right circumstances and these men performed extraordinary deeds. Acts of selfless valor were commonplace during Operation Dewey Canyon, as demonstrated by the fact that four marines were awarded the Congressional Medal of Honor, three posthumously. A fourth survived the battle to receive his hard-earned medal from the president.

Of the three young men awarded the medal posthumously, one was a good friend from my platoon. The second was from H Company of 2/9 and the third was with M Company of 3/9.

On February 5, in one of the dozens of anonymous battles during Dewey Canyon, on a mountain called Co Ka Leuye (known by the military as Hill 1175), a friend, fellow squad member, and very good man by the name of Thomas Noonan was killed. Hill 1175 was part of a steep series of ridges near the border with Laos. In heavy rain, battling mud and slippery stone slopes with the aid of ropes, we ascended the mountain, taking heavy fire. Our goal was to take out an NVA communications line that ran along the ridgeline and to hold the critical high ground. The upper portion of the mountain had a steep seventy-degree slope that required use of ropes for ascent. What was to be a fairly routine operation to secure the ridgeline and take out the communications hardware turned into a nightmare. Due to heavy enemy resistance, running out of food, running dangerously low on ammunition, and having taken several casualties, resulting in dead and wounded that needed to be carried down the steep mountain in the rain and through heavy fire, the situation became desperate.

On the way back down the NVA ambushed us, including an artillery barrage. The North Vietnamese were well protected behind boulders and we were in the open. Noonan ran through the bullets, saving four marines who had been hit. He died in his final lifesaving attempt. Four other marines, including another close friend and squad mate, died in that battle on Hill 1175 and eighteen more were badly wounded.

Tom was a very friendly man, funny, fun to be around, and a great storyteller. We called him Uncle Tom because at age twenty-five he was quite a bit older than most members of the platoon. I can clearly recall a number of times when several of us, usually including Noonan, occupied a shelter half on a muddy mountain top in the rain. There we'd sit in the mud under the rain cover smoking, playing cards, and telling stories—mostly of home and our lives prior to Vietnam. Shelter halves formed pup tent-types of covers, without the walls. We seldom spoke of the present, except about the usual rumors of things that happened and of what we were supposed to be doing in the coming days and weeks and talked little of the future.

Tom told us the story about how he came to enlist in the Corps. In his own words he said he was once a hippie and one night he made a bet with someone about something which is lost to history. The wager was that the loser would join the Marine Corps. Tom lost the bet and, true to his word, joined the Corps at age twenty-three or twenty-four, after college graduation. He was posthumously awarded the Congressional Medal of Honor for his actions on Hill 1175. It was an honor being a fellow Marine and knowing and serving with Tom. I have visited his grave in New York City, just as I have visited the graves of other friends made in combat and who died in combat.

As noted earlier, most firefights or battles of this sort went totally unnoticed by the press and the writers of history books. Hill 1175 was an exception because a reporter from the *Sea Tiger*, a small newspaper printed by and for the III Marine Amphibious Force, accompanied a rescue mission that came in to attempt to reach us and help extricate us from this life and death situation. He talked to several officers and men afterwards and wrote a good article about it that I later saw. I still have that original newspaper, dated March 7, 1969. I came across it when we were at LZ Stud for a short period and saved it. I knew that, whatever it took, I had to get that paper home; I did, mailing it home from Vandegrift. The article starts out with: "The men were exhausted. They had eaten the last of their rations some fifty hours before and despite an ordeal that few men in their generation will ever experience, their morale was high."

* * *

There was no safe area. The NVA not only fought on the ground on South Vietnamese territory near the Da Krong and A Shau Valleys, they attacked from across the Laotian border. Artillery bombardments and hit and run attacks from Laos were routine. Since Laos was allegedly a neutral country, their sovereignty had been respected by American ground forces. Rules of engagement, however, permitted commanders to take *necessary counteractions against Viet Cong and North Vietnamese Army forces in the exercise of self-defense and to defend their units against armed attacks with all means at their disposal.* That language provided sufficient basis to justify Dewey Canyon marines crossing the border into Laos.

Army Lt. Gen. Richard G. Stilwell, commanding XXIV Corps, of which the Third Marine Division was a part, wanted specific authorization from the Military Assistance Command, Vietnam (MACV) to conduct a cross-border attack for defensive purposes. On February 20, he recommended to the commander of the III Marine Amphibious Force that a limited raid into NVA Base Area 611 in Laos, to a depth of five kilometers along a twenty-kilometer front, be authorized. The proposal was endorsed and forwarded to General Creighton W. Abrams at MACV headquarters in Saigon the same day.

While top commanders debated the political advisability of an incursion into Laos, Colonel Barrow took matters into his own hands. On the afternoon of February 21, he ordered 2/9's Company H commander to set up an ambush that night along Route 922 in the NVA's Base 611. Marines had been in position to observe truck movement on the road and had called in artillery fire missions on it, but the NVA traffic continued.

At dusk on February 22, two platoons from Company H went into Laos a distance of over half-a-mile. The men stayed off trails, moving along a creek bed and a ridgeline. When they reached a small river running parallel to Route 922, a platoon commander and a sergeant went ahead to determine a good ambush site. The NVA swept the area with a spotlight but the marines remained undiscovered.

With an ambush site located, the marines set up an ambush, set out some claymore mines, and waited. A number of vehicles were allowed to pass while the ambush was being established. The North Vietnamese were using Route 922 in both directions. Having already had several pieces of artillery captured by marines, they were pulling crew weapons into Laos for safety. At the same time, the NVA continued to move truckloads of supplies and troops forward.

In the middle of the night, lights of eight trucks were seen on the road moving from the west. The first three trucks entered the killing zone and the claymore mine was fired at the second truck, setting it ablaze and killing its occupants. The first truck also started burning and the third vehicle was forced off the road. The marines poured automatic weapons fire at the NVA trucks and called in artillery. After firing for several more minutes, the marines moved back across the road and crossed the border back into South Vietnam. The ambush was a success, destroying three trucks filled with supplies and killing eight NVA troops while sustaining no casualties themselves.

The success of the ambush led Colonel Barrow to request a continuation of operations within Laos. Barrow told headquarters that "my forces should not be here if ground interdiction of Route 922 is not authorized." General Abrams agreed to a limited incursion again on February 24. Two companies of the Second Battalion moved into Laos along Route 922, staying there until March 1.

Second Battalion marines moved rapidly up Route 922, trying to force the NVA into the path of 1/9 and 3/9, who were still in South Vietnam. Along the way, 2/9 engaged in significant firefights with enemy troops and captured several artillery pieces, as well as large quantities of ammunition and other supplies.

Officially, 2/9 had eight men killed and thirty-three wounded while operating in Laos. Concerned about political repercussions, Abrams insisted that discussion of the incursion be severely restricted.

During one firefight on the west side of the border, Corporal William D. Morgan of H Company 2/9 showed the courage and selflessness of so many young American soldiers in Vietnam by single-handedly assaulting an enemy bunker to save fellow marines. One of the squads of Cpl. Morgan's platoon was temporarily pinned down and sustained several casualties while attacking an NVA force in a heavily fortified bunker complex. Seeing that two of the wounded marines had fallen in a position exposed to the enemy fire and that all attempts to evacuate them were halted by automatic weapons fire and rocket-propelled grenades, Cpl. Morgan maneuvered through the dense jungle undergrowth to a road that passed in front of the bunker complex that was the principal source of enemy fire. Aware of the consequences of his action but thinking only of the welfare of his injured companions, Cpl. Morgan initiated an aggressive assault against the hostile bunker while shouting directions and encouragement to the wounded men and others in his unit. While charging across the open road he was clearly visible to the hidden NVA who turned their fire in his direction and mortally wounded him. His diversionary tactic enabled the remainder of his squad to retrieve their casualties and overrun the North Vietnamese position. His heroic actions saved the lives of two fellow marines and were instrumental in the subsequent defeat of the enemy. He was posthumously awarded the Medal of Honor, with the place of action listed as being southeast of Vandegrift Combat Base, a true statement.

About two years after I was home, I was stunned to read the *Detroit Free Press* one day and see the entire front page filled with a story and pictures from what was called the Winter Soldiers Hearings, being held by anti-war Vietnam vets in Detroit. This group made accusations of war crimes allegedly committed by US troops. One of the events they used to support their allegations were these defensive forays by 2/9 across the border to attack the Ho Chi Minh Trail. Some of the vets making allegations of war crimes during Dewey Canyon were fellow members of 2/9.

* * *

Fighting raged throughout February, under difficult conditions. On February 24 the Second Battalion successfully captured Route 548. This was a strategically important victory as it slowed movement of enemy troops being sent in as reinforcements. Encountering NVA machine gun emplacements along the road so that no portion of it was unprotected made capture of the supply route dangerous and difficult. The picture of those machine gun emplacements, and the deadly fire that poured from them, is indelibly burned into my mind. But that was the norm for American forces in this part of the country. Nothing came easy.

Nothing happened during that period that gave much reason for hope. Conditions were difficult and dangerous, and no end was in sight. Perhaps it was just the cumulative effect of months of war and physical and emotional trauma, but during this period I was occasionally very depressed. C rations came with packets of four cigarettes. I smoked at that point in my life and those cigarettes served as a touch of home that, in a strange way, provided relief from the stark reality of the situation. One night, on a remote mountain top in late February, I was feeling especially low. Despite being dead tired and not on guard duty or on patrol, I couldn't sleep. The weather was bad, I was despondent, many of my friends were dead or wounded, and it seemed that there was no hope. I spent much of that night sitting in the mud with my back against a tree, smoking one cigarette after another, simultaneously wondering and fearing what the future held. That unforgettable night was the low point of the months spent in the north. It wasn't unusual. Most grunts had similar episodes of despair and helplessness. But a few hours or a day at best was all that was allowed for such contemplations, then it was back to the business at hand.

The intractableness of the situation was something that weighed on everyone. There was nothing one could do but survive day to day. In normal life, if a person finds their personal circumstances to be intolerable, they can do something about it. They can quit a job, move to a new location, end a relationship, whatever. A person has some ability to remove themselves from a bad situation. In a war zone there are no options. Only the dead or badly wounded get to leave. And of course, that's how it must be in a military unit. The decision to go or stay can't be voluntary. But the reality of what that means makes life for combat soldiers more difficult than civilians can possibly appreciate. Grunts adopted a basic survival mentality. We determined to do whatever was necessary to survive one day at a time and hoped that we'd live to see the end of our deployment.

War fighters often are depicted in print or videos as a group of men, all similar in appearance and in purpose. Individuality is lost in the impersonal depiction of units rather than individuals with names and stories. While we fought as a disciplined unit, we were actually hundreds of individuals. Though we were admonished to not make close friends in combat units, we did. War isn't just about the big picture; it's also about individuals who had lives and dreams and stories of their own. Some of my strongest memories are of the unique qualities of specific young men that I had the privilege of knowing and whose stories deserve to be told.

There was a man in Golf Company who had a terrific voice and loved to sing. There were many evenings digging in on a stark and lonely mountain top in the cloudy drizzle when he'd sing out loud. Singing was his attempt to find goodness and beauty in even the unpleasant conditions that made up our lives. He was approved for R&R in Hawaii and, once there, immediately got on a plane and flew to Los Angeles to see his wife and newborn son. When he got back to our unit, he talked endlessly about his son and of their future life together. He was killed a couple weeks later. The military had restrictions on flying home from Hawaii, but it was done fairly often regardless, especially by men who lived on the west coast.

There was another fine young man in our squad that was a good friend who we called *Aviation* as his nickname. He earned his name because he joined the USMC with the understanding from his local recruiter that if he joined for four years, he stood a better chance of getting accepted into the aviation unit. Obviously, he was made a grunt instead. He was from northern Michigan and we talked often about getting together back in *the world*. He was killed on Hill 1175. I've paid respects to him at his gravesite and touched his name numerous times at various monuments where his legacy is carved in stone. He was one of the few marines in the unit who knew how to play euchre and was truly one of the world's good guys. The planet would have been a better place had he lived.

Another young marine in Golf Company had an Eastern European name that we jokingly said had every letter of the alphabet in it, thus we called him *Alphabet*. Like Aviation, he was a friend. He had a good voice and was part of our mountain top chorus. He was also killed during Dewey Canyon.

Giving nicknames to friends was a way to avoid getting too close. Even though friendships were genuine and important, not using their given name kept a bit of separation in the event of their death.

Yet one more example of the quality of the blood that was shed in Dewey Canyon was a young man who was a handsome, all-American boy that everyone liked. He was athletic and probably could have played professional sports. In one of the many battles, he was hit in the head by a bullet. We were fighting side-by-side when this happened. He was still alive, so I threw him over my shoulder and carried him to a safer location where a corpsman could attend to him. Offering words of encouragement as we carefully made our way through the trees, I could feel the back of my shirt getting wet. Despite my assurances to him to the contrary I knew he was dying. When I set him down, he was dead, and my shirt was soaked with a blood and brain mixture.

There was something extremely powerful about being the person who was the last one to see and to help a dying man. There was so much unspoken communication and understanding along with words of encouragement and support. In the above instance we both knew what was happening. This scene was played out tens of thousands of times during the war. The key was to be there for the other. It was a powerful thing, hearing a young man's last words and witnessing his last breath. These are normally end of life events at which only a person's closest family is honored to be present. Friends forged in the flames of combat fill this role in a war zone.

Rank made no difference when it came to respect and friendship, nor to courage and heroic deeds for the purpose of protecting fellow Americans on the battlefield. Privates and lieutenants were equally selfless and courageous in their mission to protect the lives of their comrades.

Many combat unit leaders, commissioned or non-commissioned, rightly earned a reputation of leadership ability and courage based on their actions, not just their words. Such leaders often brought years of service and experience to the battlefield. This was the case with Lt. Wesley L. Fox, a Korean War combat veteran who was commander of Company A of the First Battalion, Ninth Marine Regiment.

February 22 was a dismal rainy day that prohibited air support and gave the enemy cover of low clouds and fog. It was also a day of heavy fighting by all three Ninth Marine battalions. The A Company of 1/9 saw especially heavy action that day, and Lt. Fox's heroic and intelligent actions saved the day.

In the northern A Shau Valley, Fox's company came under intense fire from a large well-concealed enemy force. Lt. Fox assessed the situation and conferred with his platoon leaders to devise a plan of attack. As they executed their plan, the NVA counterattacked and Fox was wounded along with all the other members of the command group except the executive officer. Despite the injury, Lt. Fox continued to direct the activity of his company. Advancing through heavy enemy fire, he personally took out one enemy position and ordered an assault against other fortified bunkers. When his executive officer was mortally wounded, Fox reorganized the company and directed the fire of his men and eventually drove the NVA forces into retreat. His courage and leadership in the face of grave personal danger inspired his marines to such aggressive action that they overcame all enemy resistance and destroyed a large bunker complex. Wounded again in the final assault, Lt. Fox refused medical attention. He established a defensive position and supervised the preparation of casualties for medical evacuation. Lieutenant Fox received the Medal of Honor from President Nixon on March 2, 1971, at which point he was a captain. He died in 2017.

But courage didn't depend on rank. Private First Class Alfred M. Wilson, of M Company, Third Battalion, Ninth Marine Regiment, was another marine who exemplified the best of the valor and selflessness of young Americans in Vietnam. He was awarded the Medal of Honor posthumously for several heroic deeds. His courageous acts included the greatest gift possible, the gift of life to his comrades. Wilson ultimately sacrificed himself by falling on a grenade to save those near him.

On March 3, 1969, while returning from a reconnaissance mission in the vicinity of Fire Support Base Cunningham in Quang Tri Province, the First Platoon of Company M came under intense automatic weapons fire and a grenade attack from a well-concealed NVA force, pinning down the center of the column. Pfc. Wilson, acting as squad leader, maneuvered his squad to form a base of fire and act as a blocking force while the point squad moved to outflank the enemy. During the ensuing fire fight, both his machine gunner and assistant machine gunner were seriously wounded and unable to operate their weapon. Realizing the importance of recovering the M-60 machine gun and maintaining a heavy volume of fire against the enemy, Pfc. Wilson, with complete disregard for his own safety, followed by another marine, ran across the fire-swept terrain to recover the weapon. As they reached the machine gun, a North Vietnamese soldier threw a grenade at the marines. Reacting instantly, Pfc. Wilson fired a burst from his M-16 rifle, killing the enemy soldier. Observing the grenade fall between himself and his comrade, Wilson, fully realizing the inevitable result of his actions, shouted to his companion and unhesitatingly threw himself on the grenade, absorbing the full force of the explosion. His heroic actions inspired his platoon members as they aggressively attacked and defeated the enemy. He bravely gave his life for his comrades. Selfless courage and dedication to fellow marines and to the Corps was the norm in the Ninth Marine Regiment.

These few examples are but a small representative slice of the kind of men that represented America in the hell that was Vietnam. They, and so many others, represented the best of who we were.

\* \* \*

The end reality of combat is the large number of dead and wounded comrades that results. Helping wounded friends on the battlefield and handling the bodies of the dead is a facet of combat that isn't generally discussed. In reality, it is an integral part of war. Every effort was made to get non-ambulatory wounded men to a relatively safe area so they could be attended to by a corpsman, or at least out of harm's way. As soon as possible, the dead were carried to an area behind the lines. What this unspoken duty meant is that over time every grunt helped carry many badly wounded or dead comrades to safety. This action created a deep bond that is impossible to explain.

One of the most sacred and fundamental creeds in the Corps is that a fellow marine is never left behind, dead or alive. It isn't an exaggeration to say that we went to extraordinary lengths to ensure that every man returned with us when we left a battle site. This meant going to considerable danger and effort to retrieve and carry the dead and wounded, but there was no question but that it would be done. Perhaps it was because we normally operated in small units and knew each other quite well, or maybe this level of selfless dedication is what *espirit de corps* really means when you take away the bravado and romantic gloss and get down to nitty gritty realities. But the fact remains that we were a tight-knit group and had confidence that if a marine were in trouble, he would not be abandoned.

It was a strange brotherhood. There were certainly men there that in the real world would not have been friends. There were guys you wouldn't like and would have nothing to do with and people who rubbed you the wrong way or that had attitudes or personalities that grated. Everyone knew that we wouldn't all be buddies over a beer back home, but in the Vietnam jungle we would die for one another, it was that simple.

In a way that is impossible to fully explain, friends in combat units bonded closer than brothers. There was an unspoken level of fellowship and mutual caring that exceeded any relationship I've had before or since outside of my immediate family.

* * *

There were still some old French and Viet Minh mine fields in this area from the early 1950s and perhaps even of World War II vintage. Mine fields of this sort are often not removed following wars and they remain to kill and maim for decades to come. Their very presence is a stark indication of how long blood has been shed in the Vietnam countryside.

When walking across an open hillside that was largely overgrown with small brush, a marine in my company stepped on one of these old mines. I remember this specific incident clearly because he was scheduled to rotate back to the States in just a few days. The end of my own thirteen-month assignment was also getting closer and I was becoming increasingly nervous about being badly injured or killed when I was finally beginning to feel that there just might be a chance to get home again.

The mine didn't kill this particular Marine but, like so many other casualties, he lost his legs. I have often wondered how many vets there are that spent the rest of their lives walking with artificial legs, having prosthetic arms, or were confined to wheelchairs. The number of men who lost limbs or suffered paralyzing injuries was depressingly high. The rate of amputations and crippling injuries for Vietnam was 300 percent higher than in World War II. The speed by which helicopters could transport a severely wounded soldier from the battlefield to a main hospital in the rear unquestionably saved the lives of many that would have died on a WWII battlefield. People sometimes only consider the cold statistic of the more than 58,000 that were killed and the nearly two thousand missing; they don't think about the many more tens of thousands that were seriously wounded and had their lives changed forever.

There were many instances in which a new replacement was killed or seriously wounded their first week in country. Similarly, there were many instances in which someone who had served their thirteen months or nearly so, was killed or seriously wounded with just a few days left in country. The latter was especially tragic, and we all feared it.

Dog tags are small metal identifiers with basic identification and blood type. They are carried by every marine and soldier. We were issued two of them. A unique tidbit that only grunts understand is the fact that while one dog tag was hung around the neck on a chain, we always kept the other tag tied in with our bootlaces. This was so that severed legs could be identified. Loss of legs to explosives was all too common. Sometimes, however, there was little left of a body if a large explosive device such as a rocket or large artillery round exploded close to a soldier. In these instances, the second dog tag was critical. It has always bothered me that the several Vietnam War monuments I've visited in various states, showing infantrymen in combat settings, don't show a dog tag in the boot lace. It just shows that a grunt was not on the advisory or design panel.

* * *

Of course, time spent in Nam wasn't consistently bad. There was horseplay, games, cards, singing songs, or time spent just relaxing. No matter the location, there was time for telling stories and jokes. That the jokes had to be crude seemed to be the only criteria that mattered. We made the best of the situation any way we could. We may have been grunts in a combat situation, but we were still teenagers or college-age at the oldest, and a good time was never far from our minds.

Our options were limited, however. One of the more memorable activities was the small group singing we did in the rain on foggy hill tops. Of course, while some of us had a few hours off others from the unit were on guard duty or patrolling the local area. Our turn to do both would come a few hours later.

We sang *a cappella*. Under the shelter of the tarps, with the sound of the rain often in the background, we sang songs like Simon &

Garfunkel's "Homeward Bound," the Animals' "We Gotta Get Out of This Place" (the grunts' anthem), car racing songs by the Beach Boys and Jan and Dean, various songs by the Rolling Stones and The Beatles, and many more. To this day there are certain songs that will bring a tear to my eye and a chill down my spine every time I hear them. There are movies about the Vietnam War that depict scenes showing grunts in foxholes with radios, tape players, or guitars. Those scenes did not depict reality and weren't possible unless a person was at a main base. When in the field, not only was it infeasible to carry such items (which would be destroyed in the swamps or rain at a minimum), they also interfered with the freedom of movement necessary in combat. A grunt had more than enough items and weight to carry in difficult terrain without adding the weight of bulky musical instruments to their load. Such items were common in rear units and were possible at the larger forward bases, but not during those lengthy periods when we were on foot.

On a regular basis one of our group was killed or seriously wounded and they'd be gone, just like that. There was actually little emotion shown on those occurrences, as we knew it would happen again and it could be one of us the next time. That doesn't mean we didn't feel the emotional pain, we just couldn't afford to show those emotions, as that destroyed a soldier after a while. There were a few heartfelt conversations in which we vowed that we would never forget those killed. We knew that, other than by immediate families, the young men killed in Vietnam were quickly forgotten by America. We promised each other that we would never forget one another and what we had experienced together. To that end, there are young marines that I have thought about every day in the ensuing years. I have also visited the gravesites of numerous former friends who died 10,000 miles from home. I'm not unique in this effort to honor the memory of wartime friends. Many Vietnam veterans do this. America would move on and Americans would forget, but fellow veterans will never forget.

We dealt with the stark reality of death through euphemisms. For instance, a friend was never killed, he was wasted, zapped, or blown away. Psychologically, not using the word *killed* made it easier to talk about somebody's death. On my helmet I wrote the words *You haven't really lived until you have nearly died*. Near death experiences give a person a perspective about life that most don't have. Foot soldiers know a lot about such things.

There were tight bonds between many of the young grunts on the front lines. It was clear that we were not there for *God and Country*, we were there for each other. We were all that we had. This reality brought us closer together than normal war experiences. We knew that back home most people weren't giving us a passing thought as they lived their comfortable lives. We were all aware that the war wasn't a cause that unified the nation and strengthened its resolve the way World War II did. There was no rationing or scrap metal drives to help the war effort. There were no war bond rallies to help fund the war. Americans were not personally involved in the war effort. We knew that, in fact, more than a few were hoping that the North Vietnamese would prevail. We didn't look for nor did we receive hope, support, or encouragement from the home front. We knew we were in this on our own and that we were involved in a political and social event that was to change our country forever, and most of us feared that the change would not be for the better.

\* \* \*

There are many memories and impressions that vets carry with them from time in-country. They're those sorts of mental images and recollections that add texture to the memories even after all these years. There are things that one sees in a war zone that won't be seen anywhere else in life, and rightly so. It's hard to erase those pictures. There are sounds and smells that are unique to the experience. There are sights that burn themselves into memory and never let go. For instance, it was a spooky sight, but fairly often one saw a helicopter flying low through the fog-filled valleys and over the mountains, below the clouds, with a long cable dangling back below the chopper. Tied onto this cable were the bodies of two or three dead American soldiers. These choppers couldn't land in the rough jungle terrain, so they lowered a cable and bodies were attached. I thought at the time how fortunate it was that parents and family members didn't have to see their sons and brothers from the point of their death to their arrival home in a casket. That interim period was not pretty.

* * *

March 18 marked the official end of Operation Dewey Canyon. Though the official multi-unit operation ended, little actually changed. The Ninth Marines were to remain in northern I Corps and carry on the fight for a few more months. As part of President Nixon's Vietnamization strategy, more of the fighting was turned over to ARVN units. The Ninth Regiment left Vietnam in July 1969.

Tactically, Operation Dewey Canyon was an unquestioned success. General Richard Stilwell reported to military command in Saigon that Operation Dewey Canyon "ranks with the most significant undertakings of the Vietnam conflict in concept and results." The ability of the North Vietnamese Army to operate was at least temporarily significantly hindered and many supplies were destroyed. Operation Dewey Canyon was a clear, but costly, victory. Though 130 marines were killed and 932 wounded, enemy losses were much higher. At least 1,617 NVA were confirmed killed and many more wounded. We captured 500 tons of arms and munitions including sixteen artillery pieces, sixty-five antiaircraft guns, and 120,000 rounds of AA ammunition. Twenty-four 57mm recoilless rifles, twenty-five mortars with thousands of shells, 966 rockets and an astounding 50,000 hand grenades were captured. Clearly the enemy had stockpiled enough weapons for a massive planned offensive, which Operation Dewey Canyon prevented. No doubt thousands of lives of South Vietnamese and Americans were saved. The uncontested use of the Laotian border area and adjacent roads by the North was also eliminated for a several-month period. The Ninth Marine Battalions were awarded Presidential Unit Citations for extraordinary service.

As with other major combat initiatives, our victory lasted only as long as we stayed there. We, of course, moved on. The temporary success of our efforts in the NVA stronghold illustrated perhaps the most frustrating aspect of the Vietnam War strategy. Throughout the long war, battles were fought and the prize obtained, only for the American military to abandon the site and the enemy to quickly move back in. We lacked manpower to occupy land once it was captured. Our policy of capturing strategic sites and then leaving to go fight elsewhere doomed us to fight the same battles again. This was true in all parts of the country. In the Khe Sanh and A Shau region, for example, major operations followed on the heels of prior efforts. The 101st Airborne Division assaulted the region again just two months later in Operation Apache Snow. Lancaster II was preceded by Lancaster I. Operation Dewey Canyon was followed by Apache Snow and two years later by Dewey Canyon II. The US Army fought the bloody and infamous Hamburger Hill battle near the A Shau Valley just two months after Dewey Canyon ended. This scenario was repeated frequently across the country and over the period of the war.

This strategy was a morale buster. We were well aware that military targets we fought hard to win were often abandoned back to the control of the enemy, so what was it all about? Why die for a piece of land that was likely to be abandoned afterward? American military leaders and Washington politicians were measuring success based on numbers of dead enemy bodies, not territory captured. Grunts at the center of the carnage knew that this was a profoundly stupid way to wage a war. Even the average Pfc. knew that simply inconveniencing the enemy for a period by temporarily disrupting their supply logistics or denying them use of a sanctuary for a few months wasn't going to win the war in the long run. North Vietnamese leaders, the Viet Cong, and the Viet Minh before them, had made it clear that they were willing to pour men and women into the fight, and for as long as necessary, regardless of the cost in human life. We needed a true campaign, whereby land was held after it was successfully fought over and the enemy denied its use permanently.

The record of combat by the NVA and VC was actually quite poor. They lost almost every battle they fought against us, but they knew our Achilles Heel was the inability to retain what we won. They bided their time, went back and licked their wounds, and returned again.

The Viet Cong and North Vietnamese Army had several strategic advantages that we could never enjoy. They obviously shared a common culture and language and could thus easily blend in and communicate with the locals. Their supply lines were measured in hundreds or dozens of kilometers, not thousands of miles across the Pacific Ocean. They had long since acclimated to the climate and environment of Vietnam and had built up resistance to endemic diseases and maladies that Americans had no familiarity with or resistance to. But most importantly, they had one quality, one strategic weapon, that we would never have: patience. The North Vietnamese leaders and people knew that it could take years, perhaps even decades, before their goal of assimilating the two countries might be achieved. As a society they were totally dedicated to commit whatever resources and manpower were needed to wait out the Americans and win the war. If it took ten, twenty, thirty, or even more years that was fine. They would keep up the fight as long as necessary. They did their homework. They knew that we would never stay in Vietnam, spending our nation's blood and treasure as long as would be necessary to win. They recognized that at some point the patience of the American people would grow thin, the American government's support of the war would end, and our politicians would find a way out of the quagmire. We weren't the first foe they had fought in this manner. Their history of waging this sort of war had been successful for them for a thousand years. They had little fear of our weapons because they knew they possessed the most important weapons absolutely critical in any war: patience and the unflagging support of the nation.

* * *

A tradition in USMC rifle units was keeping what was called a *short-timer's calendar*. The calendar was actually a drawing in the shape of the cartoon character Snoopy, famous then as the imagined *World War I Flying Ace* that battled the Red Baron in aerial combat over France. The calendar was subdivided into a hundred small boxes, and during a person's last one hundred days left in country, a numbered box was shaded in each day, from one hundred down to one and a wake up. Corps orders at the end of one's deployment read *Return to CONUS* (return to the continental United States). It was actually logistically quite difficult to fill in a short timer's calendar in the field because of the inability to keep the paper dry and intact. That was easier said than done. The closer to the last day in country found grunts happier and at the same time more worried. A person was just as likely to get killed or wounded during their last month as in the first. Deployment tours for marines were approximately 400 days. All branches of the military had a version of the short-timer's calendar. Some used thirty days as the countdown point but the marine units I'm familiar with used Snoopy and one hundred days. Everyone I knew in 2/9 that was getting short kept a calendar.

Not only did Operation Dewey Canyon end on March 18, that was also my official Return to CONUS date. My thirteen months were up! I had somehow survived eleven major combat operations and countless days of hostilities and danger on the battlefield. Now to find a way to leave. After thirteen months of doubt, it appeared that I would in fact live to see home and family again.

Normally unit commanders did their best to have marines removed from the front lines a few days before their rotation date. In mid-March I was told that I could leave on a helicopter that had room. Bad weather and enemy activity prevented birds from landing nearby, so I spent my last week in the thick of the fighting on the mountains. This was, of course, frustrating and worrisome. I also had an infected tooth that was giving me a good deal of pain, and that didn't help the situation. The only way out of the region was by chopper. There was no safe overland transportation. A couple of times medivac choppers tried to land in clearings we made on a mountain top, but NVA gunners just down the hillside and on nearby hilltops drove them away with rifle and machine gun fire, mortars, and RPGs.

Finally, the weather cleared a bit and two medivac choppers were called in to attempt a landing. It worked out. The dual rotor CH-46 troop carriers were able to land safely. The wounded and dead were loaded, and, after a few quick goodbyes, I ran onto one of the choppers. We lifted off the mountaintop and went laterally so that in a few seconds we were over a deep valley. From the hillside below we started taking a lot of rifle fire. The chopper was hit several times and the door gunner right next to me and a marine on my other side were both hit. Suddenly the chopper stopped and started dropping like a huge rock. I clearly recall screaming *"Goddamn it this can't be happening! Oh, fuck no, this can't be happening!"* I wasn't alone. Inside the apparently doomed chopper it was total pandemonium. Men were cursing and screaming while the door gunner attempted to spray some gunfire to hopefully give us a bit of cover. One man was silently praying. I was too angry to pray. I tried to will this terrible unthinkable event to stop through sheer force of focused anger. In a matter of a few seconds we experienced more frustration than some experience in a normal lifetime. I could not accept that we were all going to die in a few seconds in a huge fireball, on my way out of the country after thirteen months of hell.

Miraculously after eight or ten seconds, though it felt much longer, the pilot was able to manage the out-of-control descent such that the

WILLIAM M. MURPHY 183

chopper's fall was slowed considerably and some forward movement occurred. It was a very rough process and I remember thinking for a moment that if the crash landing didn't kill us, the chopper falling apart in midair certainly would. But gradually things smoothed out enough so that forward motion was maintained and we limped slowly at near treetop level back to LZ Stud. It was a harrowing flight. Hardly a word was spoken; we were all too stunned.

Helicopters are both incredibly tough and at the same time vulnerable. A bullet in the many gears, hydraulic lines, fuel lines, electronics, or other key components can bring these magnificent machines down in a flash.

I assume we were hit with rifle fire or possibly an NVA 12.7 mm antiaircraft machine gun, which were deadly in mountaintop settings such as this. At over two hundred pounds, the heavy .51 caliber guns weren't common in much of the lowlands of South Vietnam at that point in time, but the NVA used them extensively in the Central Highlands, near the DMZ, and along the Ho Chi Minh Trail complex. These Russian-made guns were responsible for a sizable portion of the nearly 10,000 aircraft shot down in Indochina, the great majority of which occurred in South and North Vietnam. Helicopters and low flying planes, such as those used by forward air controllers, were the most common targets.

Experienced chopper pilots in Vietnam were extremely competent. They were often the target of hostile fire but were undeterred in their fearless service to the grunts. Most helicopter pilots and crew believed that they were there first and foremost to aid those of us *carrying a rifle and backpack*, in their words. These pilots were skilled and courageous beyond the normal definition of these words. It is impossible to tabulate how many lives they saved by coming into a battle zone under fire to take away badly wounded soldiers.

I took another chopper later from Vandegrift to Dong Ha and then a military plane down to Da Nang. I was alone, which was one of the regrettable realities of the war. Soldiers normally went to Vietnam by themselves or in small unrelated groups, and they often came home alone.

When we rotated back to the states, we left all our friends behind still facing danger in the jungles, swamps, and mountains of South Vietnam.

Most participants in the conflict took home mementoes of the adventure. Most of these souvenirs were small reminders ranging from a packet of C rations to rifle magazines. I was able to take a few such artifacts home with me, items that I thought might be of interest to family or friends, or important to me in later years. These objects included the ubiquitous engraved Zippo cigarette lighter and various patches and documents. A few mementos collected on the battlefield are the most poignant. They include a bayonet from an assailant's rifle, an enemy canteen from another, and some other small memorabilia. It required significant effort to carry items such as these in the field, so what most grunts brought home were small items that could be stuffed in their backpack without interfering with more important supplies. When I checked out on my last day in country, a sergeant completed the war souvenir forms that I then signed, making everything legal.

I left the country a day or two later on a commercial Continental Airlines flight. We didn't go straight back to the US, rather, we spent a week in Okinawa at the Marine base being retrained on how to live and act as civilians. Time in Okinawa was a short effort at a transition to normal life. A week was far too brief to reacclimate from combat to home because only superficial changes in behavior could be taught. A sergeant jokingly reminding us that we couldn't go around shooting people once we got back home was one of those shallow, almost meaningless, efforts. Reminding us to properly use a toilet was cursory at best. What couldn't be taught was how to discard those traits and responses needed to stay alive in combat situations. Hyper-attentiveness, immediate reflex responses to loud noises, sleeping very lightly for survival sake, constant worry and readiness for what could happen at any moment, these behaviors had little value in a normal civilized society. The long-term impacts of being around death on a near-daily basis, rage and anger at a level not experienced by average civilians, constant and very real fear of pain and of a terribly maimed body that will affect the remainder of one's life, these realities were not easily erased. What couldn't be removed in a week's time were the haunting memories burned into one's brain, the fear, the loneliness, the grief over lost friends one watched die, or the life-long connection of certain sounds or smells with terrible events. The list of the behaviors and results of combat that needed to be addressed for successful reacclimatizing was long indeed. Unfortunately, no one has found a way to treat these deep-rooted behaviors and fears, certainly not in one short week. So, the basics and the obvious things were discussed and it's called good-enough.

Okinawa was easy duty. Nobody there was going to fuck with a bunch of grunts just returning from The Nam.

# CHAPTER 9

# RETURN TO CONUS
# TO A DIFFERENT WORLD

Following our week of education to enhance assimilation back into American society, a group of us boarded an Air Force plane at Kadena Air Force Base in Okinawa. We were to fly to Travis Air Force Base in California. The plane was filled with happy young men on their way home. Moods fluctuated between exuberance and reflective silence. In reality, it was too much to absorb. We had made it. We survived Vietnam and we were on our way home. The singular dream and hope that we dared wish for during our darkest hours had come true.

Unlike our experience on the C-141 taken thirteen months earlier in the opposite direction, everything was different. We enjoyed small comforts like food, water, and seats and of utmost importance was the fact that we were not carrying weapons of war in our hands.

I saw the sunrise over the California coast just as we were arriving. It was a wonderful sight. The fact that the sun was rising struck me as being symbolic. It was the start of a new brighter period in the lives of those of us on the plane returning from Vietnam. That long dark chapter in our lives was over.

The last half-hour of the flight was a bit bewildering. We were scheduled to land at Travis Air Force Base northeast of San Francisco. Because it was just daybreak it was foggy and we were in the clouds and fog while descending. I was in a window seat and recall finally breaking out of the clouds near the tops of low hills. We were all anxious to see The World up close out the windows. For whatever reason, when the plane was below the fog in the early phase of landing, the pilot poured on the power. The plane shook violently, slowly increasing speed and altitude. We flew across the airstrip, slowly gaining altitude but still low enough to clearly see the ground on the opposite side of the airbase. There was no explanation as to the sudden change of plans and once at a safe altitude again the pilot announced that the flight had been diverted to Los Angeles International Airport. This was not good news. Most of us wanted to avoid civilian contact due to the expected antiwar and antimilitary reception.

There were loud cheers and a few tears when the plane touched down in Los Angeles; we were home once again. In the LAX terminal reality regarding the unpopular war raised its ugly head as we received unfriendly stares and a few nasty comments, including at least one shout of 'baby killer' as we walked through the busy terminal. To add an additional surreal touch, the song "Hair," by the group The Cowsills, was playing over terminal loudspeakers. "Hair" was an iconoclastic theatric and musical celebration of the antiwar hippie lifestyle. It was as far removed from the life that we had been living as was possible to achieve. It was a fun song to listen to, but it made us all the more aware of our status as veterans coming home from war, rather than part of mainstream America.

As was the case two years earlier when we arrived at LAX as recruits, we were met at the airport by a green Marine Corps bus. The attitude of the driver was quite different this time as we made the trip through LA traffic south to Camp Pendleton. We had quite a bit of down time at Pendleton. We used it for paperwork, taking care of any necessary health issues, and various low-stress physical exercise and other activities designed to keep us busy and out of trouble, including additional acclimation classes.

Several job recruiters showed up to let us know about companies that were hiring. Many, logically, were from California and the west. Some opportunities sounded enticing and further strengthened my thoughts about moving to the West Coast.

I had originally enlisted in a special two-year program that the Corps initiated to get more volunteers because they were perilously short of manpower due to excessive casualties. Though not quite a guarantee, a two-year enlistment came with a high likelihood of being assigned to an infantry 0300 class MOS, which increased the likelihood of being sent to Vietnam. Two years earlier it was a chance I was willing to take, though I questioned it frequently while in-country. Those of us with just a few weeks or a month or two left were to be discharged early. If a marine didn't have enough time for another tour in Vietnam, assignment to another duty station, or was not a specialist whose skills were needed, they no longer had value to the Corps, and it was cheaper to release them.

Upon discharge every service member is issued one of the most important documents he or she possesses, Form DD-214. This form officially documents basic information about a person's service, including overseas assignments, awards, and more. It also has a box to identify special skills learned in the military that could have value in the person's civilian life. Such experience ranged from aircraft mechanic to x-ray technician. The DD-214 for grunts apprised potential future employers that we had bright futures as *firearms technicians.*

When the big day eventually came, those being discharged were taken by familiar green bus once again to LAX to board planes to our various home destinations. Upon arrival at the airport terminal most of us went into restrooms to change into civilian clothes. Unlike today, when soldiers proudly return from deployment in full uniform and are enthusiastically greeted by strangers with the mantra *Thank you for your service*, it was the opposite in the latter part of the Vietnam War. We concealed our status as returning war veterans to avoid trouble. We wanted no part of the hassles and insults that being in uniform would almost certainly result in. It is hard to imagine the animosity directed at military personnel a half-century ago. *Welcome home* and *Thank you for your service* were supportive statements that very few Vietnam veterans heard upon their return home, or for years afterward.

It certainly made us wonder what it was all about. Why were those thousands of young men living and dying the way they were overseas when nobody seemed to give a damn back home? How was it that the wrath of a nation had turned against its own sons who did nothing more than their duty? It was very hard to understand, let alone accept the situation as reality.

I flew the friendly skies of United back home. Landing at the local airport, I was met by family members, the norm for most returning vets. A bystander would have thought returnees had been away to college, not a war zone. It was a strange experience. Homecoming would have felt much more appropriate if I had arrived with a unit of marines, all returning home together. But like virtually every other Vietnam War veteran before and after me, I returned anonymously and alone, careful to keep my service a secret.

After being home just a couple days I learned that two childhood friends were killed in Vietnam while I was there. This was a difficult emotional situation, because for years we had been involved in the same activities and played many baseball and football games together on area farms. Having friends I had made in combat killed was bad enough, but when personal friends from one's hometown were killed, it was a hard blow. My family made a decision not to tell me about their deaths when they were killed, the same rationale that I used when I kept my letters upbeat rather than truthful.

The first few weeks were more difficult than I assumed they'd be. Most things in my hometown remained exactly the same as two years earlier. Most everyone was living life just like before. Didn't they know that there was a war going on that had changed everything and altered lives completely? There were tough acclimation issues to sort out, because though life went on as usual, I had become a very different person inside. I felt like an old man, worn out and sad, with all the happiness wrung out of me. The laughter and good times that used to be just under the surface seemed difficult to reach. I slept poorly and worried a lot, though never quite certain as to the causes of my anxieties. I was back in The World and therefore everything should be fine, but it wasn't and I didn't know why. The concept of post-traumatic stress disorder wasn't on anyone's radar at that time.

Most Vietnam vets rushed into work in an effort to restore normalcy. Work offered the opportunity to move on with life. For many, work also presented the opportunity to buy the kind of car that had been a fond wish for years. Returning Vietnam veterans played a significant role in driving the niche markets of muscle cars and motorcycles in the late 1960s and early 1970s. Ordering a new Chevelle Super Sport, with payment for the car supplemented by the money I had been sending home, held great promise to help me move on. But even this normally happy occurrence was tainted by the war.

As a result of what most might consider the natural response of seeking emotional release and celebrating after surviving the experience, Vietnam vets paid a price. A few days before my car was scheduled to arrive, I went to the insurance agency that my family used for decades to obtain necessary insurance coverage. My siblings and I had gone to school with the kids of the agency owner, and I was happy to see a young man that I graduated from high school with sitting behind the desk when I walked in. After some small talk I told him what I needed in the way of car insurance. After reviewing various books he told me what the premium was for six months. It was an outrageous amount for the time period, far more than what I knew other family members paid. In shock and immediate anger, I told him there was no way in hell that I was going to pay that amount. He explained that insurance companies charged Vietnam veterans a significant surcharge for two years following their return home due to what insurers labeled as *assumed reckless behavior*. It was another instance of the lack of recognition, let alone respect, of the service of returning Vietnam veterans. What did society expect of young men returning from a war zone? Of course some exuberant behavior was likely and a small number would carry that exuberance too far. Some did. I had a Vietnam vet friend who died in a car crash due to speed. Such behavior by returning veterans occurred after every war in modern American history. But to use the broad brush and paint every returning veteran with the same assumed guilt was wrong. Of the various irksome realities encountered upon returning home, this particular incident for some reason was among the most infuriating. It was a clear case of adding insult to injury. I found a somewhat cheaper policy elsewhere. Several vets I spoke with said they had the same experience.

Wartime experience had unexpected negative consequences involving friendships and other relationships. Attitudes and activities that once brought friends together were no longer present. As the months went by, combat experiences were the invisible but very real wall that separated returning vets from former friends and acquaintances. I witnessed this phenomenon prior to enlisting in the Corps when a young man who graduated two years before me returned home a very different person after spending a tour as a Marine grunt. It didn't occur to me then that the same thing could happen to me. The Vietnam experience and the time away created a chasm disconnecting one's youthful past from their future. Vietnam didn't bridge the two parts of our lives, it separated them completely and permanently. Much of life that existed prior to deployment just didn't matter anymore.

\* \* \*

It has been true throughout history that combat veterans view the world differently upon returning home. They also don't tell stories of things that occurred to them or their comrades. The realities of combat as they affect human beings and their frail bodies are not casually spoken of, and they damned sure are never joked about. The rules of conversation for returning grunts follow strict proscriptions, not through any formal declaration but due to basic humanity. It's a rare exception indeed for a vet to want to reflect on or talk about the *good old days* of their combat experiences.

These events are so unnatural in human life that it isn't possible to fully or accurately explain the actions and feelings or even briefly mention them with any expectation that the listener can truly comprehend what's being said. Nobody could understand, and basic respect requires confidentiality for what happened to comrades, so it's best to just say nothing. Even when combat vets happened to be together, they honored the unspoken code of silence. Nothing good could be gained by comparing notes and the only result would be reopened wounds. I once spent many days working with an Army infantryman and the topic of Vietnam was never raised except once, when he said he'd do whatever it took to make sure his newborn son never went to war.

Even if a veteran wanted to share accounts of their experiences, there was almost no one to talk with. America as a whole was trying to forget the national Vietnam nightmare and for the most part had no interest in returning vets or their stories.

With the passage of time the reluctance that Vietnam combat veterans had in putting their innermost thoughts and memories in the public realm for all to see was solidified. Throughout their postwar lives, years of experience made these survivors well aware that the general public, work acquaintances, and even friends cared little or not at all for what they experienced. Most vets concluded early in their post-Vietnam life that there was nothing to be gained and perhaps much to lose by sharing memories and events that had no meaning for almost everyone else. Many vets felt stained and damaged. Though not accepted by vets, there was the feeling that by having played any role in the Vietnam War we were guilty by association and therefore at least partially responsible for the whole sordid affair. Comments thoughtlessly made by people in everyday life made it clear that many Americans felt Vietnam veterans shared blame and were tarnished in the process.

Mired in a dilemma, Vietnam veterans simultaneously felt pride in having served in honorable military organizations, doing the thankless job we were asked to do, but also feeling aversion to what that task entailed and feeling isolated from the larger society as a result of having participated in this national military, political, and societal phenomenon called the Vietnam War. It seemed as if we just didn't fit in. Most decided to literally shut up about the entire war experience for the remainder of our lives. Many vets took it a step further. For some, the way to move on and assimilate was to virtually deny the experience and pretend that it didn't occur. This was accomplished by a near total separation from their military experience. Not only to not talk about it, but to not even think about it in an attempt to leave it all behind and move on. Hanging on to the memories carried little benefit.

If someone talked too much and too easily about their alleged exploits in the war, the listener can be quite certain that it was make-believe. A person that never saw the front lines was the teller of those tales.

War leaves indelible scars and all war veterans carry unwanted emotional baggage that is never discarded. A combat veteran's most powerful memories aren't only of family members or the many blessings of their life. Lasting for decades, barely concealed under the surface, are easily triggered memories of violent death, dismemberment, and jagged ends of white bones protruding through torn and bloody flesh; screams from terribly injured young men pleading for help, some calling for their mothers; the smell of men's guts spilled on the ground and on your clothes; the sound of gunfire followed by screams of pain; and the muffled explosions that meant another young American had activated a mine—noise for which there is no internal mute button. Mind numbing fear and personality changing feelings of passion, anger, and hate are forever buried deep in the mind.

Post-Traumatic Stress disorder was a fancy new term used instead of *battle fatigue* or *shell shock*, phrases used in World War I and World War II to describe the deleterious effect that constant combat and pervasive danger has on combatants. Vietnam vets did not escape the emotional trauma that plagued their fathers and grandfathers. A large study published in 1981 by the Center for Policy Research and the City University of New York concluded that soldiers who served in Vietnam were "plagued by significantly more problems than their peers." These problems ranged from alcoholism and drug abuse, to unemployment, depression, and suicide.

Two phenomena that have been largely forgotten with the passage of time were the large number of vets who simply dropped out of society or committed suicide. Many Vietnam vets moved to wilderness areas and just dropped out of public view. Suicide levels were well above average for the population age. Suicide among war veterans is nothing new but it was largely unnoticed and ignored until recent years.

* * *

One of the more difficult realities awaiting returning vets was the inability to properly reacclimate into society. This of course wasn't unique to Vietnam, but on the other hand, there was less attention paid to emotional issues because returning vets simply melted back into society on a one-by-one basis upon their return. Entire units didn't return *en masse* like they did after other wars. Soldiers returning from Vietnam came home not as proud vets returning to a welcoming country, but rather as war veterans disguised as civilians so as to better blend in. They then had to resume life among people who either didn't give a thought to the war or were actively anti-war and by extension unsupportive of their countrymen that served in the war. In either case, returnees received little in the way of empathy or support and were often recipients of outright disdain from the general public.

It is just barely an exaggeration to say that one week a soldier was at war and the next he was home trying to put his life back together. This acclimation process is hard enough even when society is supportive of the military and returning soldiers. Vietnam vets weren't looking for pity or a handout, they wanted nothing more than what their fathers received when they came home from war: support from their country and some recognition for the job they did and sacrifices they made.

This absence of recognition is yet one more facet of the Vietnam experience that is different than almost all other conflicts the country has been involved in. There was no real feeling of pride or accomplishment, only the private comfort of knowing you survived. There was much less of the post-war camaraderie and solidarity that veterans of earlier wars enjoyed. There were two marines in 2/9 who I considered to be good friends. I still have a picture of the three of us together. We talked about getting together if we got back home. We never did. I later checked and didn't see their names among those killed, so I assume they made it back at least alive. There were many like us who just wanted to forget it all and resume our lives once back in the states.

The heaviest loads are carried by those that served in combat situations and involve the fundamental underpinning of warfare, killing the enemy. Taking another human's life is a disturbing emotionally complex action that goes against everything we instinctively feel as a person and that we've been taught since childhood.

Even in a kill-or-be-killed situation doing something that you know is going to maim or kill another person is troubling in a way that's impossible to explain. Putting a human being in your rifle sights for the purpose of killing him or throwing a hand grenade that you know is going to horribly injure someone are among the most unnatural acts a person can perform. Contemplating such acts, and actually doing them, are another constant stress before, during, and for years after the occurrences. Killing from a distance, whether by bombs dropped by airplane pilots or as the result of an artillery round fired several miles away, is very different than eye-to-eye encounters.

It's quite amazing that so many veterans can leave a war zone where they had to kill other humans and then come home and live the rest of their lives as if those combat realities never happened. Untold thousands of people have pulled it off and it strikes me as an exceptional survival trait that allows humans to have to perform such unnatural deeds and then put it behind them so that those forced into that situation can successfully function in families and in society.

Violent movies are no longer appealing to many veterans as a result of their experiences. Combat vets in particular know all too well what bullets and shrapnel do to the fragile human body. That reality is hard to turn into a form of entertainment. Veterans know the real pain involved because they felt it themselves or saw friends who endured it and their lives forever changed. Such realities are hard to forget even when it's only pretend bullets and fake explosions on the screen.

* * *

Exposure to the several varieties of potent herbicides used in the war zone continues to be one of the more controversial issues haunting Vietnam vets. Though the most common product was code-named Agent Orange because of the orange stripes on the barrels, other mixtures were also used. Regardless of the specific materials the toxicity of the substances is unquestioned. It was vastly more deadly than over-the-counter herbicides available commercially.

Defoliant was used along infiltration routes along the Cambodia and Laos frontiers, and in secluded forested areas where the enemy maintained bases in South Vietnam. These were the same locations that saw the most action by American troops. The health problems documented from exposure to the chemical have plagued many thousands of vets and Vietnamese civilians for decades, leaving physical reminders of the worst kind. Many combat veterans suffered from chronic conditions ranging from COPD to nerve damage and various cancers. Most died significantly sooner than the average life expectancy. Offspring of vets and Vietnamese alike frequently show signs of Agent Orange exposure. The incidence of deformities is higher than normal and there appears to be little doubt but that the toxic chemicals in the applied herbicides are to blame. The Red Cross puts the number of Vietnamese who suffer direct or indirect health problems from firsthand or hereditary exposure at more than one million.

To this day veterans who were involved in a health monitoring program with the Veterans Administration get the glossy orange-colored Agent Orange Newsletter from the VA. These semi-annual reminders of the war discuss the many health issues connected with exposure to the industrial strength herbicides used in Vietnam. The results of on-going research into the several diseases known to be caused by exposure to the herbicides are regularly updated in the newsletter.

\* \* \*

High unemployment levels were a chronic problem for returning vets. Several factors combined forces to exacerbate the problem and the timing for vets was unfortunate. As the war ended there were serious economic, political, and social issues that combined to create a perfect storm scenario. The OPEC oil embargo and poor economy caused problems throughout society but affected vulnerable vets the most. Veterans lacked seniority in work settings and most lacked college degrees earned by those who had not gone to Vietnam. A changing economy also hurt. Most veterans weren't prepared for the new high technology economy.

Despite the circumstances they faced, the vast majority of returning Vietnam veterans eventually resumed a normal life. Their experience didn't deter them, it made them stronger and more determined to succeed. Most vets learned from their experiences. They didn't dwell on what happened to them, but rather viewed their experiences from the perspective of what happened for them, turning the experience from negative to positive. Every terrible day, every sight and sound of death or injury, every moment of anger and depression—these were gifts in a sense. They made us stronger and more resilient, able to face the realities of everyday life. I couldn't count the number of times that I just shook my head upon hearing someone complain about what to them was a major concern but what in reality was a minor issue of very little consequence. I'd think to myself, *If they only knew what real problems were.*

Vietnam veterans became doctors and mechanics, lawyers, and electricians. We built America's cars and drove trucks. As teachers we taught our young, perhaps from a perspective of maturity and understanding of human nature lacked by some. As parents we were able to understand the value of fragile lives and love our families deeply.

Vietnam veterans learned the lessons of social and political responsibilities. We gained an appreciation and love of the American way by seeing the other side. We saw how valiantly and desperately people were willing to fight to save their country and way of life, imperfect as it may have been. We were humbled by those who had little but were willing to risk it all. It gave us a renewed appreciation for our many blessings.

These men and women have been a major part of American society over the past fifty years and contributed greatly to the economic, moral, and social fabric of our nation. The hard-won qualities and strength of character that these Americans carry with them has helped our country in ways that are impossible to measure. Vietnam vets are proud to be part of a group of people that stood tall when called upon to serve. Through it all, Vietnam vets never forsook their country; it was the country that largely abandoned the vets.

* * *

As Vietnam vets straggled home, they did not join organizations like the Veterans of Foreign Wars (VFW) or American Legion at nearly the rate of earlier veterans. What reason was there to join such groups to reminisce with total strangers twice your age about what was widely perceived by the nation as a failed mission? Society had made it quite clear that ours wasn't an undertaking for which we and the American people could be proud or have a sense of a job well done. So why deepen the frustration by joining with folks who basked in the glory of the last good war and who enjoyed a nation's honor and respect? We had neither. An incident that cemented my impressions about how we were perceived was the reaction I received circa 1975 when I approached one of the organizations for war veterans about membership. The WWII vet behind the desk made it clear that he didn't consider Vietnam vets in a high regard due to their conduct in the war, having lost the war was how he phrased it. He said that his organization was primarily comprised of veterans of World War II and Korea. Thirty years passed before I finally joined one of these organizations.

This gentleman's comment about losing the war represented a falsehood that Vietnam veterans have had to live their entire life refuting. The American military did not lose the war. Throughout the years of combat NVA and VC forces lost virtually every battle of any size or significance. Every offensive they attempted was decisively defeated at a great loss of manpower and materiel for Communist forces. Their casualties were dramatically higher than those of American and allied forces.

America did not lose the war. North Vietnam and their allies did not defeat America; they outwaited us. When the Paris Peace Treaty was signed in 1973, South Vietnam was still an independent state, a status that would have ended decades earlier but for American involvement. It was only after American forces left South Vietnam that the North, and their powerful allies, were able to stream across the border unopposed and conquer South Vietnam.

We veterans knew that we fought as courageously as any American forces in the history of our country. We knew that we fought with honor and dedication to our mission, despite also knowing that we did not have the support of our country to a large part. We served honorably regardless. They say that integrity is doing the right thing even when no one sees and no one cares. Such was the case with American forces in Vietnam; we served with distinction, honorably and courageously, even though few Americans saw or cared.

\* \* \*

Due to the several year interruption in their post-high school lives many vets faced an obstacle when seeking employment or competing for promotional opportunities during their careers, especially in jobs requiring college degrees. Most of their peers at work were men and women who had gone the normal route from high school into the work force or to college, perhaps even to graduate school for additional employability. They didn't have the disruptive break caused by military service or the war. Obtaining a degree while working full time and raising a family is a tough way to go, but many thousands of Vietnam vets earned their college degrees in that manner. I met many of these hard working, determined vets during my years in the classroom. We were usually the oldest students in the class and instructors viewed us with mixed emotions. While they respected our work ethic and intense desire to obtain a degree, they were used to dealing with young students that sat quietly, not questioning what was being taught. Given their life experiences, vets didn't sit quietly. They challenged and questioned assumptions or the use of personal opinions presented as factual information. Our presence created a fascinating mix of personalities and ages.

Many veterans have long felt that colleges and universities should grant credits for military service. There is certainly no denying that a person learns much about every aspect of life and how to work as a team and accomplish goals by serving in the military, especially if that service included combat experience. But in any event, I know of no veteran who held it against their peers or employer for their situation. Most felt that they played the hand they were dealt and made the best of it. There was no whining or finger pointing. It's not anyone's fault that I and my fellow Marines decided to join the Corps; that was entirely our decision, based on our personal views of service and patriotism. I've proudly lived with the decision I made and had the privilege of knowing and working with many others who felt likewise.

Vietnam veterans themselves and support groups filled the void that was lacking in the way of recognition and welcome. An excellent example was the annual *Ride to The Wall* Memorial Day weekend event. Starting in 1988, the Rolling Thunder motorcycle group organized these nationwide rides which end at the Vietnam Memorial Wall in Washington DC. The event honors veterans and spotlights the continuing Missing in Action and Prisoners of War issue. The run evolved into the largest single day motorcycle event in existence. Two Vietnam veterans started the motorcycle pageant as a way to focus on the plight of Vietnam vets and to show solidarity for all veterans. I was proud to participate in several of these runs. The emotional impact of seeing tens of thousands of flag waving motorcyclists and an equal number of cheering spectators welcoming veterans as they rode through DC was a marvelous thing. The event lasted twenty-one years.

Washington DC Police lead the Memorial Day Rolling Thunder
Ride to The Wall through the city. Photo by author.

Around the year 2010 groups organized *LZ* events in many states. They were called *LZ Lambeau, LZ Michigan, LZ Maryland* and so on. They were welcome home and appreciation events, described as an opportunity to publicly say *Thank you and Welcome Home* to aging Vietnam veterans. In addition to various displays, speakers, vendors, and motorcycle events, each LZ had the Traveling Wall, a half-size portable Vietnam Memorial Wall, on site.

For several years I attended USMC birthday events at a local bar that had a big celebration each year on the tenth of November. This was a good place to go to talk or not, but to at least be among some fellow grunts. One of the first times I went, a man asked me what unit I had been with. I told him the Twenty-Seventh and Ninth Regiments. When I said G 2/9 he just looked at me and said *"Holy fuck! The Walking Dead! You guys had some bad shit up there, didn't you?"* I deflected the question by stating that all units in I Corps experienced bad shit. The *Walking Dead* title was actually ascribed to the First Battalion of the Ninth Marines.

But while it's important to honor the past and remember those who served, I gradually felt it wasn't a good thing to relive it. I really didn't want any part of telling or hearing war stories. I saw the original live play; that was enough. I wasn't alone in the desire to not make discussion of the war part of my social life. There were many vets who didn't participate in organizations or events in which the war was going to be a topic.

* * *

The many needs of Vietnam veterans were not being met by the federal government. America was moving beyond the war and was focused on other things and Vietnam vets lacked a unified voice. As time went by and the desire to join or organize grew, Vietnam specific organizations were formed. Their function was not only fraternal but strategic. It became clear that the only way veterans would receive attention from lawmakers and public agencies was if they spoke in an organized manner. Arguments based on service, equity, and justice were not enough. Agencies would respond to the needs of Vietnam veterans only if an organization representing them had political strength through numbers. Several organizations were ultimately formed. Some focused on the struggle to be heard. Others formed because of a desire to continue to serve the nation and its troops.

In 1978 a handful of Vietnam veterans traveled to Washington, DC in an attempt to form an advocacy organization devoted to the needs of those who had served in Vietnam. Shortly thereafter the Council of Vietnam Veterans was created. By the summer of 1979, the Council transformed into Vietnam Veterans of America. With more than 85,000 members, it became the largest and most effective Vietnam veterans organization. It is the only congressionally-chartered national veteran's organization dedicated to Vietnam-era veterans and their families. The motto of VVA is *Never again shall one generation of Americans abandon another*. It is a profound statement of intent by people who understood firsthand the harm caused by societal ambivalence.

Another organization that was formed by and originally largely staffed by Vietnam veterans who had a desire to serve new war veterans is the Patriot Guard Riders. Like the VVA, the PGR was committed to support a new generation of veterans. Their motto was *Standing For Those Who Stood For Us* and that never again would the sacrifices of war veterans be forgotten.

Founded in 2005, its original purpose was to shield families of fallen service members from the Afghanistan and Iraq Wars from protestors that disrupted the memorial and funeral services of those soldiers. The protestors were not rallying against the wars but rather social issues, in particular the issue of homosexuality. They connected the death of soldiers as a sign of God's wrath imposed on America for alleged social ills.

Originally formed as a motorcycle-based group, PGR riders formed protective honor lines to separate families and guests from protestors. Members stood outside in silent respect as the funeral service took place inside the facility, preventing protestors from interrupting the service. The mission of the group expanded to include first responder funerals and funerals for all veterans, not just those killed in action. Perhaps the most visible manifestations of the organization are the impressive yet respectful motorcycle escorts from the place of the funeral service to the burial ground—frequently a national cemetery.

With the passage of years, traditional veteran organizations became much more inviting to Vietnam veterans. Given the number of Vietnam veterans, it appears that the percentage of membership that are Vietnam vets is below what one would expect. That might be at least partially attributed to the fact that as a nation we are no longer as interested in joining fraternal or service organizations as our parents and grandparents were. I believe there is also a reticence on the part of Vietnam vets to join these groups at this point in their lives; it's too late.

Perhaps the proudest legacy of Vietnam vets is how we vigorously supported veterans of the Afghanistan and Iraq Wars and all military personnel today. Vietnam vets played active roles in every way, from troop departure events to welcoming home ceremonies at airports and bases. We served as escorts in funerals, led fundraisers for families, and overall have been there for today's veterans in every manner possible.

Caring about the plight of veterans continues to be a problem in America. Veterans organizations alone can't adequately take care of the needs of the men and women that the country has sent off to war or other dangerous duties. Our society has to learn to accept that the cost of a military deployment doesn't end when the troops finally return home. American citizens may want to immediately forget the war and move on with their lives, but that's not how it works. Associated costs of war that society has a moral obligation to pay will remain for at least an entire generation. Disabled soldiers and their dependents must be cared for. Thousands of badly wounded vets will require medical care their entire lives and society has a moral and legal duty to provide compassionate and adequate care. It was the American people, after all, who sent the young man or woman away to war on their behalf. They can't just forget about the veteran once they are done fighting the country's battles.

* * *

The post-Vietnam era saw several movies that seemed to go out of their way to portray soldiers in Vietnam negatively. All for the entertainment and economic value that could be had by making combat troops in particular look cruel, out of control, and even psychopathic. Unfortunately, the creators of one of the most influential movies, *Platoon,* deemed it necessary to make the murderous Sgt. Barnes character and his lackeys appear to be the norm in Vietnam. They weren't. They were far from the norm.

I sadly recall my secretary telling me about her daughter's comments upon seeing the movie, which the producers proudly claimed portrayed *the real thing.* Upon seeing the movie, her daughter, a high school senior at the time, told her mother that "Vietnam veterans were every bit as evil as the Nazis in World War II. All they did was rape, plunder, and murder." Her mother reluctantly relayed the incident to me the next day. How unfortunate that writers, directors, and producers let the desire for profit outweigh truth, and as a result led an entire generation to believe that Vietnam veterans were little more than uncaring criminals taking advantage of a license to kill. Far too few young Americans recognized the false impressions perpetuated about the war and the men who fought in it as the outrageous falsehoods that they are.

The impact of Vietnam vets being negatively portrayed during the war by Hollywood and others came home to roost years later, when I was fifty years old. Four of us were in a car returning from a conference. The conversation somehow stretched to involve the Vietnam War. One of the passengers, a woman who was about the same age as my prior secretary's daughter, made a strongly disparaging and broad-brush comment about Vietnam vets. I was stunned and spent the rest of the trip explaining the truth to her. She was apologetic, having no idea that I was one of the group she had such strong negative feelings about. In our conversation it became obvious that her opinions were formed by what she had seen and heard in the media and from her peers. By the time we arrived home her attitude had changed considerably and to this day I count her as one of my friends.

Because of the controversies surrounding the Vietnam experience even after the end of the war, there was never an end point for Vietnam veterans. Public discourse over many years regarding *the lessons of Vietnam* were generally negative in nature, what we should not do versus the positive lessons learned. A final insult was former Defense

Secretary Robert McNamara's 1995 memoir in which he described the Vietnam War as being "wrong, terribly wrong." It was McNamara's recommendations to President Johnson in 1965 and 1966 that vastly increased troop levels in Vietnam. For those of us that ended up there because of his decisions, his blanket damnation of the entire affair was perhaps the ultimate slap in the face and repudiation of all that we experienced and the good we tried to do.

The roles played by McNamara and other high-level decision makers, made known by the Pentagon Papers, added another level of anger and frustration for Vietnam vets. The movie *The Post*, released in 2017, was difficult to watch if one served in Vietnam. Damning information about the conduct of the war was known while many young Americans were there fighting and dying.

* * *

Many veterans went into law enforcement, from the same sense of public service that we possessed in Vietnam. Careers in criminal justice placed veterans in frequent situations in which they were again at the receiving end of angry and even hateful insults from generational peers. The societal rendering and philosophical split caused by the war lasted for a decade after the fighting ended. Officers often came face-to-face with residual anger and civil disobedience attitudes that young people of our age possessed. This phenomenon was a continuation of the schizophrenic generation reality. These young people were the same age we were. They were our generation. They were our peers. We presumably were on the same side. In Vietnam we would have fought side by side. But to many the police were the enemy and called *pigs*. Vietnam vets and non-vets viewed the world quite differently during the turbulent post-war period.

An even more troubling generational situation that returning vets faced was seeing the flag of North Vietnam and banners of the Viet Cong displayed by youthful protestors at antiwar protests and various other antigovernment rallies. Seeing fellow Americans arrogantly flying the flag of an enemy that killed and maimed thousands of other young Americans, our comrades on the battlefield, was extremely difficult to accept. The tectonic fault lines that so deeply divided our generation, the Vietnam generation, were manifested in many ways and for many years. It's easy to imagine how devastated returning veterans from the Iraq and Afghanistan wars would have felt had they witnessed large groups of their American generational peers displaying banners of ISIS and Al Qaeda. When display of the enemy's flag was compounded by vocal support for that hostile entity, the emotional wound was even deeper.

Many, perhaps most, Vietnam era servicemen thought that Vietnam was a noble cause, even if not a war of national defense. We were helping people who were unable by themselves to save their country and way of life from an invasion by North Vietnam, which was largely a proxy nation for the Soviet Union and China in the effort to spread communism. We were fighting to keep a nation free from subjugation. There were millions of people in South Vietnam that desperately did not want to be under the harsh laws and doctrines of the North. Millions of people simply wanted to live according to their customs and be able to practice their religious beliefs without persecution by atheistic dictators from Hanoi, Moscow, and Beijing. But was that reason enough for us to intervene and for tens of thousands to die? To this day I do not know. I'm afraid I lack the wisdom to answer that awesomely difficult question. If North Vietnam had honored the Paris Peace Accords and not invaded the South while the ink was still wet on the paper, there could have been peace. Had that been the case and if the people of South Vietnam were able to live their lives in peace while remaking their own country, the sacrifices and deaths perhaps would have been worthwhile. The freedom of millions of people is a goal worth fighting for. But the North, with the backing of the Russian and Chinese behemoths, had no intention of letting the population of the South live in peace. Secretary of State Henry Kissinger must have struggled mightily as he put pen to paper to rationalize in his own mind that he was condemning South Vietnam to conquest and at the same time negating the blood, sweat, and tears of hundreds of thousands of young Americans and their families.

Once we were committed to fight for the people of South Vietnam, veterans of that war gave it their all. They fought and died so that people they didn't know might live in freedom and, ultimately, peace. But the issue of Vietnam always seems to complicate rather than clarify. The decision was made in the early 1950s to become involved. And we honored that decision. But there was an alternative course of action and that was for America to not become involved in the politics of Vietnam. The war did not have to happen. Unlike World War II, which was truly a war to save the world from international fascism and the loss of freedom, the Vietnam War could have been avoided with different decisions in the war's formative years. Roosevelt's desire to end French colonial control after World War II could have been accepted. Had FDR lived, he might have prevailed and America would have responded differently to pressures from France to maintain their colony. France and America might have given greater consideration to Ho Chi Minh's efforts to work with world powers immediately after World War II toward the establishment of independent countries in Southeast Asia. Presidents Truman and Eisenhower did not have to support, and then take over France's war after their defeat in the name of an anti-communist policy. They could have allowed events to occur as they would have without outside interference and involvement. In 1964 Congress did not have to issue President Johnson broad, arguably unlimited, authority following the inconsequential Gulf of Tonkin incident. Cooler heads and clearer thinking might have prevailed, urging caution and restricting the country's response, not throwing the gates to war wide open. Once committed, especially after the 1964 congressional action and early troop buildup, withdrawal became almost impossible. Vietnam vets have spent their lives wondering *what if?* This generation of veterans has also spent their lives hoping and praying that the country never again goes to war for reasons other than protecting the homeland.

The plight of prisoners of war and those missing in action was a war-related issue that united most Americans even while the war was raging. This concern led two college students, Carol Bates Brown and Kay Hunter, to create the concept of POW/MIA bracelets. They formed Voices in Vital America (VIVA) on Veterans Day in 1970, using the idea of metal bracelets, each bearing the engraved name of a missing or captured servicemember, to draw attention of their plight. The program became quite popular and was the topic of discussion on many media events across the country, especially after the war's end when the number of missing became apparent. Interest in the program waned by the early 1980s, but there were Americans who wore a bracelet for many years afterwards, taking it off only if the missing soldier's remains were found and repatriated. I purchased a bracelet circa 1974, and a great disappoint for me was losing it while on a motorcycle trip a few years later. I regret losing it and regret not buying another to replace it.

The Paris Peace Accords ending America's involvement in Vietnam were signed on January 27,1973. Lt. Col. William B. Nolde was the last American killed during the war; he was killed by an artillery shell at An Loc, sixty miles northwest of Saigon, only eleven hours before the truce went into effect.

The settlement included a cease-fire throughout North and South Vietnam. The Accords called for the eventual reunification of Vietnam through peaceful means. The United States agreed to the withdrawal of all remaining US troops and advisors, numbering about 23,700, and the dismantling of all US bases within sixty days. North Vietnam agreed to release all US and other prisoners of war. Most Americans assumed that the great majority of those held as POWs or labeled as missing would be repatriated. According to the best information available from the battlefield, 2,646 Americans were unaccounted for, and presumed either missing in action, killed but the body not recovered, or held as prisoners of war. Five hundred ninety-one POWs were repatriated as part of Operation Homecoming. The government and hopeful families across the country were predictably disappointed. The reality of about 2,000 missing men was a bitter pill and resulted in the creation of an accounting mission by the military to find those missing Americans. Many Americans and military personnel at the time believed that some, perhaps many, of the missing were still being held as prisoners in remote prison camps throughout Southeast Asia, perhaps not under the direct control of Hanoi. The thought of American sons and brothers being held in cruel jungle camps played on the minds of many. This concern brought the VIVA MIA/POW bracelet program to the mainstream for several years. This fear also helped create the logo for the POW/MIA movement; a tormented soldier held in a bamboo cage, typical of prisoner camps run by the VC.

Article Eight of the peace accord called for mutual assistance among the several parties in accounting for missing Americans, but deadly conditions on the ground in North and South Vietnam, Cambodia, and Laos limited access to the entire region.

From February 1973 to March 1975, teams from the United States and South Vietnam conducted joint, but limited, searches for Americans missing in South Vietnam. These searches were somewhat successful with the status of sixty-three servicemen confirmed. Twenty-three of these had died in captivity in North Vietnam. Five had been killed in Laos. Search efforts were stymied when US Army Capt. Richard M. Rees was killed by guerrilla fighters while conducting search efforts on Dec. 15, 1973. This event caused restrictions on the ongoing recovery work. On April 30, 1975, searches ended completely when North Vietnam forces captured South Vietnam.

The US resumed its recovery efforts in the early 1980s with high-level contacts between Washington and Hanoi. General John Vessey Jr. was appointed as a special presidential emissary on POW/MIA issues in 1987 to find ways to account for those still unaccounted for. The Vietnamese permitted American teams to search throughout the country starting in September 1988. Parallel arrangements were reached in Laos and Cambodia around the same time and occasional targeted investigations were done in China. Continuous joint searches began in April 1988 in Laos, and in October 1991 in Cambodia. In February 1992, the US organized its accounting efforts into the large-scale field operations which continue to this time. The efforts have been very successful despite extremely difficult conditions. Since 1973, the remains of more than 1,000 Americans killed in the Vietnam War have been identified and returned to their families for burial with full military honors. One thousand five hundred eighty six Americans are still classified as missing in action from the Vietnam War.

\* \* \*

All Vietnam veterans remember three milestones that resulted in powerful emotional responses. The first was on January 27, 1973 when the Paris Peace Accords were signed. The second was Operation Homecoming and the release of American Prisoners of War, which took place over a three-month period in the spring of 1973. Vietnam veterans across the country wept as they watched those 591 amazing men walk, limp, or be carried off the planes that brought them home. Imagining what they endured, some for as long as eight and a half years at the hands of their captors was overwhelming. The entire nation wept for joy when these men were finally reunited with their families. The long nightmare was finally, really, over.

The third major event was April 30, 1975, the horribly depressing day when the unopposed North Vietnamese Army completed their capture of the South and Saigon fell. The pictures of helicopters frantically removing the last of the marines from the embassy rooftop and leaving hundreds of desperate Vietnamese friends and allies behind to suffer at the hands of their captors was extremely distressing. America always exited its wars with celebrations and parades, not scenes of chaos and life and death desperation. The picture of those helicopters and of the people on the roofs with their outstretched arms desperately seeking a way out, is forever burned into the brain of every Vietnam veteran. Those scenes of disarray and despair were what we all fought and so many thousands died to prevent. Veterans felt so sorry for all the people we let down who now had to face an uncertain and difficult future. We also wondered, though of course we knew the answer, where the world's outrage was, given the fact that North Vietnam so blatantly violated the peace treaty they signed that supposedly ended the war two years earlier. Vietnamization worked well for us but it didn't work worth a damn for the South Vietnamese.

What the Paris Accords accomplished in reality, of course, was to allow America to declare that we accomplished our objective and hand the war over to the Vietnamese. How ironic. Almost exactly forty years earlier the Geneva Peace Accords paved the way for France to make their own exit from the country of Vietnam, passing the baton of responsibility for the quagmire on to America.

Perhaps the most visible and important occurrence in the post war period, for both the veterans of the war and the entire American population, was construction of the memorial wall. Officially known as the Vietnam Veterans Memorial, known simply and reverently by veterans as *The Wall*. The beautiful black granite monument stands in honor of the 58,220 men and eight women who gave their lives in the war. In 1980 Congress authorized a nonprofit organization, the Vietnam Veterans Memorial Fund, Inc., led by Vietnam vet Jay Scruggs, to raise funds and build the memorial. On November 13, 1982 the unique structure was dedicated. More than five million people visit the memorial every year to honor those Americans who gave their lives and to remember that period in our history. Only the Lincoln Memorial sees more visitors.

The Wall is much more than a monument. It is a sanctuary. It is a memorial. It is a haven where the grieving and troubled can find comfort, support, and peace. It is hallowed ground. If ever there was a place or idea that brought Americans together and helped bury the ashes of discord generated by the flames of this war, it is The Wall.

Ceremony at the
Vietnam Memorial
on Veterans Day,
2008.

Photo by the
US Army

For several years following the end of the war, American politicians, military leaders, pundits, professors and others spoke of *the lessons of Vietnam*; those things that America supposedly learned from the experience. It appears that any lessons learned stayed with us for less than ten years.

An important, perhaps the most important, lesson that Americans hoped our government acquired was that war, and all of the death and destruction that attends it, must not be used in lieu of diplomacy or to achieve political or diplomatic goals. War is meant as a last resort to protect our homeland or the defense of critical allies pursuant to established legal treaties. War must always be the absolute last resort and any gain of going to war must clearly offset the great human costs that will occur. Since the formal end of the Vietnam War, America has been involved in one military engagement, or outright war, after another. Indeed, there often was no pause between wars. Since 1981 the American military has become involved (to one degree or another, but seriously enough to require deployment of young Americans to dangerous locations) in dozens of events in at least thirty-five locations on the globe, ranging from Afghanistan to Zaire. Perhaps the lesson of diplomacy first and war only as an extreme last resort was not accepted by American politicians and decision-makers, as we had hoped at the close of the Vietnam War.

Another lesson was that to be successful, war must have the nation's support. A third was that military superiority does not guarantee victory. The country as a whole must be on board in support of a military action for the long term, and behind the military personnel being sent into harm's way. Justification for the hostile action must not only be legally and morally valid, it must be clearly defined, explained, and have an exit strategy. Citizens have a right to expect these things. Further, politicians and citizenry alike must be ready to pay the price of war, in all of its costly currencies. If not, the death of America's youth on foreign battlegrounds will be of little benefit, and America will be weakened and torn asunder like it was during the Vietnam War. Hubris, arrogance, and a sense of military superiority have no place in our decision-making process. A humbling lesson from Vietnam is that military superiority, high-tech equipment, and tonnage of bombs dropped does not necessarily lead to the desired results.

These lessons, too, seem to have fallen between the cracks. Our military deployments and engagements have earned the label *forever wars*. They are fought by a professional military comprised of voluntary enlistees, leaving the vast majority of America and Americans untouched by the costs of a deployment or conflict. The end of compulsory military service was seen as a way to placate the mood of America a half-century ago, but it has had the unfortunate effect of insulating much of America from the actions of our leaders. When less than one-half of one percent of the population serve in the military and are affected by decisions to go to war, the remaining nearly 99 percent can become dangerously apathetic.

A final lesson that should be learned from all wars is that General William Tecumseh Sherman's statement that *war is hell* wasn't an exaggeration. It was an understatement.

# VIETNAM ERA FACTS
# AND FIGURES

Note: These figures are based on the government's official number of killed in action. As MIA remains are repatriated, this number changes. An audit performed in 2019 showed that there is a total of 58,276 names now qualified to be engraved on the wall.

| Year of Death or Declaration of Death | Number of Records |
|---|---|
| 1955–1959 | 4 |
| 1960 | 5 |
| 1961 | 16 |
| 1962 | 53 |
| 1963 | 122 |
| 1964 | 216 |
| 1965 | 1,928 |
| 1966 | 6,350 |
| 1967 | 11,363 |
| 1968 | 16,899 |
| 1969 | 11,780 |

| | |
|---|---|
| 1970 | 6,173 |
| 1971 | 2,414 |
| 1972 | 759 |
| 1973 | 68 |
| 1974 | 1 |
| 1975 | 62 |
| **Total** | **58,220** |

| Age of KIAs | Number of Records |
|---|---|
| 17 – 19 | 11,398 |
| 20 – 22 | 28,598 |
| 23 – 29 | 11,972 |
| 30 – 39 | 4,927 |
| 40 – 49 | 1,156 |
| 50 or older | 125 |
| Unknown/Unreported | 144 |

| Home State or Territory of KIA | Number of Records |
|---|---|
| Alabama | 1,208 |
| Alaska | 57 |
| Arizona | 619 |
| Arkansas | 592 |
| California | 5,575 |
| Canal Zone | 2 |
| Colorado | 623 |
| Connecticut | 612 |
| Delaware | 122 |
| District of Columbia | 242 |
| Florida | 1,954 |
| Georgia | 1,581 |
| Guam | 70 |
| Hawaii | 276 |
| Idaho | 217 |
| Illinois | 2,936 |
| Indiana | 1,534 |
| Iowa | 851 |
| Kansas | 627 |
| Kentucky | 1,056 |
| Louisiana | 885 |
| Maine | 341 |
| Maryland | 1,014 |

| Massachusetts | 1,331 |
|---|---|
| Michigan | 2,657 |
| Minnesota | 1,077 |
| Mississippi | 636 |
| Missouri | 1,418 |
| Montana | 267 |
| Nebraska | 396 |
| Nevada | 149 |
| New Hampshire | 226 |
| New Jersey | 1,487 |
| New Mexico | 395 |
| New York | 4,119 |
| North Carolina | 1,613 |
| North Dakota | 199 |
| Ohio | 3,094 |
| Oklahoma | 987 |
| Oregon | 710 |
| Pennsylvania | 3,147 |
| Puerto Rico | 345 |
| Rhode Island | 209 |
| South Carolina | 895 |
| South Dakota | 192 |
| Tennessee | 1,295 |
| Texas | 3,415 |
| Utah | 361 |

| | |
|---|---|
| Vermont | 100 |
| Virgin Islands | 15 |
| Virginia | 1,305 |
| Washington | 1,047 |
| West Virginia | 733 |
| Wisconsin | 1,161 |
| Wyoming | 119 |
| Other (non-US home of record) | 125 |
| **Total** | **58,220** |

| Records by Race—KIAs | Number |
|---|---|
| American Indian/Alaska Native | 226 |
| Asian | 139 |
| Black or African American | 7,243 |
| Hispanic One Race | 349 |
| Native Hawaiian or other Pacific Islander | 229 |
| Non-Hispanic/ more than one race | 204 |
| White | 49,830 |
| Total Records | 58,220 |

| Records by Paygrade—KIAs | Number |
|---|---|
| Enlistee (Grades E1–E9) | 48,717 |
| Officers (Grade 001–008) | 6,604 |
| Warrant Officers (Grades W01–W04) | 1,277 |
| Undefined Code or Blank | 1,622 |
| Total Records | 58,220 |

| Military Service Branch—KIAs | Number of Records |
|---|---|
| Air Force | 2,586 |
| Army | 38,224 |
| Coast Guard | 7 |
| Marine Corps | 14,844 |
| Navy | 2,559 |
| **Total** | **58,220** |

| Country Where Death Occurred | Number |
|---|---|
| Cambodia | 523 |
| China | 10 |
| Laos | 728 |
| North Vietnam | 1,120 |
| South Vietnam | 55,661 |
| Thailand | 178 |

| Missing in Action Year | Number of MIAs |
|---|---|
| 1973 | 2,646 |
| 2020 | 1,586 |
| Number of Remains Recovered | 1,060 |
| **Repatriations of MIAs** | **Number of MIAs Repatriated** |
| From Vietnam | 728 |
| From Laos | 287 |
| From Cambodia | 42 |
| From China | 3 |

| Allied Nations KIAs | Number |
|---|---|
| Australia | 426 |
| New Zealand | 37 |
| Philippines | 9 |
| South Korea | 5,099 |
| Taiwan | 25 |
| Thailand | 351 |

Data from the National Archives (Military Records and Research unit) and the Defense POW/MIA Accounting Agency.

# GLOSSARY

**AAA**—anti aircraft artillery.

**Ace of spades**—symbol of death, a good luck talisman, or a symbol of that war. Worn especially by Grunts on their helmet, it was the trademark of Vietnam war fighters.

**Actual**—the Marine unit commander. Used to distinguish the commander from the radioman when the call sign is used.

**Advanced infantry training**—specialized infantry training taken after basic training.

**AFVN**—Armed Forces Vietnam Network radio station.

**Agency**—the Central Intelligence Agency.

**A-gunner**—assistant gunner.

**AHB**—assault helicopter battalion.

**AID**—Agency for International Development.

**Airborne**—soldiers that are qualified as parachutists.

**Air Cav**—air cavalry, helicopter-borne infantry, helicopter gunship assault teams.

**Airmobile**—helicopter-borne infantry.

**AIT**—advanced infantry training.

**AK-47**—Soviet-manufactured Kalashnikov semi-automatic and fully automatic combat assault rifle, 7.62-mm. Weapon of the communist forces.

**ALPHA**—military phonetic for the letter A.

**Ammo dump**—location where live ammunition is stored.

**Amtrack**—amphibious armored vehicle used by marines to transport troops and supplies, sometimes armed with a .30-caliber machine gun.

**Angel track**—armored personnel carrier used as an aid station.

**AO**—area of operations.

**APC**—armored personnel carrier. A track vehicle used to transport Army troops or supplies, usually armed with a .50-caliber machine gun.

**APO**—Army post office located in San Francisco for overseas mail to Vietnam.

**ARA**—aerial rocket artillery. A Cobra AG-1H helicopter with four XM-159C 19-rocket (2.75 inch) pods.

**Arc light**—code name for B-52 bomber strikes along the Cambodian and Vietnamese border. These operations shook the earth for ten miles away from the target area.

**Article 15**—section of the Uniform Military Code of Justice. A form of non-judicial punishment.

**Arty**—shorthand term for artillery.

**Arvin**—soldier in the ARVN, or the ARVN itself.

**ARVN**—Army of the Republic of Vietnam; the South Vietnamese Regular Army.

**A-team**—basic ten-man team of the US Special Forces. The A-teams often led irregular military units that were not responsible to the Vietnamese military command.

**AWOL**—absent without leave; leaving a post or position without official permission.

**Azimuth**—A bearing from north.

**B-52**—US Air Force eight-engine high-altitude bomber. Officially called the Stratofortress. It can carry up to 70,000 pounds of weapons.

**Ballgame**—an operation or a contact.

**Band-aid**—medic.

**Bandoliers**—cloth belts to hold rifle ammunition or loaded magazines, sometimes used to mean belts of machine gun ammunition.

**BAR**—Browning automatic rifle. A .30-caliber magazine-fed automatic rifle used by US troops during World War II and Korea. Not used in Vietnam for most of the war.

**Base camp**—a resupply base for field units and a location for headquarters of brigade or division-size units, artillery batteries, and airfields. Also known as the rear area.

**Basic**—basic training.

**Battalion**—a military unit composed of a headquarters and two or more companies, batteries, or similar units.

**Battery**—an artillery unit equivalent to a company. Six 105mm or 155mm howitzers or two eight-inch or 175mm self-propelled howitzers.

**Battle-sight zeroing**—process of adjusting a weapon's sights and windage to an individual soldier so the weapon, when fired, will hit the object of aim.

**BCD**—bad conduct discharge.

**BDA**—bomb damage assessment.

**Beans and dicks**—military C-ration hot dogs and beans meals.

**Beaten zone**—area where the majority of bullets will strike when a machine gun is laid-in to cover a part of a defensive perimeter or part of an ambush zone.

**Beehive round**—an explosive artillery shell that delivered thousands of small projectiles instead of shrapnel.

**Berm**—perimeter line of a fortification, usually raised above surrounding area.

**Big Red One**—nickname for the First Infantry Division.

**Bird**—any aircraft, but usually refers to helicopters.

**Bird dog**—forward air controller, usually in a small, maneuverable single-engined propeller airplane.

**BK amputee**—below-the-knee amputation of the leg.

**Blood trail**—a trail of blood on the ground left by a fleeing man who has been wounded.

**Bloods**—term used by and for African American soldiers in Vietnam.

**Blooper**—the M-79 grenade launcher. A 40-millimeter, shotgun-like weapon that shoots spin-armed small grenades. Also known as a *blooker*.

**Blue feature**—used in reference to any water feature because of the color used to designate water on topographic maps.

**Body bag**—plastic bag used to transport dead bodies from the field.

**Body count**—the number of enemies killed, wounded, or captured during an operation. The term was used as a means of measuring the success and progress of the war.

**Boom-boom**—sex, as in the offer of sex by a woman or pimp.

**Boondoggle**—any military operation that hasn't been completely thought out. An operation that is absurd or useless.

**Boonie hat**—soft hat worn by a boonie rat in the boonies.

**Boonie rat**—combat infantryman.

**Boonies**—infantry term for the field; jungles or swampy areas far from the comforts of civilization.

**Boot**—a soldier just out of boot camp; inexperienced, untested.

**BOQ**—bachelor officer quarters; living quarters for officers.

**Bouncing Betty**—antipersonnel mine with two charges: the first propels the explosive charge upward, and the other is set to explode at about waist level.

**Bowl**—pipe used for smoking dope.

**BRAVO**—military phonetic for the letter B.

**Breaking squelch**—disrupting the natural static of a radio by depressing the transmit bar on another radio set to the same frequency.

**Brigade**—a tactical and administrative military unit composed of a headquarters and one or more battalions of infantry or armor, with other supporting units.

**Bro**—a Black soldier. Term used by other Black soldiers.

**Bronco**—twin-engine observation aircraft equipped with rockets and miniguns.

**Bronze Star**—US military decoration awarded for heroic or meritorious service not involving aerial flights.

**Brother**—a fellow Black Marine; sometimes used as slang for all Black males.

**Brown bar**—a lieutenant; denotes the single bar of the rank. In the field, officers wore camouflage rank which was often brown or black instead of brass.

**Brown water Navy**—term applied to the US Navy units assigned to the inland boat patrols of the Mekong River delta.

**BS**—bullshit, as in chewing the fat, telling tall tales, or telling lies.

**Buckle**—to fight. *Buckle for your dust* means to fight furiously.

**BUFF**—big ugly fat fucker, slang for a B-52.

**Bug juice**—military issued insect repellant.

**Buku**—from French word *beaucoup;* many, large, much.

**Bummer**—bad luck or unfortunate set of circumstances.

**Bush**—infantry term for the field.

**Bust caps**—Marine Corps term for firing a rifle rapidly.

**C-4**—plastic, putty-textured explosive used by military engineers and highly desired by infantry soldiers. Small pieces burned with a hot flame when lit. It was used in small pieces to heat C-rations in the field.

**C-54**—largest of the American helicopters, strictly for cargo. Also called Flying Crane or Skycrane.

**C-123**—small cargo airplane.

**C-130**—large propeller-driven Air Force planes that carry people and cargo called the *Hercules*. Also used as a *Puff* or *Spooky* aerial weapons plane.

**C-141**—very large cargo airplane called the *Starlifter*.

**CA**—combat assault. The term is used to describe dropping troopers into a hot LZ.

**Cache**—hidden supplies.

**Cammies**—camouflage uniforms.

**C and C**—command and control helicopter used by reconnaissance or unit commanders.

**CAP**—civil action program. US military personnel working with Vietnamese civilians.

**CAR-15**—a carbine rifle.

**Carbine**—a short-barreled, lightweight automatic or semiautomatic rifle.

**Caribou C-7A**—small transport plane for moving men and material.

**CAS**—close air support. Firepower from helicopters or fixed-wing aircraft directed at the enemy close to American units.

**Cav** —cavalry; the First Cavalry Division (Airmobile).

**CC**—company commander.

**CG**—commanding general.

**Chao**—from the Italian word *ciao*; hello or goodbye, depending upon the context.

**CHARLIE**—military phonetic for the letter C.

**Charlie**—Viet Cong; the enemy.

**Chas**—Viet Cong; the enemy.

**Cherry**—slang term for youth and inexperience; a virgin; a boot.

**Chi-com**—Chinese communist.

**Chi-com mine**—Chinese mine; can be made of plastic.

**Chieu Hoi**—the *open arms* program, promising clemency and financial aid to Viet Cong and NVA soldiers and cadres who stopped fighting and returned to South Vietnamese government authority.

**Chinook**—CH-47 cargo helicopter.

**Chop chop**—slang for food.

**Chopper**—helicopter.

**Choppered**—to be taken somewhere by a helicopter.

**Chuck**—the Viet Cong; the enemy.

**CIB**—combat infantry badge. An Army, later Marine, award for being under enemy fire in a combat zone, worn on both fatigues and dress uniforms.

**CIDG**—South Vietnamese Civilian Irregular Defense Groups.

**CINCPAC**—Commander in chief of all American forces in the Pacific region.

**Civilian Irregular Defense Group**—American financed, irregular South Vietnamese military units which were led by members of Special Forces A-teams. Members of these units were Vietnamese nationals but were usually members of ethnic minorities in the country.

**Clacker**—a small hand-held firing device for a claymore mine.

**Claymore**—an antipersonnel mine used by the infantry which, when detonated, propelled small steel cubes in a sixty-degree fan-shaped pattern to a maximum distance of 100 meters.

**Clearance**—permission from both military and political authorities to engage the enemy in a particular area.

**Click**—a kilometer in distance.

**Cluster fuck**—any attempted operations which went badly; a disorganized operation.

**Clutch belt**—cartridge belt worn by marines.

**CMH**—Congressional Medal of Honor. The highest US military decoration awarded for conspicuous gallantry at the risk of life above and beyond the call of duty.

**CO**—commanding officer.

**Cobra**—an AH-1G attack helicopter. Also known as a gunship, it is armed with rockets and machine guns.

**Cochinchina**—the French name for its southern Vietnamese colony, encompassing the III Corps and Mekong Delta rice-producing lowlands, which earlier were part of Cambodia.

**Co Cong**—female Viet Cong members.

**Code of Conduct**—military rules for US soldiers taken prisoner by the enemy.

**Comics**—topographic maps.

**Commo**—shorthand for *communications*.

**Commo bunker**—bunker containing vital communications equipment. Usually included in the last redoubt of established defensive positions.

**Commo wire**—communications wire.

**Company**—a military unit usually consisting of a headquarters and two or more platoons.

**Compound**—a fortified military installation.

**Concertina wire**—Coiled barbed wire used as an obstacle

**Connex container**—Corrugated metal packing crate, approximately six feet in length.

**Contact**—Firing on or being fired upon by the enemy.

**CONUS**—continental United States.

**COSVN**—Central Office of South Vietnam. Communist headquarters for military and political action in South Vietnam.

**Counterinsurgency**—Antiguerrilla warfare.

**Country team**—The staff and personnel of an American embassy assigned to a particular country.

**CP**—Command post.

**CP pills**—Anti-malarial pills.

**CQ**—Charge of quarters. An officer officially in charge of a unit headquarters at night.

**C-rations**—combat rations. Canned meals for use in the field. Each usually consisted of a can of some basic course, a can of fruit, a packet of some type of dessert, a packet of powdered cocoa, a small pack of cigarettes, and two pieces of chewing gum.

**Crispy critters**—burn victims.

**CS**—a gas which burns the eyes and mucus membranes; also known as tear gas.

**Cumshaw**—unofficial trading, begging, bartering, or stealing from other branches of the service.

**Cyclo**—motorized rickshaw.

**Dac Cong**—Viet Cong special forces.

**Daily-daily**—daily anti-malarial pill.

**DCI**—the director of Central Intelligence; the CIA.

**De-Americanization**—early term for Vietnamization.

**DELTA**—military phonetic for the letter D.

**DEROS**—date of expected return from overseas. The day all American soldiers in Vietnam were waiting for.

**Det Cord**—detonating cord. A rope-like explosive that can be wrapped around structures or trees to destroy or fell them. The entire length of cord explodes instantaneously.

**Deuce-and-a-half**—two-and-a-half ton truck.

**Dew**—marijuana.

**DH5**—Viet Cong claymore mine.

**DH10**—Viet Cong claymore mine.

**DI**—Marine boot camp drill instructor. Called a *drill sergeant* in the Army.

**Diddy-bopping**—walking carelessly.

**Didi**—slang from the Vietnamese word *di*, meaning "to leave" or "to go."

**Didi mau**—Vietnamese for "go quickly."

**Dink**—derogatory term for an Asian.

**Dinky dau**—to be crazy.

**District team**—American personnel assigned to act as advisors to Vietnamese military and civilian officials at the district level.

**District mobile company**—the major Viet Cong fighting unit organized within each district in Vietnam. The district mobile company was assigned to carry out various assignments from direct offensive operations to sabotage and terrorism.

**DMZ**—demilitarized zone. The dividing line between North and South Vietnam established by the 1954 Geneva Accords.

**Doc**—medic or corpsman.

**Dong**—unit of North Vietnamese money equal to roughly a penny in worth.

**D-ring** - a D-shaped metal snap link used to hold gear together.

**Dri-slide**—a highly-desired commercial firearms lubricant and waterproofing substance that was sprayed on and immediately dried to the touch. It didn't attract dirt like oily lubricants.

**Drops**—reduction in length of tour caused by overall reduction and withdrawal of American forces from Vietnam.

**Dung lai**—Vietnamese for "stop!"

**Dustoff**—medical evacuation by helicopter.

**E-Tool**—small, foldable shovel and pick, usually strapped onto the backpack, used primarily to dig fighting holes, and other excavation work as necessary.

**Eagle flights**—large air assault of helicopters.

**Early-outs**—a drop or reduction in time in service. A soldier with 150 days or less remaining on his active duty commitment when he

DEROSed from Vietnam also ETSed from the army under the early out program.

**ECHO**—military phonetic for the letter "E."

**Elephant grass**—tall, razor-edged tropical plant indigenous to certain parts of Vietnam.

**Eleven Bravo**—the MOS of an Army infantryman.

**EM**—enlisted man. Enlisted grades E1 – E9.

**EOD**—explosive ordinance disposal. A team that disarms explosive devices.

**E-tool**—entrenching tool. Folding shovel carried by infantrymen.

**ETS**—date of departure for overseas duty station; estimated time of separation from military service.

**Evac'd**—evacuated.

**Expectants**—casualties who are expected to die.

**F-4**—Phantom jet fighter-bombers. Range: 1,000 miles. Speed: 1400 mph. Payload: 16,000 lbs. The workhorse of the tactical air support fleet.

**FAC**—forward air controller; a person who coordinates air strikes.

**Fatigues**—standard combat uniform, green in color.

**FB**—firebase.

**FDC**—fire direction control center.

**Fire base**—Temporary artillery encampment used for fire support of forward ground operations.

**Firefight**—a battle, or exchange of small arms fire with the enemy.

**Fire Track**—flame-thrower tank.

**Five**—radio call sign for the executive officer of a unit.

**Flack jacket**—heavy fiberglass-filled vest worn for protection from shrapnel.

**Flaky**—to be in a state of mental disarray, characterized by spaciness and various forms of unreasoning fear.

**Flare**—illumination projectile, hand-fired or shot from artillery, mortars, or planes.

**Flechette**—a small dart-shaped projectile clustered in an explosive warhead. A mine without great explosive power containing small pieces of shrapnel intended to wound and kill.

**FNG**—fucking new guy.

**FO**—forward observer. A person attached to a field unit to coordinate the placement of direct or indirect fire from ground, air, and naval forces.

**FOB**—forward operating base.

**Foo gas**—a mixture of explosives and napalm, usually set in a fifty-gallon drum.

**Fours**—F-4s.

**FOXTROT**—military phonetic for the letter "F"

**Frag**—fragmentation grenade; shortened form of "fragging."

**Fragging**—the murder of an officer by his own troops, usually by a grenade.

**Freedom Bird**—the plane that took soldiers from Vietnam back to The World.

**Free fire zone**—free strike zone. Persons in this geographic area were assumed to be the enemy unless there was evidence to the contrary.

**Free strike zone**—tactical operations region where everyone was deemed hostile and a legitimate target by US and allied forces.

**French fort**—a distinctive triangular structure built by the hundreds by the French.

**Freq**—radio frequency.

**Friendly fire**—accidental attacks on US or allied soldiers by other US or allied soldiers.

**FUBAR**—fucked up beyond all recognition (sometimes *repair* is used instead of *recognition*), used to describe any badly disorganized operation.

**Fucked up**—wounded or killed. Also, to get stoned, drunk, or to be foolish or do something stupid.

**Fugazi**—fucked up or screwed up.

**Funny papers**—topographic maps.

**FWMAF**—Free World Military Assistance Forces. The Allies.

**G-3**—division level tactical advisor; a staff officer.

**Gamma Globulin/GG shots**—medicine given by an injection, usually in the buttocks, thought to strengthen the immune system and improve resistance to disease. The shots were quite painful and were given every few months in Vietnam. Administered by corpsmen in the field.

**Garand**—M-1 rifle.

**Ghosting**—goldbricking or sandbagging; screwing off.

**GI**—government issue. Usually refers to an American soldier.

**Glad bag**—slang term for body bag.

**GOLF**—military phonetic for the letter 'G'

**Gook**—derogatory term for the Viet Cong. Originally derived from Korean slang for *person* and passed down by Korean war veterans.

**Green Berets**—US Special Forces.

**Greens**—Army Class A uniform.

**GR point**—graves registration point. That place on a military base where the identification, embalming and processing of dead soldiers takes place.

**Grids**—map broken into numbered thousand-meter squares.

**Grunt**—infantryman. Originally slang for a Marine fighting in Vietnam but later applied to any solder fighting there; a boonierat.

**GSW**—gunshot wound.

**The Gun**—M-60 machine gun.

**Gung ho**—enthusiastic (usually about military matters).

**Gunship**—armed helicopter.

**GVN**—government of South Vietnam.

**HALO**—high-altitude, low-opening jumping for insertion of troops behind enemy lines. The jump is begun from 15,000 feet.

**Ham and motherfuckers**—ham and lima beans C-ration meal. An unpopular choice of meal.

**Hamlet**—A small rural village.

**Hammer and anvil**—an infantry tactic of surrounding an enemy base area, then sending in other units to drive the enemy out of hiding.

**Hand frag**—fragmentation grenade thrown by a soldier.

**HE**—high explosive, normally referring to artillery shells, as opposed to smoke or other marker rounds. HE rounds were used when firing for effect.

**H&I**—harassment and interdiction. Random artillery fire directed at suspected locations of enemy troops or possible movement of enemy troops in an area.

**Hardstand**—a pierced steel plate (PSP) platform over sand. Mortar application.

**Heart**—a Purple Heart award for a wound or the wound itself.

**Heat tabs**—flammable Trioxane tablet used to heat C-rations. Always in short supply.

**Hercules**—a C-130.

**HHC**—headquarters and headquarters company.

**Higher-highers**—the honchos; the command or commanders.

**HM**—Navy hospital corpsman; a medic.

**Hmong**—a dominant Laotian hill tribe generally opposed to the North Vietnamese and Pathet Lao communists. Many were driven into exile after the Pathet Lao, and the NVA and VC, were victorious in Laos and Vietnam in 1975.

**Ho Chi Minh slippers**—sandals made from tires. The soles are made from the tread and the straps from inner tubes.

**Hoi-Chanh**—Vietnamese Communist soldiers and cadre who rallied to the South Vietnamese government under the Chieu Hoi amnesty program.

**Honey-dippers**—people responsible for burning human excrement.

**Honky**—African American vernacular term for white people.

**Hooch**—a hut or simple dwelling, either military or civilian. Usually made of Bamboo and palm or other natural materials. Also spelled hootch.

**Hoochgirl**—Vietnamese woman employed by American military as maid or laundress.

**Hook**—a radio or radio handset.

**Horn**—radio microphone/headset.

**Hot**—area under fire.

**HOTEL**—military phonetic for the letter H.

**Hot LZ**—a helicopter landing zone under enemy fire.

**Howitzer**—a short cannon used to fire shells at medium velocity and with relatively high trajectories.

**HQ**—headquarters.

**Huey**—nickname for the single rotor UH-1 series helicopters. They were used for many purposes, primarily as medivac and supporting gunship functions.

**Hump**—march or hike carrying full gear and rucksack; to perform any difficult or unpleasant task.

**I Corps**—the northernmost military region in South Vietnam.

**II Corps**—the Central Highlands military region in South Vietnam.

**III Corps**—the densely populated military region between Saigon and the Highlands.

**IV Corps**—the marshy Mekong Delta southernmost military region.

**III MAF**—third Marine Amphibious Force, primarily responsible for military action in I Corps.

**IG**—Inspector General of the US Army.

**Illum**—an illumination flare, usually fired by a mortar or artillery weapon.

**Immersion foot**—condition resulting from feet being submerged in water for a prolonged period of time, causing cracking and bleeding.

**In-country**—in Vietnam / serving in Vietnam.

**Increments**—removable charges attached to mortar fins. If they become wet, the mortar round misfires and falls short.

**INDIA**—military phonetic for the letter I.

**Insert**—to be deployed into a tactical area by helicopter.

**Iron Triangle**—Viet Cong dominated area between the Thi-Tinh and Saigon rivers, next to Cu Chi district.

**JAG**—judge advocate general, the legal department of the armed services.

**Jam/Jamming**—The process whereby a rifle is made nonfunctional because a bullet became stuck while being loaded into the breech. It required physical removal of the jammed round before the rifle could work again.

**Jet jockey**—Air Force fighter pilot.

**Jody**—The person who wins your lover or spouse away while you are in Nam. From the marching song or cadence count, "Ain't no use in goin' home/Jody's got your girl and gone/sound off . . ."

**John Wayne**—P-38 can opener for canned food. Also used as a verb to describe the actions of someone who exposes himself to danger.

**JULIET**—military phonetic for the letter J.

**Jungle boots**—footwear that looks like a combination of combat boot and canvas sneaker used by the US military in a tropical climate, where leather rots because of the dampness. The canvas structure speeds drying after crossing streams or rice paddies.

**Jungle utilities**—lightweight tropical fatigue uniform.

**K**—kilometer.

**K-bar**—combat knife.

**KCS**—Kit Carson scout.

**KIA**—killed in action.

**Killing zone**—the area within an ambush where everyone is either killed or wounded.

**Kill zone**—the radius of a circle around an explosive device within which it is predicted that 95 percent of all occupants will be killed should the device explode.

**KILO**—military phonetic for the letter K.

**Kit Carson scout**—former Viet Cong who act as guides for US military units.

**Klick**—a kilometer in distance.

**Kool-Aid**—killed in action.

**KP**—kitchen police; mess hall duty.

**L**—a type of ambush set-up, shaped like the letter L.

**LAAW**—light anti-armor weapon. Sixty-six millimeter, hand-held self-contained rocket for use against armor or bunkers.

**Lager**—a night defensive perimeter.

**Lao Dong**—the Vietnamese Workers Party.

**Leg**—slightly contemptuous term used by airborne-qualified troops when they are talking about regular infantry.

**Lifer**—career military person. The term is sometimes used in a derogatory manner.

**LIMA**—military phonetic for the letter L.

**Lima-lima**—land line. The term refers to telephone communications between two points on the ground.

**Litters**—stretchers to carry dead and wounded.

**Little people**—The VC or NVA. A perjorative.

**Lit-up**—fired upon; shot and killed or wounded.

**LMG**—light machine gun. The Soviet-made RPD, a bipod-mounted, belt-fed weapon similar to the American M-60 machine gun. The RPD fires the same cartridge as the AK-47 and the SKS carbine.

**Log Bird**—logistical helicopter, generally referring to resupply flights.

**LP**—listening post. A two- or three-man position set up outside the perimeter, which acted as an early warning system against attack.

**LRRP**—long range reconnaissance patrol. An elite team usually composed of five to seven men who went deep into the jungle to observe enemy activity without initiating contact.

**LSA**—small arms lubricant.

**LST**—troop or tank landing ship.

**LT**—lieutenant.

**Lurps**—members of long range reconnaissance patrols.

**LVT**—landing vehicle, tracked, also known as amtracs. They carried troops or vehicles onto the shore or over land.

**LZ**—landing zone, usually a small clearing secured temporarily for the landing of helicopters. Some remained in use during the course of an offensive operation.

**M-1**—World War II vintage American rifle.

**M-14**—wood stock rifle used in early portion of Vietnam conflict. 7.62 caliber.

**M-16**—the .223 caliber 5.56 mm US military rifle used in Vietnam beginning in 1966. Successor to the M-14. The rifle had a hard plastic stock and forearm. Standard magazines held 20 rounds.

**M-60**—the standard lightweight machine gun used by US forces in Vietnam, using a 7.62 NATO/.308 caliber cartridge.

**M-72**—a 66mm light anti-armor weapon (LAAW).

**M-79**—a US military hand-held grenade launcher.

**MA**—mechanical ambush; a euphemism for an American-set booby trap.

**MACV**—military assistance command / Vietnam. American joint service military command unit that had responsibility for and authority over all US military activities in Vietnam.

**Mad minute**—a weapons free-fire practice and test session.

**Main Force Battalion**—the primary Viet Cong fighting force within each province of South Vietnam. These units were often large enough and well enough equipped to participate in direct attacks on large Vietnamese and American installations and units.

**Mama san**—slang used by American servicemen for any older Vietnamese woman.

**MARS**—military affiliate radio station used by soldiers to call home via signal corps and ham radio equipment. It was undependable and rarely used by front line troops.

**Mas-Cal**—mass casualty.

**MASH**—mobile army surgical unit.

**MAT**—mobile advisory team. Five-man teams of American advisors who were assigned to live and work in the Vietnamese villages.

**Marker round**—the first round fired by mortars or artillery, used to adjust the following rounds onto the target. Sometimes WP rounds.

**MCRD**—Marine Corps recruit depot. Boot camp locations.

**Mechanized platoon**—a platoon operating with tanks and/or armored personnel carriers.

**Med Cap**—Medical Civil Action Program in which US medical personnel would go into the villages to minister to the local populace.

**Medivac**—medical evacuation from the field by helicopter.

**MFW**—multiple frag wounds.

**MG**—machine gun.

**MIA**—missing in action.

**Mighty mite**—commercial air-blower used for injecting gas into tunnels.

**MIKE**—military phonetic for the letter M.

**Mike-mike**—radio term for millimeter.

**Million-dollar wound**—a non-crippling wound serious enough to warrant return to the US.

**Minigun**—electronically controlled, extremely rapidly firing machine gun, most often mounted on aircraft to be used against targets on the ground.

**Mr. Charles**—the Viet Cong or NVA; the enemy.

**MI team**—military intelligence team.

**Monday pills**—anti-malarial pills taken once a week.

**The Monster**—a PRC-77.

**Montagnard**—tribes of mountain people inhabiting the hills and mountains of central and northern Vietnam.

**Mortar**—a muzzle-loading cannon, with a short tube in relation to its caliber, that throws projectiles with low muzzle velocity at high angles. The 60mm and 81mm were the most commonly used in Vietnam. Large, four-deuce (4.2-inch) mortars were located at main bases.

**MOS**—military occupational specialty.

**MP**—military police.

**MPC**—military payment certificates. The currency, also known as *scrip*, US soldiers were paid with.

**Mule**—small, motorized platform originally designed to carry a 106-millimeter recoilless rifle, but most often used for transporting supplies and personnel in base area.

**Nam**—Vietnam.

**Napalm**—a jellied petroleum substance which burns fiercely and is used as a weapon against personnel.

**Navigator**—the person in a column responsible to ensure direction of travel and to count steps so that distances can be determined.

**NCO**—a noncommissioned officer, usually a squad leader or platoon sergeant. E4 – E9.

**NDP**—night defensive position.

**Net**—radio frequency setting, from the word *network*.

**Next**—person who was the next to rotate home.

**Nickel**—the number five, used in any context.

**NLF**—National Liberation Front.

**No sweat**—easy, simple, no problem.

**NPD**—night perimeter defense.

**Number one**—the best.

**Number ten**—the worst.

**Number ten thousand**—a description of how bad things can be.

**Nung**—tribespeople of Chinese origin from the highlands of North Vietnam. Some who moved South worked with the US Special Forces.

**Nuoc—mam**—fermented fish sauce used by the Vietnamese as a condiment.

**NVA**—North Vietnamese Army.

**OCS**—officer candidate school.

**OD**—olive drab, a camouflage color.

**Opcon**—operational control.

**OSCAR**—military phonetic for the letter O.

**OSS**—Office of Strategic Services.

**Over the fence**—crossing into Cambodia or Laos.

**P**—slang for the Vietnamese piaster. One piaster was worth one cent or less.

**P-38**—a small, collapsible can opener for opening food cans, most commonly known as a *John Wayne* in the USMC. It allegedly received this nickname because the actor was shown using the device in a WW2 training film.

**PAPA**—military phonetic for the letter P.

**Papa san**—term used by US servicemen for any older Vietnamese man.

**Papa Sierra**—slang for platoon sergeant.

**Pathet Lao**—the Laotian communists who, from their inception, have been under the control of the Vietnamese Communist Party.

**PBR**—river patrol boat. Navy designation for the fast, heavily armed boats used for safeguarding the major canals and rivers and their tributaries in South Vietnam.

**Perimeter**—outer limits of a military position. The area beyond the perimeter belongs to the enemy.

**PF**—popular forces; South Vietnamese National Guard-type local military units.

**Pfc.**—private first class/E-2. Enlisted rank.

**Phoenix**—intelligence-based campaign to eliminate the Viet Cong infrastructure.

**Piss-tube**—a vertical tube in the ground protruding far enough to urinate into.

**Platoon**—a subdivision of a company-sized military unit, normally consisting of three or more squads. Generally, around forty-five men made up an infantry platoon.

**Pogue**—derogatory term for military personnel employed in rear echelon support capacities, usually used by marines.

**Point man**—the forward-most, or point, man or element on a combat patrol.

**Poncho liner**—highly valued Nylon insert for the military rain poncho, used as a blanket.

**Pop smoke**—to ignite a smoke grenade to signal an aircraft.

**Popular Forces (PF)**—local South Vietnamese militia, often part time, whose primary responsibility was to help defend rural villages. They bore much of the fighting but were often poorly trained and equipped.

**Pos**—slang for position, usually meaning a friendly location.

**POW**—prisoner of war.

**PPB**—platoon patrol base. Forward outpost from which squad- or platoon-sized patrols are run for a period of days to a week or two.

**PRC-25**—portable radio communications, Model 25. A back-packed FM receiver-transmitter used for short-distance communications. The range of the radio was five to ten kilometers, depending on weather and terrain. Large nonportable antennae can extend the range to twenty to thirty kilometers.

**PRC-77**—heavy radio similar to the PRC-25, but with a cryptographic scrambling/descrambling unit attached. Transmission frequencies on the PRC-77 constituted what was called *the secure net.*

**Prick 25**—common name for the PRC-25 radio.

**Profile**—a prohibition from certain types of military duty due to injury or disability.

**Province chief**—governor of a state-sized administrative region.

**PTSD/Post Traumatic Stress Disorder**—development of harmful behavioral practices after experiencing a psychologically traumatic event. Symptoms involve frequently reimagining the event, numbing of responsiveness to or involvement with others, difficulty sleeping or relaxing, exaggerated startle responses, lack of concentration, memory impairment, and guilt feelings.

**QUAD-50s**—a four-barreled assembly of .50 caliber machine guns.

**Quantico**—Marine training base in Virginia.

**QUEBEC**—military phonetic for the letter Q.

**RA**—regular Army; prefix to the serial number of enlistees.

**Rack**—bed or cot.

**Radioman**—person responsible to carry the two-way communication radio for a unit, usually including company, platoon, and squad levels. They normally stayed close to the unit commander to receive and relay communications.

**Rallier**—a defector from the Viet Cong.

**R and R**—rest and recreation. A vacation from the war for a soldier of typically five days, including travel. It included out of country locations.

**Rangers**—elite commandos and infantry specially trained for reconnaissance and combat missions.

**RBF**—reconnaissance by fire.

**React**—one unit coming to the aid of another under enemy fire.

**Recon**—reconnaissance. Surreptitiously going into contested lands to identify enemy activity.

**Recondo school**—a training school in-country for LRRPs. The largest was at Na Trang, where the training action was taken against the Seventeenth NVA Division.

**Red alert**—the most urgent form of warning, it signals an imminent enemy attack.

**Red bird**—A Cobra helicopter.

**Red Legs**—slang for artillery. In the Civil War, Union artillery men had red stripes on their pants.

**Reeducation camps**—political prisons and labor camps of varying degrees of severity and size that comprised the Soviet-style gulag system throughout communist Vietnam.

**Regiment**—a military unit usually consisting of four battalions.

**Regional Forces**—militia units organized within each district in South Vietnam to engage in offensive operations against local Viet Cong forces. RF units were better paid and equipped than PF units and could be assigned duties anywhere within the home district.

**REMF**—pronounced *remf*, meaning rear-echelon motherfucker. Term used primarily by infantrymen for military personnel assigned to rear bases, away from front lines.

**Repo depo**—replacement detachment.

**RF/PF**—regional and popular forces. The South Vietnamese National Guard-type units. Regional forces were company-size and protected district areas. Popular forces were platoon-size and guarded their home villages.

**RIF**—reconnaissance in force; a heavy reconnaissance patrol. After the war, RIF came to mean reduction in force; an administrative mechanism for retiring career soldiers before the end of their twenty-year term.

**Ringknocker**—a graduate of a military academy; the term refers to the ring worn by graduates.

**Rock'n'roll**—firing a weapon on full automatic, which was rarely done.

**ROK**—Republic of Korea. Used in reference to a soldier from Korea.

**ROKMC**—Republic of Korea Marine Corps. Korea sent marines to South Vietnam.

**ROMEO**—military phonetic for the letter R.

**Rome plow**—mammoth bulldozer used to flatten dense jungle.

**RON**—remain-overnight operation.

**Rotate**—return to the US at the end of a tour in Vietnam.

**ROTC**—Reserve Officers Training Corps. Program offered in many high schools and colleges, aimed at preparing students to become military officers.

**Round eye**—American or European person, usually when referring to a woman.

**RPD**—a light, 7.62 mm Russian machine gun with a 100-round, belt-operated drum that fires the same round as the AK-47. The Chinese version was called the Type 56. Common weapon of the VC.

**RPG**—rocket-propelled grenade; a Russian-made portable antitank or anti-personnel grenade launcher.

**RTO**—radio telephone operator. The man who carried his unit's radio on his back in the field; a radioman.

**Rucksack**—backpack issued to infantry.

**Ruff puff**—derogatory term used by Americans for RF/PF.

**Rules of engagement**—the specific regulations for the conduct of air and surface battles by US and allied forces during the Vietnam war.

**Rumor control**—The most accurate source of information prior to the actual occurrence of an event.

**S-1**—personnel.

**S-2**—intelligence.

**S-3**—operations.

**S-4**—supply.

**S-5**—civil affairs.

**Saddle up**—to put on one's pack and all other necessary gear and get ready to head out on patrol or to march.

**Salt**—a seasoned marine or soldier with several years of experience. Rank is not critical, only years in service matter. The term is derived from the faded utilities they proudly wear, in comparison to the new, unfaded uniforms worn by new marines and soldiers.

**Salt tabs**—tablets of salt (sodium chloride) thought to restore electrolytes to the body during periods of exertion and sweating caused by heat.

**Salvo**—firing a battery in unison.

**Sampan**—small Vietnamese boat used by civilians for fishing or other livelihood purposes.

**SAF**—small arms fire.

**S and S**—supply and service; designation of a support unit.

**Sapper**—a Viet Cong or NVA commando, usually armed with explosives.

**Satchel charges**—pack used by the enemy containing explosives that is dropped or thrown, often to breach a fence or wall.

**Scrip**—military payment certificates.

**Scuttlebutt**—rumors or loose talk among troops speculating as to what is going to happen.

**Seabags**—heavy canvas duffel bags.

**SeaBees**—Navy construction engineers.

**SEAL**—highly trained Navy special warfare team members (sea, air, land force).

**Search and destroy**—an operation in which Americans searched an area to locate the enemy and to destroy enemy facilities and supplies.

**SEATO**—Southeast Asia Treaty Organization.

**Semper Fi**—short for Semper Fidelis, the Marine Corps motto. Stands for *always faithful.*

**SERTS**—Screaming Eagle Replacement Training School.

**SF**—Special Forces.

**Shake'n'bake**—sergeant who attended NCO school and earned rank after only a very short time in uniform.

**Shamming**—goofing off or getting by with as little effort as possible.

**Shaped charge**—an explosive charge, the energy of which is focused in one direction.

**Shelter half**—a tarp that served as a sort of tent. It served a variety of other purposed as needed.

**Shit burning**—the sanitization of latrines by kerosene incineration of excrement.

**Short**—a term used by everyone in Vietnam to tell all who would listen that his tour was almost over.

**Short-timer**—soldier nearing the end of his tour in Vietnam.

**Short-timer's stick**—when a soldier had approximately two months remaining on his tour in Vietnam, he might take a long stick and notch it for each of his remaining days in—country.

**Short timer calendar**—a drawing, often of Snoopy, with one hundred boxes to shade in to count down the days from 100 to zero and return to CONUS.

**Shrapnel**—pieces of metal sent flying by an explosion.

**SIERRA**—military phonetic for the letter S.

**Silver Star**—US military decoration awarded for gallantry in action.

**Sit-rep**—situation report.

**Six**—unit commander, from the company commander on up.

**Six-by**—a large flat-bed truck, usually with wooden slat sides enclosing the bed and sometimes a canvas top covering it. Used for carrying men or anything else that would fit on it.

**Skate**—a task that required little effort or pain; verb form means to take it easy.

**SKS**—Simonov 7.62 mm semi-automatic carbine.

**Sky**—to leave.

**Sky crane**—large, double-engine helicopter used for lifting and transporting heavy equipment.

**Sky out**—to flee or leave suddenly.

**Slackman**—the second man back on a patrol, directly behind the point. This person often had navigation responsibilities.

**Slant**—derogatory term for a Vietnamese person.

**Slick**—a UH-1 helicopter used for transporting troops in tactical air assault operations. The helicopter did not have protruding armaments and was, therefore referred to as *slick*.

**Slope**—derogatory term for an Asian person.

**SMG**—submachine gun.

**Smoke grenade**—a grenade that releases colored smoke used for signaling.

**SNAFU**—situation normal, all fucked up.

**Snake**—a Cobra helicopter.

**SOI**—signal operating instructions. The booklet that contained all of the call signals and radio frequencies of the units in Vietnam.

**Solacium payment**—standard amount paid by the US government to Vietnamese civilians when US forces were deemed responsible for a wrongful civilian death.

**SOP**—standard operating procedure.

**Sopwith Camels**—slang term for a light, fixed-wing reconnaissance aircraft.

**Soul brother**—a black soldier.

**Spec-4**—specialist, fourth class. An Army rank immediately above private, first class. Most enlisted men who had completed their individual training and had been on duty for a few months were spec-4s. Probably the most common rank in the Vietnam-era Army.

**Spec-5**—specialist, fifth class. Equivalent to a sergeant.

**Spider hole**—camouflaged covered hole or pit capable of concealing a sniper.

**Spooky**—propeller-driven aircraft, often C-130s, with a minigun mounted in the door. Capable of firing 6,000 rounds per minute. Also used to refer to gunship helicopters with miniguns.

**SP pack**—cellophane packet containing toiletries and cigarettes, which was sometimes given along with C-rations to soldiers in the field.

**Squad**—a small military unit consisting of less than fifteen men.

**Staff sergeant**—an E-6, the second-lowest noncommissioned officer rank.

**Stand-down**—an infantry unit's return from the boonies to the base camp for refitting and training. Later, a unit being withdrawn from Vietnam and redeployed to the US.

**Starlifter**—a C-141, the largest military cargo transport airplane in the Air Force inventory.

**Starlight scope**—an image intensifier using reflected light to identify targets at night.

**Steel pot**—the outer metal cover of the standard military helmet.

**Strategic hamlet program**—a controversial pacification and village self-defense program implemented by the Diem government that attempted to turn all sixteen thousand South Vietnamese hamlets into fortified compounds.

**Strobe**—hand-held strobe light for marking landing zones at night.

**Syrette**—collapsible tube of morphine attached to a hypodermic needle. The contents of the tube were injected by squeezing it like a toothpaste tube.

**TA-50**—individual soldier's standard issue of combat clothing and equipment.

**TAC**—tactical air strikes; fighter bombers.

**Tail-end charlie**—last person or unit in a column.

**T and T**—through and through wound, one in which a bullet or fragment has entered and exited the body.

**Tanglefoot**—single-strand barbed wire strung in a meshwork pattern at about ankle height. The barrier was designed to make it difficult to cross the obstructed area by foot and was usually placed around permanent defensive positions.

**TANGO**—military phonetic for the letter T.

**Tango boat**—US Navy designation for an armored landing craft mounted with 50-caliber machine guns and a 40-caliber anti-aircraft gun used for direct fire.

**TC**—tactical commander.

**Tet**—January holiday celebrating the Buddhist lunar New Year, which marks Buddha's birthday.

**Tet Offensive**—a major uprising of the National Liberation Front and NVA characterized by a series of coordinated attacks against military installations and provincial capitals throughout Vietnam. It occurred during the lunar New Year at the end of January 1968.

**Tee-tee**—slang for very small.

**Thermite**—a mixture of powdered aluminum and metal oxide, which produces great heat for use in welding and incendiary bombs.

**Three**—radio call signal for the operations officer.

**Three-quarter**—a three-quarter-ton truck.

**Tiger suits**—camouflage fatigue uniforms.

**Tight**—good friends.

**TO and E**—table of organization and equipment.

**TOC**—tactical operations center.

**Top**—a top sergeant/first sergeant – E-8.

**TOT**—time on target. A prearranged mortar or artillery barrage set to occur at a specific time in order to coordinate with an infantry assault.

**Trach**—a tracheotomy, where an opening into the windpipe is made to facilitate breathing.

**Tracer**—rounds of ammunition chemically treated to glow or give off smoke so that its flight can be followed.

**Tracks**—any vehicles that move on tracks rather than wheels.

**Triage**—the procedure for deciding the order in which to treat casualties.

**Trip flare**—a ground flare triggered by a trip wire used to signal and illuminate the approach of an enemy at night.

**Tropic Lighting**—the US Twenty-Fifth Infantry Division.

**Turtles**—new replacements. Primarily an Army term, they were called turtles because it took so long for them to arrive.

**Two**—radio call signal of the intelligence officer.

**Two-niner-two**—the RC-292 ground plane antenna, which was used to extend the range of the MAT and the district team's PRC-25.

**UCMJ**—Uniform Code of Military Justice, the legal code of the military.

**Unbloused**—pants not tucked into boot tops.

**UH-1H**—Huey helicopter.

**UNIFORM**—military phonetic for the letter U.

**US**—prefix to serial number of Army draftees.

**USAF**—United States Air Force.

**USARV**—US Army, Republic of Vietnam. The command of operations unit for all US military forces in Vietnam, based in Long Binh.

**USMC**—United States Marine Corps.

**USO**—United Service Organization, provided entertainment to US troops.

**USOM**—US Operations Mission, funded US programs during the early American involvement in Vietnam.

**V**—a type of ambush set-up, shaped like the letter.

**VA**—Veterans Administration.

**VC**—Viet Cong, National Liberation Front fighters.

**VCI**—Viet Cong infrastructure. It was the aim of the Viet Cong to have a complete government in place when their victory was finally won. Communist cadres were secretly assigned positions as village chiefs, police officers, district-level officers, province-level officers, and national-level officers. The VCI were the shadow government of the National Liberation Front.

**VFW**—Veterans of Foreign Wars, an American service organization.

**VICTOR**—military phonetic for the letter V.

**Victor Charlie**—the Viet Cong.

**Viet Cong**—The Communist-led forces fighting the South Vietnamese government. The political wing was known as the National Liberation Front, and the military was called the People's Liberation Armed Forces. Both the NLF and the PLAF were directed by the People's Revolutionary Party, the southern branch of the Vietnamese Communist Party, which received direction from Hanoi through COSVN, which was located in III Corps on the Cambodian border. After 1968, as negotiations began in Paris, the NLF established the Provisional Revolutionary Government.

**Viet Minh**—Viet Nam Doc Lap Dong Minh Hoi, or the Vietnamese Allied Independence League, a political and resistance organization established by Ho Chi Minh before the end of World War II, dominated by the communist party.

**Vietnamese Popular Forces**—South Vietnamese local militia forces.

**Vietnamization**—US policy initiated by President Richard Nixon late in the war to turn over the fighting to the South Vietnamese Army during the phased withdrawal of American troops. The term was coined by Nixon's Secretary of Defense, Melvin Laird to replace the policy of *de-Americanization*.

**Ville**—Vietnamese hamlet or village.

**VNAF**—South Vietnamese Air Force.

**VSI**—very seriously ill. The Army designation for those troopers who may die without immediate and definitive medical care.

**VVA**—Vietnam Veterans of America. Vietnam veterans organization.

**VVAW**—Vietnam Veterans Against the War. Organization formed by Vietnam veterans who gathered to protest American involvement in Vietnam.

**Wake-up**—as in *ten and a wake-up*, the last day of a soldier's Vietnam tour.

**Walking wounded**—wounded who are still able to walk without assistance.

**Walter wonderful**—Walter Reed Army Hospital in Washington, DC.

**Wasted**—killed.

**Water taxi**—small engine-powered boat with a sheltered passenger compartment. These native craft plied the major canals and rivers of Vietnam and provided a means of transportation from one village to the next.

**Web gear**—Canvas belt and shoulder straps for packing equipment and ammunition on infantry operations.

**Weed**—marijuana.

**WHISKEY**—military phonetic for the letter W.

**White bird**—a LOH.

**White phosphorus (WP)**—type of explosive round from artillery, mortars, or rockets. The rounds exploded with a huge puff of white smoke from the hotly burning phosphorus and were used as marking rounds or incendiary rounds. When white phosphorus hit the skin of a living creature it continued to burn until it had burned through the body. Water did not extinguish it.

**WIA**—wounded in action.

**Willy Peter (WP)**—white phosphorus.

**Winter Soldier Hearings**—meetings and staged hearings held in 1971 by the group Vietnam Veterans Against the War, asserting charges of war crimes by the US and allies.

**Wood line**—row of trees at the edge of a field or rice paddy.

**World, The**—The United States.

**WP**—white phosphorus/willie peter.

**X**—type of ambush set up, shaped like the letter.

**XO**—executive officer, the second in command of a military unit.

**X-RAY**—military phonetic for the letter X.

**YANKEE**—military phonetic for the letter Y.

**YD**—geo-position 100,000 meters by 100,000 meters square from the Universal Transmercator (UTM) Grid Zone 48Q. A UTM dispenses with latitude and longitude in favor of a system of six-digit metric coordinates that allow the user of the map to determine a location within 100 meters.

**Zapped**—killed.

**Zipperhead**—derogatory term used to describe the Vietnamese.

**Zippo raids**—military operations that involved burning down rural hooches suspected of use by VC or their supporters. Zippo cigarette lighters were often used to ignite the huts.

**Zit**—derogatory term for Vietnamese people.

**ZULU**—military phonetic for the letter Z.

**Zulu**—casualty report.

# RESOURCES

## CHAPTER I:

United States Department of State Archives. *The United States and the Founding of the United Nations*, August 1941–October 1945.

National Park Service. *OSS Training in the National Parks and Service Abroad in World War II.*

OurDocuents.Gov. *Tonkin Gulf Resolution* (1964)._

History.Com. *The Gulf of Tonkin Incident.* August 31, 2018.

Joint Chiefs of Staff. *Management and Review of Campaign and Contingency Plans.* CJCSI 3141.01F January 31, 2019 Enclosure A-1.

The University of Virginia, Miller Center. *Lyndon B. Johnson: Foreign Affairs._By Kent Germany.

Council on Foreign Relations. *The Water's Edge. The First US Combat Troops Arrive in Vietnam._James M. Lindsay March 8, 2015.

Karnow, Stanley *Vietnam: A History* New York City: The Viking Press, 1983. 55, 117, 135, 136 – 140, 219 – 221, 279, 310, 367 – 372, 451.

VietnamWar50th.com. *The US Army in Vietnam: 1954–1973.*

History.com. *Statistics About the Vietnam War 45th Surgical Hospital Tay Ninh Vietnam Army Units in Vietnam.*

Senate Committee on Foreign Relations Hearing. *Causes, Origins, and Lessons of the Vietnam War*, 1972. 164–165.

History.Com. *Vietnam War Timeline.*

The History Place. *The Vietnam War/Seeds of Conflict 1945–1960._*

Letter of Instructions dated May 16, 1945 to Major Thomas. *Deer Mission to Viet Minh Headquarters July–September 1945.* Special Operations Branch, Office of Strategic Services.


### CHAPTER 2:

PBS - *The Vietnam War: A Film by Ken Burns and Lynn Novick._*

University of Maryland Library. *About the Music; Vietnam War Songs Discography.*


### CHAPTER 4:

The History Place. The Vietnam War. *The Jungle War 1965–1968._*

173rdAirborne.com. *US Army Units Vietnam.*

US Army Center of Military History. *Vietnam War Campaigns.*

Karnow, Stanley. *Vietnam: A History* New York City: The Viking Press, 1983.

Spector, Ronald H. *After Tet: The Bloodiest Year in Vietnam.* New York City: The Free Press, a Division of Macmillan Inc., 1993. 1, 9, 22.

CHAPTER 5:

5th Marine Division.com. *Operation Allen Brook.*

United States Marine Corps History Division. *The Battle of Hue City.*

US Army Center of Military History. *The 1968 Tet Offensive Battles of Quang Tri City and Hue.* Erik Villard, 2008.

HistoryNET. *Valor at Dai Do.* Colin D. Heaton, 2014.

Congressional Medal of Honor Society.

Karnow, Stanley. *Vietnam: A History.* New York City: The Viking Press, 1983.

Spector, Ronald H. *After Tet: The Bloodiest Year in Vietnam.* New York, NY: The Free Press, a Division of Macmillan Inc. 1993. 47, 55.

Shulimson, Jack; Lt. Col. Blasiol, Leonard; Capt. Dawson, David; Smith, Charles; *US Marines in Vietnam – The Defining Year – 1968.* Published by the History and Museums Division, USMC, 1997. 533, 537, 539, 557.

CHAPTER 6:

Robert Cooney & Helen Michaelowski, *The Power of the People*, Philadelphia, PA: New Society Publishers, 1987._

University of Michigan. *The Anti-Vietnam War Movement at the University of Michigan 1965 – 1972.*

Flynn, George Q. *The Draft, 1940–1973.* Modern war studies. University Press of Kansas, 1993.

History.com. *The Paris Peace Accords.*


CHAPTER 7:

The American War Library. *Vietnam War Allied Troop Levels: 1960 – 1973*

The Washington Post. *China Admits Combat in Vietnam War.* May 17, 1989


CHAPTER 8:

2ndBatallion9thMarines.Org. *Hell in a Helmet_*

HistoryNET. *The Vietnam War: Operation Dewey Canyon_*

The National Interest. *USS Battleship New Jersey in Vietnam War.*

Periscope Film/YouTube. *Operation Dewey Canyon 1969._*

Spector, Ronald H. *After Tet: The Bloodiest Year in Vietnam* New York City: The Free Press, a Division of Macmillan Inc. 1993. 78, 118 -119, 122-126

Michael R. Conroy, "Personality," *Vietnam Magazine* Volume 3 No. 6, April 1991, 8

Michael R. Conroy, "Laotian Secret," *Vietnam Magazine* Volume 5 No. 2, August 1992, 42

Shulimson, Jack; Lt. Col. Blasiol, Leonard; Capt. Dawson, David; Smith, Charles; *US Marines in Vietnam – The Defining Year – 1968.* 1997. Published by the History and Museums Division, USMC: 547 – 550.

*The Marines in Vietnam, 1954–1973: An Anthology and Annotated Bibliography.* By the History and Museums Division, USMC Headquarters, Washington DC, 1985.

Congressional Medal of Honor Society.

## CHAPTER 9:

US Department of Veterans Affairs Military Health History Pocket Card/Agent Orange_

Defense POW/MIA Accounting Agency. Vietnam War Accounting._

POW-MIAFamilies.Org *History of the POW/MIA Bracelets._*

History.com. *January 27, 1973. Paris Peace Accords Signed._*

Karnow, Stanley. *Vietnam: A History.* New York City: The Viking Press, 1983. 25–26.

The Vietnam Veterans Memorial Fund.

## TABLES AND STATISTICS:

The National Archives. *Vietnam War US Military Fatal Casualty Statistics.*

American War Library. *Vietnam War Deaths and Casualties by Month.*

The Vietnam Veterans Memorial Fund.

# ACKNOWLEDGEMENTS

E very book is a team effort, and as a result, it is only proper to acknowledge those who played a role. First and foremost, I must thank my lovely wife, Susan, for her forbearance and understanding. During the many months I was sequestered in my basement office thinking, researching, and writing about a decidedly unpleasant topic, she provided unquestioned support—even when the topic put me in less than cheerful moods, which I brought into the living room with me. Consenting to read an early draft, she also made recommendations that made the book more understandable and meaningful for all readers, not just those familiar with the reality of military life and lingo. She reminded me that readers want stories in clear black and white; they don't want to have to assume or guess about key aspects.

My good friend, Mac, also provided important early input, which put me on the path of making the book meaningful for a broader audience and also helped get me over my reticence at sharing details.

The marvelous staff at Koehler Books played a larger role than they perhaps appreciate. Wendolin saw potential and had faith in the early manuscript. Becky's editorial input was stellar and critical. The transformation from draft to final form reflects her considerable talents. John and Joe provided necessary support and guidance from beginning to end. It's a talented and supportive team, and because of them, this book is published as a quality creation.

My most heartfelt acknowledgment goes to the untold thousands of young Americans that proudly and faithfully served their country during the Vietnam era and especially in the Vietnam War. I hope that after reading this book folks will better realize what a tremendous sacrifice and patriotic effort that service represented. Those young Americans were among the finest this country has ever produced. This book is for and about them.

*Bill Murphy*

CPSIA information can be obtained
at www.ICGtesting.com
Printed in the USA
LVHW020335051021
699541LV00005B/272